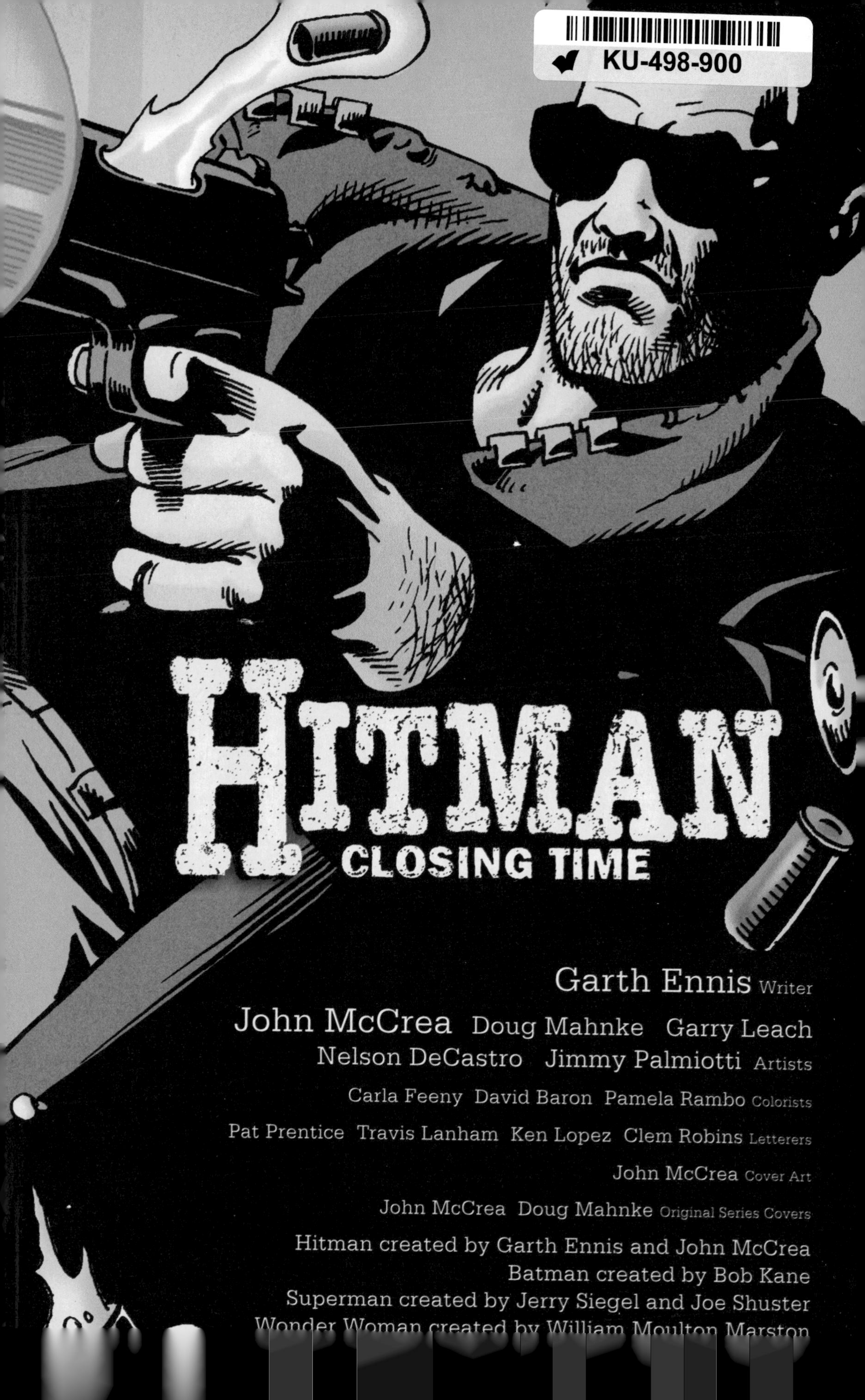

KU-498-900
HITMAN
CLOSING TIME
Garth Ennis Writer
John McCrea Doug Mahnke Garry Leach
Nelson DeCastro Jimmy Palmiotti Artists
Carla Feeny David Baron Pamela Rambo Colorists
Pat Prentice Travis Lanham Ken Lopez Clem Robins Letterers
John McCrea Cover Art
John McCrea Doug Mahnke Original Series Covers
Hitman created by Garth Ennis and John McCrea
Batman created by Bob Kane
Superman created by Jerry Siegel and Joe Shuster
Wonder Woman created by William Moulton Marston

Peter J. Tomasi **Michael Siglain** Editors – Original Series **L.A. Williams** **Harvey Richards** Assistant Editors – Original Series
Scott Nybakken Editor **Robbin Brosterman** Design Director – Books **Louis Prandi** Publication Design

Bob Harras VP – Editor-in-Chief

Diane Nelson President **Dan DiDio** and **Jim Lee** Co-Publishers **Geoff Johns** Chief Creative Officer
John Rood Executive VP – Sales, Marketing and Business Development **Amy Genkins** Senior VP – Business and Legal Affairs
Nairi Gardiner Senior VP – Finance **Jeff Boison** VP – Publishing Operations **Mark Chiarello** VP – Art Direction and Design
John Cunningham VP – Marketing **Terri Cunningham** VP – Talent Relations and Services **Alison Gill** Senior VP – Manufacturing and Operations
Hank Kanalz Senior VP – Digital **Jay Kogan** VP – Business and Legal Affairs, Publishing **Jack Mahan** VP – Business Affairs, Talent
Nick Napolitano VP – Manufacturing Administration **Sue Pohja** VP – Book Sales
Courtney Simmons Senior VP – Publicity **Bob Wayne** Senior VP – Sales

Cover color by **Carla Feeny.**

HITMAN: CLOSING TIME

DC Comics, 1700 Broadway, New York, NY 10019
A Warner Bros. Entertainment Company.
Printed by RR Donnelley, Willard, OH, USA. 6/29/12.
First Printing.
ISBN:978-1-4012-3400-3

Certified Sourcing
www.sfiprogram.org
SFI-01042
APPLIES TO TEXT STOCK ONLY

I WAS HALFWAY THROUGH MY THIRD BEER WHEN THAT STUPID BASTARD WALKED INTO NOONAN'S.
FRAG, FRAG, BASTICH ETC
I HATED HIM ON SIGHT AN' I WASN'T EVEN LOOKIN' AT HIM. HE DRESSED LIKE AN IDIOT, TALKED LIKE A MORON, AN' SMELLED LIKE HE WORE HIS BOWELS OUTSIDE HIS BODY. IT WASN'T A GOOD BEGINNIN'.
ON TOPPA THAT, HE WAS A BULLY.
AN' I ALWAYS DID HATE BULLIES.
THAT STUPID BASTICH
GARTH ENNIS WRITER
DOUG MAHNKE ARTIST
KEN LOPEZ LETTERER
CARLA FEENY COLORIST
JAMISON SEPARATOR
L.A. WILLIAMS ASSISTANT EDITOR
PETER TOMASI EDITOR
A SPECIAL THANKS TO PAT GLEASON
HITMAN created by ENNIS/McCREA
LOBO created by GIFFEN/SLIFER
AUTHOR'S NOTE: CLEARLY, THIS STORY TAKES PLACE BEFORE CERTAIN MEMBERS OF THE CAST WERE SLAUGHTERED.

WHAT'LL IT BE?
PITCHER O'YER FINEST PIGSWILL, BARKEEP! TH' MAIN MAN'S READY TO DO SOME SERIOUS DRINKIN'!

NOT THAT THIS LOOKS LIKE TH' PLACE FER IT! OF ALL THE TWO-BIT DIVES IN THIS HALF-HORSE TOWN ON THIS CRAPOLA MUDBALL PLANET, WHY THE HELL'D I HAVETA WALK INTO THIS ONE?

NAME'S LOBO, YA BASTICHES! SCOURGE A' THE GALAXY, THAT'S ME! BUNCHA HUME BASTICHES LIKE YERSELVES CAN CONSIDER ME BEIN' HERE AN HONOR!

'CEPT FOR TAFF THE SPAFF, NO-GOOD SMUGGLIN' BASTICH FROM THE ARCTURUS SYSTEM!

THOUGHT HIDIN' FROM TH' BO ON EARTH'D SAVE HIS BUTT-- GOT HIM OUTSIDE ON TH' BIKE NOW, FRAGGED! TEN THOU BOUNTY, SOON AS I GET HIM HOME!

AGGLUGLUGLGLUG
URRRPP!
KEEP EM' COMIN', GRANDAD!
WHAM!

YEAH, I'M THE BIGGEST, BADDEST
I'M GONNA TAKE A WILD GUESS AN' SAY TIEGEL DUMPED YOU AGAIN...
IN ONE.

SHE JUST CAN'T SEEM TO GET OVER THE HITMAN THING...
YOU TRY BEIN' NICE ALL THE TIME, KEEP HER FROM BRINGIN' IT UP?
I AM NICE ALL THE TIME.

BUT YOU KNOW HOW IT IS, IT ALWAYS COMES UP ANYWAY.
LIKE TONIGHT WE'RE PLAYIN' TRIVIAL PURSUIT-- I MEAN WHAT COULD BE SAFER, RIGHT? AN' THE QUESTION IS "WHO HAD A HIT WITH LOVE IS BLAND (DON'T STEP ON MY HAIR) IN 1988?"
AN' BEFORE I CAN SAY BON JOVI SHE'S LIKE, "AH! A HIT! THE WAY YOU MAKE YOUR LIVING! OH GOD, I DON'T KNOW IF I CAN RECON- CILE THIS, OH WHAT AM I DOING WITH YOU" AN' THE NEXT THING YOU KNOW I'M OUT THE GODDAMN DOOR!

IT ALWAYS TAKES A LIFETIME TO TALK HER 'ROUND, TOO...
YOU'LL BE FINE.
LISTEN, I GOTTA GO TO THE MEN'S ROOM AN' FILL THIS, OKAY? KEEP AN' EYE ON BOZO FOR ME WHILE I'M GONE.
SO I DID. A REAL CLOSE EYE.
MATTER OF FACT, HAVIN' NOTHIN' BETTER TO DO, I READ THE JERK'S MIND...
WHICH WASN'T A MAJOR UNDERTAKING, 'CAUSE WHEN IT CAME TO MINDS THIS GUY HAD THE SPECIAL JUNIOR READERS EDITION.
BOUNTY HUNTER FROM OUTER SPACE, SURE ENOUGH. INCREDIBLE STRENGTH, HIGHLY-TUNED SENSE OF SMELL, ABLE TO REGROW HIMSELF FROM A SINGLE DROP OF BLOOD AN' TALK NON-STOP CRAP IN A TOTAL VACUUM--
NOT GOOD NEWS.
WORSE WAS TO COME.
SAY! WHO'S THAT LITTLE BASTICH S'POSED TA BE?
...AN' I MEAN YOU THINK ABOUT IT: SUPERNESS, NOCTURNAL MAMMALS, WOMEN, FISH, GREEN STUFF, MARS OR FAST THINGS--WHEREVER THE TROUBLE ARISES, THE J.L.A. HAVE GOT IT COVERED!

HEY!
WHAT'RE YOU S'POSED TO BE, SHORTY! SOME KINDA SUPERHERO?

DAMN RIGHT I AM! LET GO, YA BIG CREEP! GET OFFA ME!
SIX PAC
HAW!

WHAT A DWEEB! WHAT YA KEEP HIM AROUND FER, TA SHOVE ON TOPPA TH' CHRISTMAS TREE?
UNHAND ME, EVILDOER-- OR FACE THE WRATH OF SIXPACK!
TAKE THAT! UNGHH--AN' THAT!

HAW HAW HAW! FRAGGIN' LITTLE ANKLESUCKER!
NOT IN MY PLACE, MEATHEAD--
WHOA!

THE MOOD I'M IN RIGHT NOW?
ALLOW ME.

AIN'T HAD THIS MUCH FUN SINCE THE LAST BASTICH I FRAGGED!
FIGHT FAIR, DAMN YA! LEMME GET TO MY BOTTLE AN' I'LL CUT YER FRIGGIN' EYES OUT!
I HOPE YOU KNOW WHAT YOU'RE DOIN', TOMMY...
HAVE NO FEAR.
GAKK--!
PUCKER UP, ULTRADWEEB!
TAP TAP
'SCUSE ME, MISS LOBO?
MISS?!
NO ONE QUESTIONS TH' GENDER O' TH' MAIN MAN AN' LIVES TA TELL TH' TALE! WHOEVER YA ARE, YA HUME BASTICH-- CONSIDER YERSELF FRAGGED!

WHUT TH'--
KABLAM

YAAAAAGGHH!!

THIS IS WAR!

SEE, THE WAY I FIGURED IT, THE ONLY THING THAT STUPID BASTARD SAW WAS TWO BIG BLACK NINE MILLIMETER TUNNELS-- SO UNTIL HIS EYES GREW BACK ENOUGH TO GET A LOOK AT ME, HE'D HAVE TO TRACK BY SCENT...

IT WASN'T TOO LONG 'TIL IT DAWNED ON ME THAT THIS MAYBE WASN'T SUCH A SMART IDEA AFTER ALL...
DORANS
I CAN SMELL YA, YA LIQUOR-SODDEN BASTICH! GONNA CHOKE YA ON YER OWN FRAGGIN' APPENDIX!

BUT THIS BEIN' GOTHAM CITY, IT DIDN'T TAKE TOO LONG FOR THINGS TO ESCALATE--
SPTOOF--! MONAGHAN?!

THIS IS SALAD MIKE AT DORAN'S! PUT PAULIE ON!
NO, SERIOUSLY! THIS IS GOOD!

GODAMMIT--!
SCREEECH

LITTLE DIRTBAG!
HOLY JEEZ--!

HELLO, MIKE.
YOU DO, HUH? AND WHY WOULD I BE INTERESTED IN TOMMY MONAGHAN?

WHAT, ARE YOU KIDDIN', PAULIE? HE KILLED MEN'S ROOM LOUIE! YOUR FRIGGIN' UNCLE!

MY WIFE'S FRIGGIN' UNCLE, MIKE. I COULDN'T STAND THE DISGUSTING OLD BASTARD.

COME BACK, YOU SLIME! HALT!
LET'S GET THE BASTARD--

OH SURE, IT'D DO ME PLENTY OF GOOD WITH THE FAMILIES. I DON'T NEED YOU TO TELL ME THAT.
I'M JUST THINKING OF WHAT HAPPENED TO THE LAST COUPLE OF HUNDRED GUYS WHO SCREWED WITH TOMMY, YOU KNOW WHAT I MEAN?
I...I DON'T THINK THAT'S GONNA BE A PROBLEM, PAULIE...
COMIN' FER YA, KING FRAG!!
KRRRRNNCH
HE'S KINDA GOT HIS HANDS FULL RIGHT NOW!

AND--
LAST TIME MIKE SAW HIM HE WAS HEADING DOWN PECKINPAH, JOHNNY. YOU OUGHT TO GET A GOOD SHOT AT HIM WHEN HE CROSSES ONTO HOUSTON.
GOT YOU, PAULIE.

NOW, JUST IN CASE YOU MISS, I'VE GOT--
I AIN'T GONNA MISS, PAULIE.

NO, JOHNNY. BUT JUST IN CASE YOU DO, I'VE GOT THREE CARS FULL OF SHOOTERS READY TO MOVE IN AND CUT HIM OFF.
YOU GET FIRST SHOT BECAUSE YOU'RE MY LITTLE BROTHER, JOHNNY. AFTER THAT I'M LEAVING IT UP TO PROFESSIONALS.

GET READY TO EAT A LITTLE CROW, BRO--

HE'S HERE!

STAND BY TA DOCK WITH PLANET FRAG, EARTH FEEB!
OH JEEZ--

BLAM
YES!

SPLAK
HUH?!

I--I MISSED!
IMAGINE THAT.
HIT IT, BOYS.

GET HIM!
FOR CRYIN' OUT LOUD!
SCRREEEEEEECH

BRATTABRATTABRATTABRATTA
SPING
PING
POK
POK
SPAK
SPAK
POK
PING
SPOK
PING
POK
SPING
YAAAAHH
CLOSE IN! CLOSE IN! WE GOT HIM!
UNO MOMENTO, CLYDE!
HOLY GOD!
CAN'T SEE YA--BUT I CAN SMELL YA!
SKRUNCH
OH NO--
OUT!
NO ONE BLOWS TH' MAIN BRAINS ALL OVER TH' STREET AN' LIVES TA FRAG AGAIN--

DOCTOR BO RECOMMENDS AN INTRAVENOUS DOSE O' FRAG!!
AAAAIIIIEEEEE

OH MY GOD.
JOHNNY?

SKRASSH
SKLATCH

DID YOU SEE THAT?!
SPIRIT OF CHOW YUN FAT BE WITH ME NOW...

HEY--
BLAM
BLAM
BLAM
BLAM
BLAM
BLAM
BLAM
BLAM
BLAM
BLAM
BLAM
BLAM
EEEIIIGGHHH

COME OUT, COME OUT WHEREVER YA ARE!

WHOA--!
THE FIRST BULLET-- THE ONE THAT STUPID BASTARD GOT IN THE WAY OF--I KINDA KNEW IT WAS MEANT FOR ME. I MEAN WHO'S GONNA TAKE MY SIDE AGAINST SOME CORNBALL ALIEN MECHAGODZILLA, RIGHT?
WHAT I COULDN'T FIGURE WAS WHO CALLED IN THE HIT...

BUT THE DEAD GUY TOLD ME EVERYTHING.
ONE OF PAULIE BATTS'S BOYS...!

THOUGHT YOU'DA HAD MORE SENSE, PAULIE.
HAAAIIIIEEE!!

I HAVEN'T FORGOTTEN YA, BASTICH! FRAGGIN', READY OR NOT!

BY NOW I WAS STARTIN' TO PUT A PLAN TOGETHER, BUT THAT STUPID BASTARD WAS CLOSIN' FAST...

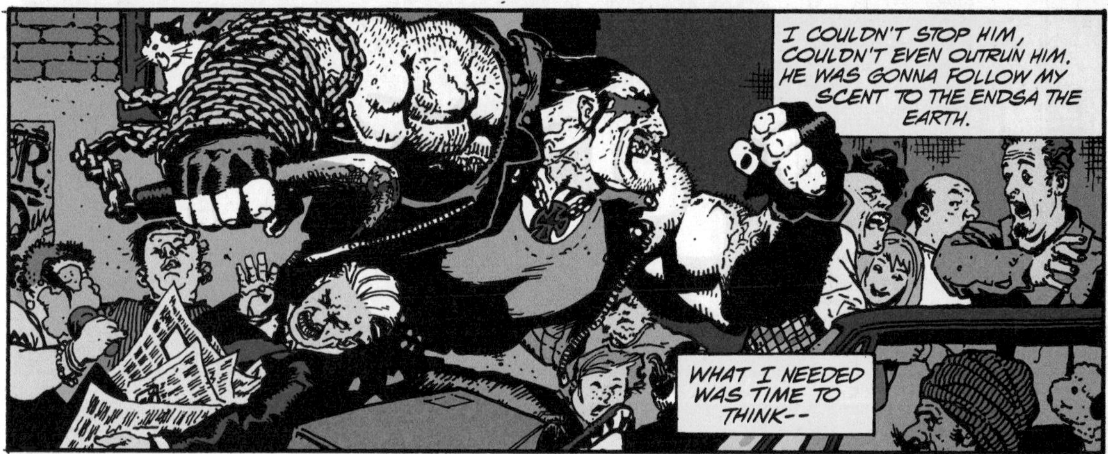
I COULDN'T STOP HIM, COULDN'T EVEN OUTRUN HIM. HE WAS GONNA FOLLOW MY SCENT TO THE ENDSA THE EARTH.
WHAT I NEEDED WAS TIME TO THINK--

PAULIES
SLOTS
TABLES
AN' THEN I SAW A WAY TO KILL TWO BIRDS WITH ONE STONE.

WELL, WELL.

EVENIN', PAULIE.

EVENIN', TOMMY.
KILL HIM.

HEADS UP, YA FEEB-BUTT LAME-O! GONNA GIVE YA A TASTE O' LOBO'S FRAG A L'ORANGE--
SLOTS TABLES
GRAND PAYOUT

SERVED WITH A SIDE DISH O' FRAG!

BUDDABUDD
UDDABUDDA
BLAM BLAM
BLAM
BLAM
BLAM
BLAM
BLAM
BLAM
BLAM
BLAM
BLAM
UH-OH...

THIS WHOLE CITY'S A GLUTTON FER PUNISHMENT.

BANZAAIII!
NOOOO
AAAGH AIEEE
HELLP AAAKK
SEAN? HEY, PUT SIXPACK ON, WILL YOU?
NO, I'M IN A MOVIE THEATRE. IT'S THE AUDIENCE, THEY'RE WATCHIN' A JOEL SCHUMACHER RETROSPECTIVE...
RRRIIIPP
SLOOTCH
HEY, HOW'S GOTHAM'S MIGHTIEST SUPERHERO?

REAL GOOD, TOMMY... JUSHT... COMIN' UP ON MY SHECOND WIND, Y'KNOW?
YEAH? YEAH, SURE I CAN HELP YA, BUDDY!

GREAT--WHOA--
I WANT YOU TO MEET ME DOWN ON FOURTH, OKAY? ON THAT CONSTRUCTION SITE, WHERE THEY'RE PUTTIN' UP THE NEW TRADE CENTER?
SPLAK
I NEED YOU TO PICK UP A COUPLA THINGS ON THE WAY--BUT FIRST OF ALL YOU GOTTA CALL YOUR BOYS, SIXPACK.

YOU GOTTA PUT THE TEAM BACK TOGETHER.
SIXPAC

FWUMP

HEY... TOMMY...
HEY, PAULIE. WE MEET AGAIN, HUH?

THAT GUY YOU GOT THERE... HE'S...REALLY SOMETHING...
THAT STUPID BASTARD? YEAH, HE AIN'T NO LIGHTWEIGHT.
YOU WANNA HEAR SOMETHIN' IRONIC, PAULIE?
SURE...
IT WASN'T ME WHO KILLED MEN'S ROOM LOUIE.
YEAH...
THAT IS... PRETTY IRONIC... TOMMY...
YOU!
GOTTA GO, PAULIE.
SEE YOU.

EVERYTHING RELIED ON SIXPACK GETTIN' IT EXACTLY RIGHT-- THOUGH WHY I WAS TRUSTIN' A CAPED DRUNK AN' A SUPERTEAM FULLA THE CRIMINALLY INSANE WAS COMPLETELY BEYOND ME...
DANGER
KEEP OUT

TURNED OUT I SHOULDA HAD MORE FAITH.
HERE IT COMES, BASTICH! GROUND CONTROL TA MAJOR FRAG!
DANGER
KEEP OUT

ALL YOURS, TOMMY!
GANGWAY--
SIX PAC
SPLOOSH

SNFF SNFF
DAMMIT! LOST TH' SCENT!

POIK POIK
...YES!
STROKE O'LUCK!

EVERYBODY READY?
YOU BETCHA! SECTION EIGHT, GO!

THE MAIN MAN'S BACK IN TH' GAME, DWEEBO! GONNA WISH YA A FRAGGY CHRISTMAS--
AN' A HAPPY NEW FRAG!

JEAN DE BATON!
UH?
JEAN DE BATON!

WHO TH' HELL IS THAT?
JEAN DE BATON-BATON!

FUH!
HOLY CRAP!

FUH-
FUH-FUH-
FUH-FUH-
FUH!

?
JEAN DE BATON!

WHO'S THERE, DAMMIT!
SIXPACK'S TEAM WAS A SIGHT TO BEHOLD. WHERE SHAKES USED HIS TERRIBLE TWITCH AN' CHRONIC STUTTER TO FIGHT CRIME, JEAN DE BATON TOOK A MORE DIRECT APPROACH...

WHO TH--
JEAN DE BATON!

JEAN DE BATON-BATON!
KRAK
HEY!!
YA LITTLE SCUZZBALL! I'M GONNA--
THE DEFENESTRATOR PLAYED HIS PART--
KRRASSH
YA UNBELIEVABLE BASTICH! PREPARE TA DIE!
SO DID FLEMGEM--
FWIP
HAWCCHTT

TOOFFT!

AAAH! AAAH! YA DIRTY LITTLE BASTICH!

SO, I'M SORRY TO SAY, DID FRIENDLY FIRE--
FRAGGIN' HELL, I THINK I SWALLOWED SOME!
STAND BACK, BOYS! I GOT THE CREEP!

DAMMIT!
ZZAK
AAARGGH! ARC DE TRIOMPHE! MERDE!!

BUT IT DIDN'T MATTER. THEY BOUGHT US THE TIME WE NEEDED.
READY?

COPACETIC, TOMMY! LET'S SMITE THE BASTARD!

AAA-EE-AA-EE-AAAAA

UNGAWA!!
OH, HELL--

SKRRRUNNCH
HNNNGHH!
TAKE 'ER UP, TOMMY! LET'S PUT THISH EVILDOIN' SUNAVABISH TA BED!
YOU GOT IT--
UH...?
SAY HELLO TO THREE TONSA *IRON JUSHTISH*, LAWBREAKER!

SO SHALL ALL CRIMINALS PERISH, THE BASTARDS!
HE'S GONNA REGENERATE. HAVE YOUR BOYS PULL HIM OUTTA THERE, WILL YOU?
YOU BRING THE CAMERA?

YEP!
THEN I GUESS IT'S TIME FOR PHASE TWO.

HEH, HEH, HEH...

BUENO...

BUENO EXCELLENTE WAS THE KEY TO MY WHOLE PLAN, THOUGH HOW I CAME UP WITH THIS ONE IS BEYOND ME.
YOU MIGHTA SEEN SOME OF HIS FILMS, IF YOU'RE UNLUCKY ENOUGH: THIS FIST FOR HIRE, MAYBE...
HEH, HEH, HEH...

OR YOU BETTER BELIEVE IT'S NOT BUTTER.
EXCELLENTE...
ROLL 'EM.

TWO HOURS LATER...
YOU GET ALL OF IT?
SURE DID!
DOGWELDER?

THE FINISHIN' TOUCH, IF YOU PLEASE.

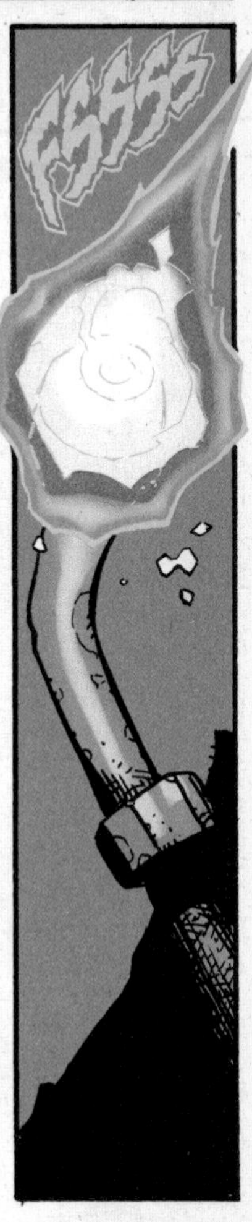
FSSSS

NOONANS
NOONANS
YA FRAGGERS!

THIS IS IT, YA HIVE O' BASTICHES! YA PUSHED TH' MAIN MAN INTO MAXIMUM FRAG!
EYES SHOT OUT! BRAINS BLOWN AWAY! MACHINE-GUNNED FULLA LEAD! BEATEN, SPAT ON, DEFENESTRATED AN' CRUSHED UNDER A GIANT STEEL GONAD! I WOKE UP FEELIN' LIKE I CHOKED ON ARCTURIAN CURRY!

AN' WHO TH' HELL WELDED THIS FRAGGIN' DOG TO MY BUTT?!

BUT WHUT I REALLY WANNA KNOW IS, WHO'S TH' DIRTY LOWDOWN SOON-T'BE-MEAT PASTE LITTLE BASTICH THAT SHOT ME AN' DRAGGED ME ALL OVER THIS SCUMSUCKIN' TOWN INNA FIRST PLACE?

THAT'D BE ME.

OH, BOY.
OH, BOY...
AIN'T TOO MANY LAMBS COME SO WILLINGLY TA TH' FRAGGIN! HEADS UP-- GONNA SCORE ELEVEN ON A SCALE OF ONE TA FRAG!
NOW WOULD BE A REALLY GOOD TIME, SEAN.

VHS
KLIK

SAY HELLO TA TH' GREEN, GREEN GRASS O' FR--
HEY...

THAT'S ME!
VHS

HEY, IS THIS WHEN I PASSED OUT? WHY AM I WEARIN' A FRAGGIN' TUX?
AN' WHO'S--

WHO TH' HELL IS THAT...?
WHUT TH' HELL IS HE DOIN'...?

GETTIN' MARRIED.
TO YOU.

WE GOT THE WHOLE CEREMONY ON TAPE.
NOT TO MENTION THE REST OF IT.
OH, AN' NEEDLESS TO SAY--

WE MADE COPIES.

WHUT?

YEAH, A WHOLE BUNCHA THEM. AN' IF ANYTHING HAPPENS TO ANY OF US, THEY'RE GONNA GET SENT TO ALL KINDSA INTERESTED PARTIES.

WHO?!
GOVERNMENT PEOPLE, FOR STARTERS. THEY GOT CONTACTS WITH A COUPLA ALIEN CIVILIZATIONS-- NEWS LIKE THIS'D SPREAD ACROSS THE GALAXY LIKE WILDFIRE. AN' THE MEDIA, THEY'RE GONNA LOVE IT. I MEAN TALK ABOUT A CLOSE ENCOUNTER, HUH?
THEN THERE'S S.T.A.R. LABS. I BET WITH ALL THE STUFF THEY DO OUT THERE, YOU'VE MESSED THINGS UP FOR THEM ONCE OR TWICE. WE EVEN THOUGHT OF SENDIN' A COPY TO THE JUSTICE LEAGUE.

YA FRAGGIN' LITTLE ANKLESUCKER, I OUGHTA GUT YA LIKE A--
GO AHEAD.

BUT THE NEXT TIME YOU'RE FIGHTIN' SUPERMAN, DON'T BE TOO SURPRISED IF HE'S LAUGHIN' HIS ASS OFF.

BASTICHES!
NOONANS
FWOOSH

TEMPER.

STILL, THAT'S THE LAST WE'LL SEE OF THAT STUPID BASTARD, HUH?
YEAH, HE'S OFF BACK TO PLANET McGOOFY OR WHEREVER THE HELL HE'S FROM...
EVENTUALLY.

EVENTUALLY?
YEAH.

AFTER YOU LEFT LAST NIGHT, SIXPACK WENT OUTSIDE AN' PISSED IN HIS GAS TANK.

FRAAAAAAAGG!!
HEH, HEH, HEH...
BUENO...
-The End-

NOONAN'S BAR, GOTHAM CITY: AS HITMAN & CO. CLOSE UP FOR THE NIGHT, THE TOWN'S MIGHTIEST DEFENDER PREPARES FOR ACTION...
CAR'S OUT FRONT. SIXPACK GONNA BE OKAY BY HIMSELF?
BE RIGHT THERE, FELLAS.

'COURSE HE IS. GETTIN' READY FOR A HARD NIGHT'S CRIMEFIGHTIN', FROM THE LOOKA THINGS.
'KAY, LET'S GO.

NUHH... BLURRR... MINDIVI... MIND...
MIND IF I JOIN YOU ON PATROL TONIGHT, SIXPACK?

BE MY GUEST, SUPERMAN!
SIX PACK
HOW TO BE A SUPER-HERO
GARTH ENNIS STORY
NELSON PENCILS
JIMMY PALMIOTTI INKS
CLEM ROBINS LETTERS
PAM RAMBO COLORS
SUPERMAN CREATED BY JERRY SIEGEL AND JOE SHUSTER

SO WHAT BRINGS GOTHAM'S GUARDIAN TO METROPOLIS?
AH, YOU KNOW. THOUGHT I'D DROP BY, SPEND SOME TIME PURSUIN' JUSTICE, FIGHTIN' THE NEVER-ENDIN' BATTLE...
SMITE SOME EVILDOERS AN' TRANSGRESSORS, I GUESS. YOU UP FOR THAT?

SOUNDS GOOD TO ME.
AHA! AN' THERE'S WHERE OUR WORK WILL BEGIN!

Eh?
WIZZZZZZ
LEXCORP!

COMIN' FOR YA, LUTHOR! YA MULTINATIONAL BAG O' SICK!

WHAT THE--?
KRESSH!
EEEEHW
SPL.ATT

SUPERMAN, WHAT ON EARTH IS THE MEANING OF THIS? WHO IS THIS--THIS RIDICULOUS CREATURE?
I'LL ASK THE QUESTIONS, CUE-BALL!
WHUMP!
GREAT SCOTT!
SKRUNCH
PICK THE BONES OUTTA THAT, WRONG-DOER!
SIXPACK, WHAT ARE YOU DOING?
YOU CAN'T JUST ATTACK LEX LUTHOR LIKE THIS! HE HASN'T DONE ANYTHING WRONG!
'COURSE HE HAS! HE'S A SUPER-VILLAIN, AIN'T HE? IT GOES WITH THE TERRITORY!
YES, BUT... HMMM.
COME WITH ME.

ROOF EXIT
I DON'T GET IT, SUPERMAN. LEX LUTHOR'S AN EVIL INTERNATIONAL MEGA-GENIUS--PROBABLY GOT A HAND IN EVERY DIRTY DEAL ON THE PLANET...
AH, YES! YOU KNOW THAT, AND I KNOW THAT--BUT WE CAN'T ACT WITHOUT PROOF, UNDERSTAND?
NOT REALLY, NO.
HAVEN'T YOU HEARD OF DUE PROCESS? CONSTITUTIONAL RIGHTS? THE LAW?
AIN'T THAT FOR COPS?
WELL, YES, BUT WE STILL HAVE TO OBSERVE THE SAME PROTOCOLS.
WE DO WORK OUTSIDE THE LAW, TECHNICALLY SPEAKING, BUT THAT DOESN'T GIVE US A LICENSE TO JUST-- JUST ASSAULT WHOEVER WE WANT...
YOU SEE, THESE...WELL, THESE SUPER-VILLAINS HAVE CHOSEN TO CROSS THE LINE. THEY HABITUALLY BREAK THE LAWS THAT SOCIETY SETS FOR ITSELF. THAT'S WHAT MAKES THEM CRIMINALS.
IF WE IN TURN CHOOSE TO FOLLOW THEM ACROSS THAT LINE--IF WE CAN'T CATCH THEM IN THE ACT, OR FIND THE PROPER EVIDENCE BEFORE APPREHENDING THEM--WE ARE EFFECTIVELY JOINING THEM.
AND ONCE PEOPLE SEE THAT ANYONE CAN BREAK THE LAW WHENEVER IT'S CONVENIENT--WELL, THEN THE ENTIRE SYSTEM BREAKS DOWN...
DO YOU UNDERSTAND NOW, SIXPACK?
SIXPACK?

SIXPACK! SIXPACK!
CCC

SIXPACK, WHERE ARE YOU?!

WHERE CAN HE BE...?
WAIT A MINUTE--

GOOD LORD!!
STRYKER'S ISLAND
MAXIMUM SECURITY PRISON
Trespassers Will Be Shot
PETROLEUM

SO SHALL ALL MISCREANTS PERISH, THE PUKES!

UNTIL THE WORLD IS FR--
FOR CRYING OUT LOUD, SIXPACK!
SKRITCH
YOU CAN'T SET FIRE TO STRYKER'S ISLAND! THE INMATES WILL ROAST IN THEIR CELLS!
WELL--YEAH, THAT'S THE GENERAL IDEA.

BUT IT'S MURDER!
WHADDAYA TALKIN' ABOUT? THEY'RE A BUNCHA CRIMINAL SCUM! ALL THEY EVER DO IS ESCAPE AN' GO BACK TO THEIR EVIL WAYS!
MAY AS WELL FRY 'EM ALL AT ONCE, SAVE EVERYONE A WHOLE MESS O' TROUBLE!

BUT-- LOOK--I MEAN--
YOU SEE, MANY OF THE PEOPLE INCARCERATED HERE HAVE FALLEN FOUL OF MISFORTUNE OR PERSONAL TRAGEDY, AND THEY'VE SIMPLY BEEN TOO WEAK TO RISE ABOVE THEIR ENVIRONMENT. THEY DESERVE A CHANCE AT PERSONAL REDEMPTION, AT REHABILITATION...
THEY DO?

...ALL RIGHT, COME WITH ME.
THERE'S SOMEONE I'D LIKE YOU TO MEET.

SO WHO'S THIS GUY YOU'RE TAKIN' ME TO MEET?
THERE HE IS NOW...
WURG...
DOOMSDAY!
HOLY JOE SMITH! STAY BACK, SUPERMAN!
BUT--
METROPOLIS COMMUNITY YOUTH CENTER
Reading: It's Fundamental
Say NO to drugs!
TRASH
I'LL HANDLE THIS!
GET THAT STITCHED, YA MINDLESS ABOMINATION!
HHNNGH!!
WUNNNGGHH
I'LL TEACH YA TO GO ON A RAMPAGE OF ALL-CONSUMIN' FURY--
NEEIIGHH!!
KRRENNNGG
POP-POP!

SIXPACK, STOP! YOU'RE KILLING HIM!
YA GOT THAT RIGHT, SUPERMAN! THE NO-GOOD BUM KILLED YOU, DIDN'T HE?
BUT THAT'S ALL IN THE PAST...!
LOOK, DOOMSDAY USED TO BE A VICIOUS GENETICALLY ENGINEERED BEHEMOTH, INCAPABLE OF EMOTIONS BEYOND HATRED AND RAGE-- BUT HE'S BETTER NOW!
HURG... BLURGGH...
METALLICA
METRO FUZZ STINK!
DOOMSDAY REFORMED, SIXPACK. FOR THE PAST SIX MONTHS HE'S BEEN RUNNING AN ENCOUNTER GROUP FOR VICTIMS OF VIOLENT CRIME.
YOU SEE, THIS IS WHAT I MEAN ABOUT REHABILITATION --ABOUT EVERYONE'S RIGHT TO A SECOND CHANCE...

OKAY, WHAT ABOUT THOSE GUYS OVER THERE?
MM?

HAND OVER YOUR LIFE SAVINGS AND VALUABLES THAT YOU'RE DUMB ENOUGH TO CARRY AROUND WITH YOU, OLD BAG!
M-M-MERCY!
NO MERCY HERE, GRAN'MA! WE NEED THE MONEY FOR METHAMPHETAMINES AN' COMIC BOOKS, SEE!
AH.

TURF! KEEP OFF!!
AND--
OH, SUPER-MAN, THANK YOU! I DON'T KNOW WHAT I'D HAVE DONE IF YOU HADN'T ARRIVED WITH YOUR BRAVE SIDEKICK!
THINK NOTHING OF IT, MRS. CONNER. YOU TAKE CARE.
EXCEPT HE'S NOT MY SIDEKICK, OKAY?
STINKIN' TRANSGRESSORS--
HERE
FONTI RULES
KILLROY WAS NEVER HERE!

GONNA PUT A STOP TO YER PREYIN' ON THE INNOCENT ONCE AN' FOR ALL!
GOOD LORD!
HOLY JEEZ!

AW...!
SSSSSSS
SIX PACK

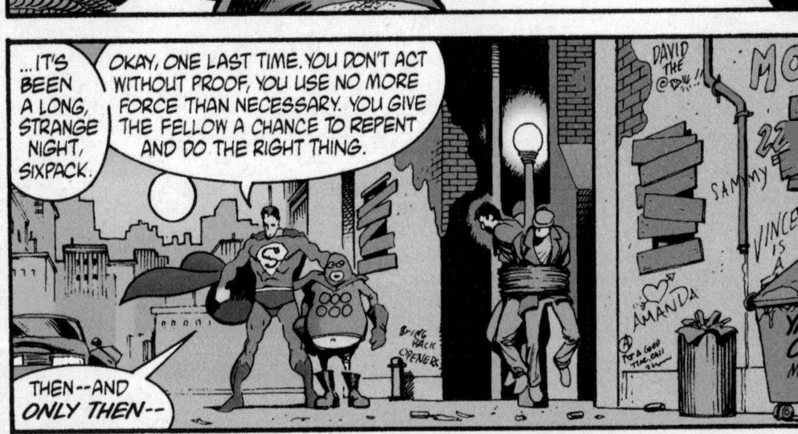
...IT'S BEEN A LONG, STRANGE NIGHT, SIXPACK.
OKAY, ONE LAST TIME. YOU DON'T ACT WITHOUT PROOF, YOU USE NO MORE FORCE THAN NECESSARY. YOU GIVE THE FELLOW A CHANCE TO REPENT AND DO THE RIGHT THING.
THEN--AND ONLY THEN--
DAVID THE
SAMMY
VINCE IS A
AMANDA

--YOU'RE CLEAR TO GO AHEAD AN' SMASH HIS FACE INTO A BLOODY PULP?
NO, SIXPACK...

YOU'LL BE A SUPER-HERO.

SUBRERO... GUZZA...GUH... WHA--?
MORNIN', SIXPACK!
UH... JUSHT GEDDA LIDDLE...FRESH AIR...
CAREFUL, PAL. I HEARD BANE'S BACK IN TOWN, SWEARIN' VENGEANCE FOR YOU KICKIN' HIS BUTT THE LAST TIME...
HEH! SHURE, FELASH...
OH, AND CAT-WOMAN PHONED AGAIN. WANTS TO KNOW WHY YOU AIN'T RETURNIN' HER CALLS.
SLEAZY BAR
NOONANS
OH, BOY.
IF ONLY THEY KNEW...
SIXPACK!!
SIXPACK
KRRUNCHH
IF ONLY THEY KNEW!
The End

McCREA 2008

O DEADLY DARKSHEID BOOAAAKK
NO CAR PARK
NEW ROCK
Simply Jeff
20 JULY - 8th AUG Vietname Water-Puppets
SOAPY SUDZ 2K
GARTH ENNIS WRITER
JOHN McCREA PENCILLER
GARRY LEACH INKER
PAT PRENTICE LETTERER
CARLA FEENY COLORIST
HEROIC AGE SEPARATOR
L.A. WILLIAMS ASST. EDITOR
PETER TOMASI EDITOR
SUPER GUY!
PART 1
HITMAN CREATED BY ENNIS & McCREA

CASHT YER EVIL WEBBA NETSH OVERA CAUL'RON AN'... AN' I'LL KICK YER ASH, YA TYRANT!
FOR I DO FRIGGIN' SHWEAR BY MINE HONOR TO... PROTECTA... FOLKSH LIVE HERE FROM... INNERG'LACTIC BASHTERDSH LIKE YERSHEFF!
AAAAH, BLACK RASHER!!
NO... NO NEEDA THANG ME, CHIP. JUSH 'NOTHER DAYSH WORK FERA NEIGHBORHOOD'SH MASHKED MARVEL...
FER... SIXPACK...
DAILY FACT
PORTILLO FROM MARS, NOT
SPORT
zzZzZzZz

HELP ME! SOME-BODY HELP ME! THEY'RE TRYING TO KILL ME!

OUTTA THE WAY! GET THE HELL OUTTA THE WAY!
WE ARE TRYNNA KILL HIM!!

HEEELLLPP!
Vince d. was 'ere
Petes Pizza
FOR CRYIN' OUT LOUD...!

GETTIN' KINDA-- HFFF-- PUBLIC-- HFFF--
I TOLD YOU WE WERE OUTTA RANGE FOR THAT FIRST SHOT...
MISS SIXTY

I DIDN'T WANT TO DO THIS! YOU FORCED ME TO DO THIS!
HUH?

HOLY CRAP!
YOU SHOULD'VE LEFT ME ALONE!

BRRRRTTTTT
WHERE THE HELL'D HE COME UP WIT' THAAATT!!

PROFESSOR HADDOCK...?
INJUN PEAK TOP SECURITY RESEARCH FACILITY

PROF IGNATIUS HADDOCK
YES, DOCTOR JACKSON?
I WAS WONDERING IF I COULD HAVE A BRIEF WORD...

INITIALIZING
IT WOULD BE MY PLEASURE, DOCTOR.
HEM HUM.
A. CROWLEY

WELL, IT'S ABOUT THIS UNFORTUNATE BUSINESS WITH YOUR LAB ASSISTANT...
THE CHAP YOU HAVE SENT THE ASSASSINS OUT AFTER?
A. CROWLEY

MONAGHAN AND WALLS, YES. CUTTHROAT SCUM, BUT THEY SHOULD BE ABLE TO KEEP A LID ON THINGS.
ANYWAY. YOUR ASSISTANT, HARRY. I... *HAD* UNDERSTOOD THAT HE ABSCONDED WITH THE DATA FROM YOUR *TESSERACT EXPERIMENT,* BUT YOUR NOTES SEEM TO SUGGEST THAT... WELL...

THAT HE *IS* THE TESSERACT EXPERIMENT, DOCTOR.

I SEE...
NO YOU DON'T. YOU UNDERSTAND NOTHING OF TESSERACT TECHNOLOGY.

THE TECHNOLOGY THAT WILL CHANGE OUR EXISTENCE *FOREVER*.

BY A PROCESS OF THEORETICAL PHYSICS FAR, *FAR* TOO COMPLICATED FOR ME TO GO INTO NOW, SCIENTISTS HAVE BELIEVED FOR SOME TIME THAT AN EXTRADIMENSIONAL SPACE--A *TESSERACT*--OF ALMOST *INFINITE CAPACITY* CAN BE CREATED INSIDE ANY GIVEN OBJECT. PUT SIMPLY, THAT A BIG THING CAN BE MADE TO FIT INSIDE A SMALL THING.
I HAVE MADE THE THEORETICAL REAL. I HAVE CONSTRUCTED A TESSERACT WITHIN THE BODY OF MY ASSISTANT.
WORLD
MAN

AND HE RAN AWAY BECAUSE...?
HE WENT SLIGHTLY MAD. THE PROCESS PROVED TO BE TOO MUCH FOR THE AVERAGE HUMAN MIND.

HE'S APT TO GET MADDER, TOO. I HOPE THESE KILLERS OF YOURS KNOW WHAT THEY'RE DOING.
HEM HUM.

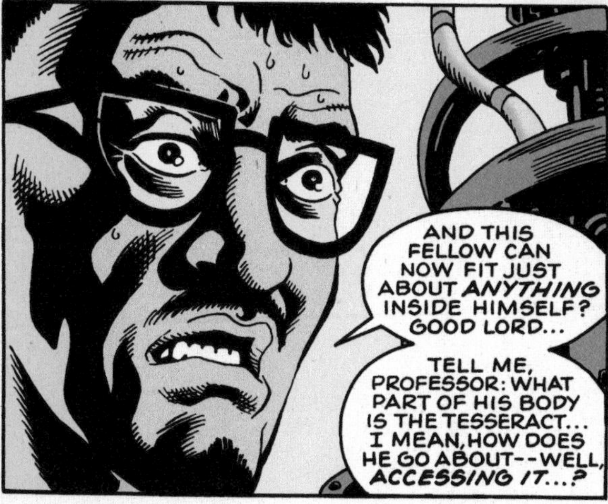
AND THIS FELLOW CAN NOW FIT JUST ABOUT *ANYTHING* INSIDE HIMSELF? GOOD LORD...
TELL ME, PROFESSOR: WHAT PART OF HIS BODY IS THE TESSERACT... I MEAN, HOW DOES HE GO ABOUT--WELL, *ACCESSING IT*...?

HOW MUCH JACKSON PAYIN' US FOR THIS?
AS OF THIS MOMENT, *DOUBLE*--

OH GOD. RUN.
WHAT?

RUN! RUN! JUST RUN, NATT!

WHEEEEEEEEBAKOOOOMM
WHERE IS HE *GETTIN'* THIS STUFF--?

HAAAIIIIEEE!!

KATZ'S That's all!
FAMOUS
DELICATESSEN
KNOWN as the Best
SINCE 1898
Z
HA!!

...TRIPLE.
DEFINITELY TRIPLE.
VRRRMMMMM

'COURSE, WE GONNA HAVE TO EARN IT FIRST...
WE'LL TAKE THAT!

ESTABLISHED 1854
... EIGHTY, NINETY, THREE HUNDRED LOOKS LIKE THIS FINE ESTABLISHMENT CAN COUNT ON THE FULL PROTECTION OF THE LAW FOR ANOTHER MONTH OR TWO...
MAN, I THINK I'M GONNA LIKE WORKIN' THE CAULDRON!

WHAT THE--?!
COP9

WHOA, SON.
WHAT? WHY?!
'CAUSE THAT WAS TOMMY MONAGHAN JUST TOOK OUR CAR.

SEAN NOONAN GOT CLIPPED BY THE MOB THREE MONTHS AGO. EVER SINCE THEN, TOMMY AIN'T EXACTLY BEEN IN THE BESTA MOODS.
SO LET'S GO HAVE A DRINK AN' WAIT A COUPLA HOURS BEFORE DISCOVERIN' THE SHOCKIN' THEFT OF OUR CAR, OKAY? THAT WAY, TONIGHT'S BODY-COUNT'LL STAY IN SINGLE FIGURES.

YOU ARE GONNA LIKE WORKIN' THE CAULDRON, KID--
BUT YOU'RE GONNA HAVETA GET USED TO IT FIRST.

WE'LL NEVER MATCH THAT THING. CUT THROUGH THE GYM AN' WE'LL GET HIM WHEN HE HITS PECKINPAH...
UH... WE DO THAT?

IN THIS?
POINT.

WE FIVE-OH.
GYM RULES
NO DRUGS SPITTING WIMPS FATTIES
PUMP
GOLDS
AAAII'EEE!!

HNNNHHH!

HNNNHHH!!

I HEREBY CALL THIS MEETING OF GOTHAM'S GREATEST HEROES TO ORDER...

AN' I WANNA APOLOGIZE FER BEIN' LATE, TOO. FRIGGIN' SERVANTS OF EVIL AMBUSHED ME, LEFT ME LYIN' INNA STREET. BASTARDS.
WE'LL START WITH ROLL CALL... *FRIENDLY FIRE?*
WASTE PIPE 63

HERE...
GOOD MAN. *JEAN DE BATON?*

OUI, MON CAPITAINE!
OKEYDOKEY... *FLEMGEM?*

HERE-- *PTOOFF!*

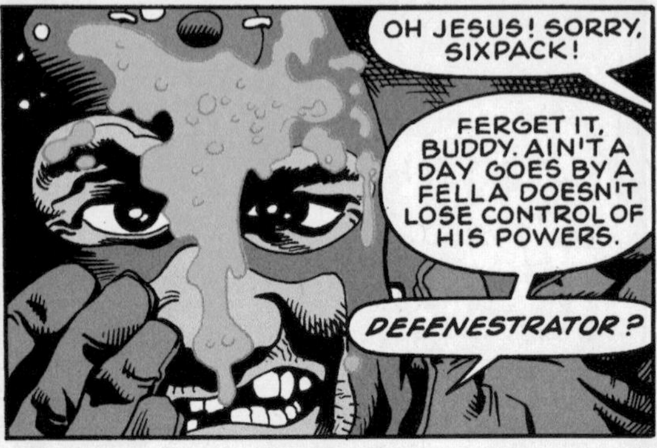
OH JESUS! SORRY, SIXPACK!
FERGET IT, BUDDY. AIN'T A DAY GOES BY A FELLA DOESN'T LOSE CONTROL OF HIS POWERS.
DEFENESTRATOR?

OKAY, WE'LL TAKE THAT AS READ... SHAKES?

FFFFFFUH! FUH! FUH!
DOGWELDER?

FSSSSS
HEY, BUDDY, AND... UH...

BUENO EXCELLENTE?
HEH, HEH, HEH...

BUENO...

UH... RIGHT. AND TOGETHER WE ARE--SECTION EIGHT...
OKAY, FIRST ITEM ONNA AGENDA--
HEY, STOP IT!

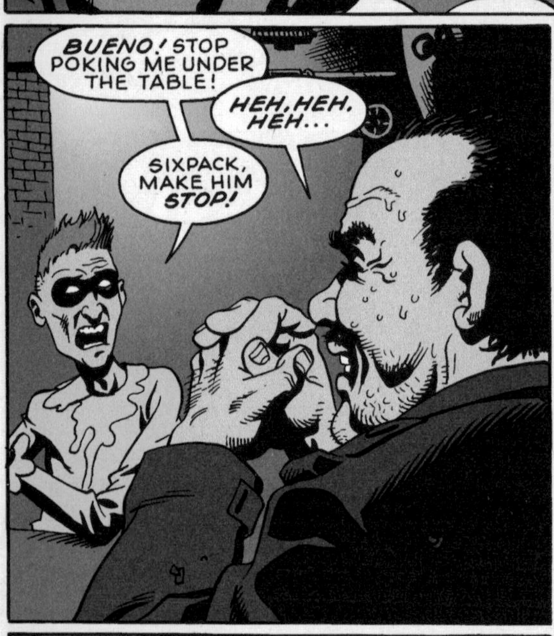
BUENO! STOP POKING ME UNDER THE TABLE!
HEH, HEH, HEH...
SIXPACK, MAKE HIM STOP!

EXCELLENTE...
COME ON, BUENO, SETTLE DOWN!

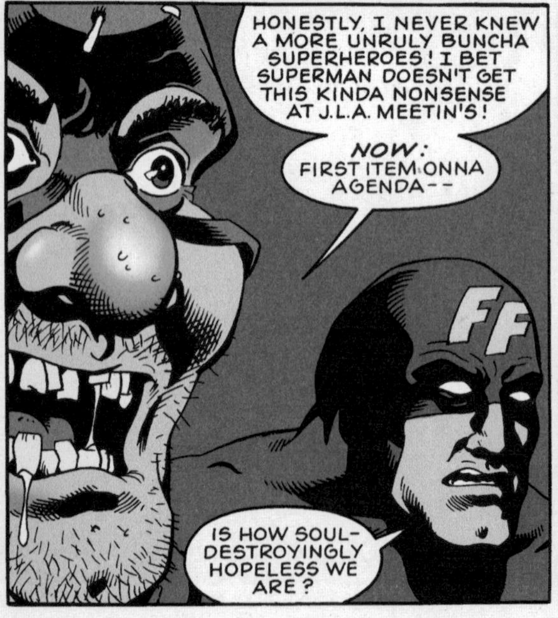
HONESTLY, I NEVER KNEW A MORE UNRULY BUNCHA SUPERHEROES! I BET SUPERMAN DOESN'T GET THIS KINDA NONSENSE AT J.L.A. MEETIN'S!
NOW: FIRST ITEM ONNA AGENDA--
IS HOW SOUL-DESTROYINGLY HOPELESS WE ARE?

SAY WHAT?
WE'RE NOT SUPERHEROES, SIXPACK! WE'RE A BUNCH OF DERANGED BASTARDS!
THIS WHOLE SITUATION IS COMPLETELY AND TOTALLY INSANE...!

LOOK AT US, SIXPACK! WE'RE PATHETIC! WE MEET UP HERE ONCE A MONTH AND TALK COMPLETE HOGWASH ABOUT FIGHTING CRIME, AND WHAT DO WE EVER ACTUALLY DO?

NOTHING!

TAKE ME, FOR INSTANCE: BORN WITH THE AMAZING POWER TO VAPORIZE EVERYTHING IN SIGHT EXCEPT THE ACTUAL TARGET! AND DOGWELDER, WHAT DOES HE DO? HE *WELDS DOGS TO PEOPLE!* NO DOUBT SUPERVILLAINS EVERYWHERE ARE PISSING THEIR PANTS AT THE VERY THOUGHT!

THE DEFENESTRATOR'S A *MENTAL PATIENT,* SHAKES-- *SHAKES,* JEAN HAS A *STICK,* FOR GOD'S SAKE, FLEMGEM SPITS ON PEOPLE-- WHICH I REALLY DON'T THINK IS GOING TO HAVE THE TITANS KNOCKING ON THE DOOR--

AND AS FOR BUENO, WELL, I DON'T KNOW ABOUT YOU, BUT SOMEHOW I CAN'T SEE HIM FIGHTING SIDE BY SIDE WITH *BATMAN AND FRIGGING ROBIN!*

YOU'RE AN ALCOHOLIC, CAN'T YOU SEE THAT? THESE ADVENTURES YOU HAVE, THIS CRIMEFIGHTING BALONEY-- IT ALL HAPPENS IN YOUR HEAD, MAN! IT ISN'T REAL!

THAT... THAT'S NOT TRUE...
CHRRIIISSSTT...!

OH SIXPACK, I'M SORRY. I DON'T MEAN TO BE SO HARSH. I JUST GET SO EXASPERATED WITH THIS--THIS SUPER-FOLLY, WHERE WE WASTE OUR LIVES PRETENDING WE'RE CHANGING THE WORLD...!
I'M TRYING TO SNAP US OUT OF IT, THAT'S ALL. AND LISTEN, SERIOUSLY: IF I'M WRONG, IF WE'RE NOT COMPLETELY DELUSIONAL, IF WE ARE SUPERHEROES--

THEN HOW COME WE'RE EIGHT GROWN MEN IN FANCY DRESS DOWN A SEWER, SITTING ROUND A TABLE, STUCK ON AN ISLAND IN THE MIDDLE OF A LAKE OF TURDS?

PTOOOFFSSHH HOLY CRAP!!

DOCTOR JACKSON?
PROFESSOR HADDOCK, THESE-- THESE NOTES OF YOURS! DO YOU KNOW EXACTLY WHAT IT IS YOU'VE *DONE*?

CREATED A REVOLUTIONARY NEW TECHNOLOGY, OF COURSE.
YES, BUT *HOW*, PROFESSOR? WHAT'S ALL THIS LATIN TEXT PRINTED ON ANCIENT PARCHMENT? AND THIS DIAGRAM MARKED *PARA-GEOMETRICAL LAYOUT OF THE NINE LEVELS OF EVERLASTING DAMNATION*?

AND WHAT ABOUT THIS, *"I PLEDGE MY ETERNAL SOUL TO THE MANY-ANGLED ONES IN RETURN FOR THE BOUNTY OF KNOWLEDGE THAT THEY GRANT ME,"* WITH *YOUR SIGNATURE* AFTER IT?
PROFESSOR HADDOCK, REALLY, SERIOUSLY, *WHO THE HELL ARE THE MANY-ANGLED ONES?!*

CALM YOURSELF, DOCTOR. WE ARE MEN OF SCIENCE.
HEM HUM.

YES... YES, I KNOW THAT, PROFESSOR. BUT SIX MONTHS AGO I NARROWLY AVOIDED BEING DEVOURED BY A TYRANNOSAURUS REX, AND THE SECURITY OF THIS PLANET CURRENTLY LIES WITH A GROUP OF MEN WHO WEAR TIGHTS AND LIVE ON THE MOON.
SO PLEASE, *PLEASE* DON'T THINK I'M BEING FRIVOLOUS WHEN I SAY THERE'S JUST A *TINY* POSSIBILITY THAT YOU *MIGHT HAVE SOLD YOUR SOUL TO THE DEVIL*...
THE DEVIL! REALLY, DOCTOR! WHAT WILL YOU COME UP WITH NEXT!
THE DEVIL OR SOMETHING LIKE THAT, I DON'T KNOW... WHERE DID YOU GET ALL THIS STUFF, ANYWAY?
I INHERITED ALL THESE RESEARCH MATERIALS FROM MY BROTHER KEVIN. NOW, IF THERE'S NOTHING ELSE--
THAT WOULDN'T BE YOUR BROTHER KEVIN WHO MYSTERIOUSLY DISAPPEARED IN 1967, ONLY FOR HIS HIDEOUSLY DISMEMBERED SKELETON TO BE DISCOVERED THIRTY YEARS LATER, WOULD IT?
YES, THAT'S HIM.
OKAY, LET'S GO THROUGH IT...
YOU FIND KEVIN'S NOTES AND YOU FOLLOW THE INSTRUCTIONS TO THE LETTER. YOU DRAW THE *PENTAGRAM*, YOU RECITE THE *INCANTATIONS*, YOU SIGN THE *CONTRACT*--
THEN WHAT HAPPENS?

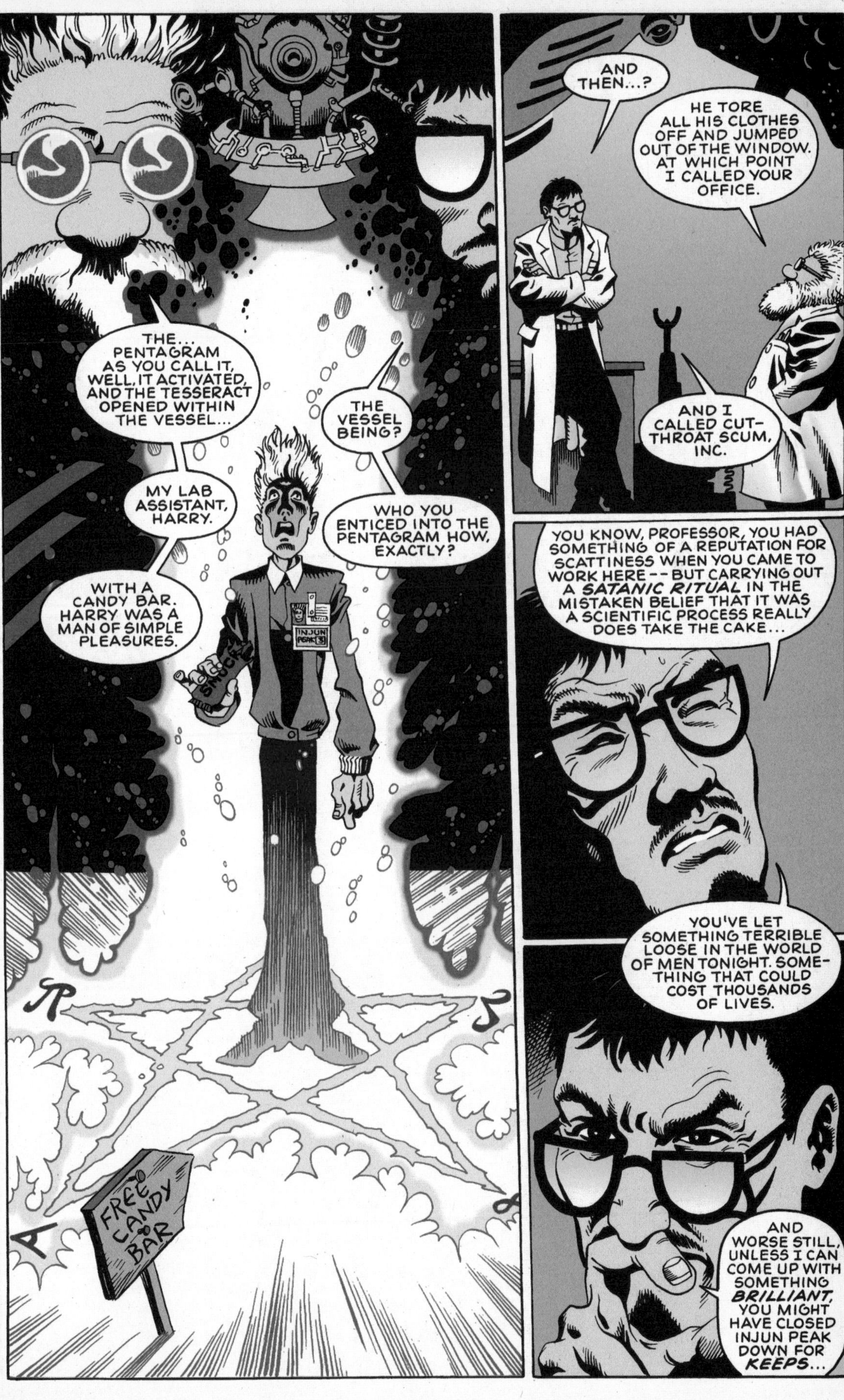
THE... PENTAGRAM AS YOU CALL IT, WELL, IT ACTIVATED, AND THE TESSERACT OPENED WITHIN THE VESSEL...
THE VESSEL BEING?
MY LAB ASSISTANT, HARRY.
WHO YOU ENTICED INTO THE PENTAGRAM HOW, EXACTLY?
WITH A CANDY BAR. HARRY WAS A MAN OF SIMPLE PLEASURES.
INJUN PEAK
FREE CANDY BAR
AND THEN...?
HE TORE ALL HIS CLOTHES OFF AND JUMPED OUT OF THE WINDOW. AT WHICH POINT I CALLED YOUR OFFICE.
AND I CALLED CUT-THROAT SCUM, INC.
YOU KNOW, PROFESSOR, YOU HAD SOMETHING OF A REPUTATION FOR SCATTINESS WHEN YOU CAME TO WORK HERE -- BUT CARRYING OUT A *SATANIC RITUAL* IN THE MISTAKEN BELIEF THAT IT WAS A SCIENTIFIC PROCESS REALLY DOES TAKE THE CAKE...
YOU'VE LET SOMETHING TERRIBLE LOOSE IN THE WORLD OF MEN TONIGHT. SOMETHING THAT COULD COST THOUSANDS OF LIVES.
AND WORSE STILL, UNLESS I CAN COME UP WITH SOMETHING *BRILLIANT*, YOU MIGHT HAVE CLOSED INJUN PEAK DOWN FOR *KEEPS*...

WAY I FIGURE IT, WE OUGHTA COME OUT JUST AHEADA HIM...
COP 9
FLOAT
'3m
HOLY JEEZ!
AAAIIEEE!!

OH MY GOD--
VRRRMM
HEY, RESPECT TO THE BLIMP IN THE HAT!

AAARRRGHH!!
BITE ME, WILL YOU?
WHUNNCHH
KRESSHHH

FELLAS, WAIT! DON'T LET IT END LIKE THIS! DON'T LET THE DREAM DIE!
GIVE IT UP, SIXPACK. IT'S *OVER*, CAN'T YOU SEE THAT?
WE DID OUR BEST, OLD FRIEND...

BUT THE WORLD HAS ALL THE HEROES IT NEEDS.

OH, *NO!* THIS LAST PAGE -- HAVE YOU READ THIS?
EH?
MONAGHAN! WE'VE GOT TO STOP MONAGHAN!
Addendum
the many angled ones will

IF HE KILLS HARRY, ALL BLOODY HELL WILL BREAK LOOSE!!

HAVE YOU SEEN THIS...?
COME, CITIZENS OF GOTHAM!

LET ME FREE YOU FROM THIS EARTHBOUND DRUDGERY! A BETTER WORLD AWAITS! A WORLD BEYOND YOUR IMAGININGS!
STEP THROUGH THIS GATEWAY-- TO FREEDOM!

OH MAN, ENOUGH IS ENOUGH...! PUT THIS FOOL OUTTA HIS MISERY AN' LET'S GO GET A BEER, OKAY?

I SECOND THE MOTION.
BADAMM

OH, *FELLAS*...
YOU KNOW WHO *THIS* LOOKS LIKE A JOB FOR...?

WHAT THE HELL... JUST HAPPENED...?

WELL I... I SHOT THE NAKED GUY, AND...
HE JUST KINDA BLINKED OUT, RIGHT? AIN'T THAT WHAT YOU SAW?
AN' *THEN*...

THEN THERE WAS THAT.

OH MAN, WHAT *IS IT*--!
AT A GUESS?
NOTHING GOOD.

NO.

NOTHING GOOD.
SUPER GUY
part two
ENNIS · WRITER
McCREA · PENCILLER
LEACH · INKER
PRENTICE · LETTERER
FEENY · COLORIST
HEROIC AGE · SEPS
WILLIAMS · ASST. ED.
TOMASI · EDITOR
HITMAN CREATED BY
ENNIS & McCREA
BAGELS A-GO
DELI
PICKLES
TATOOS WHILE U WAIT
I'M DUMB

WE ARE OF THE GAPS BETWEEN THE HELLS. FROM FALLEN ANGELS WE STOLE SACRED GEOMETRY, TWISTED IT AND MADE IT OURS.
GAS
WASH 'N' WAX
CANDY STORE
PUPSI
ECCH-ON
WE ARE THE ARCHITECTS OF THE INFERNO. THE TYRANT KINGS OF RULE AND LINE. THE SCIENCE DEMONS.

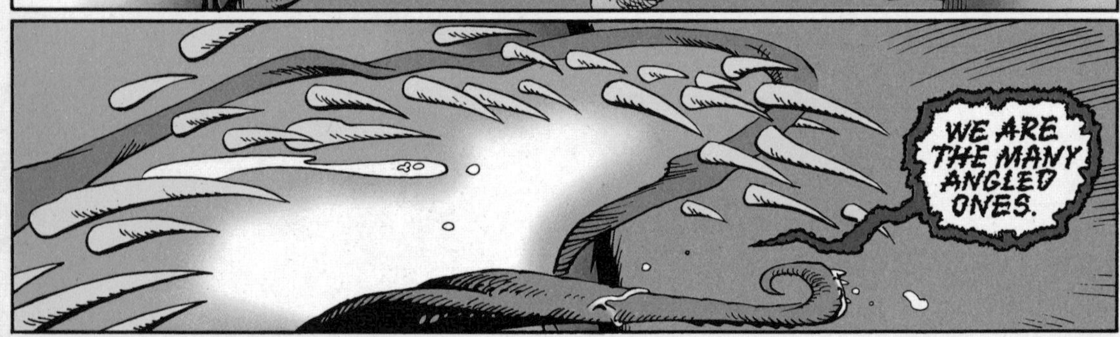
WE ARE THE MANY ANGLED ONES.

WE WERE SUMMONED TO THIS WRETCHED WORLD. WE BARGAINED WITH A HUMAN, AND BOUND OURSELVES TO SERVE HIM.
A VESSEL WAS PROVIDED, TO HOLD OUR POWER WHILE ON THIS PLANET.
OH, NO...
BUT THE VESSEL WAS TORN ASUNDER...
FAP!

AND WE ARE FREE.

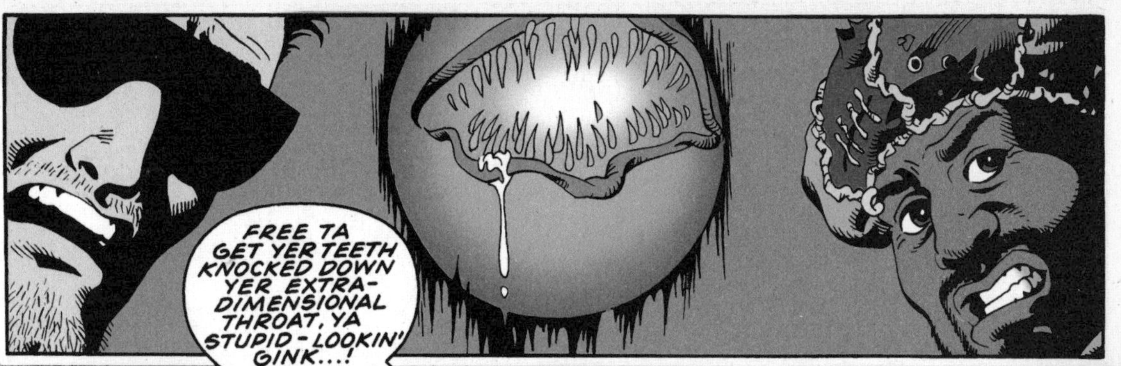
FREE TA GET YER TEETH KNOCKED DOWN YER EXTRA-DIMENSIONAL THROAT, YA STUPID-LOOKIN' GINK...!

SECTION EIGHT GO!!

WHO THE HELL ARE THOSE FREAKS?
SIXPACK, I DUNNO IF THIS IS REALLY SUCH A GOOD IDEA...

WHAT IS THIS?

IT'S THE SENSES-SHATTERIN' CLIMAX, FREAKSHOW! CRIMINALS ARE A COWARDLY, SUPERSTITIOUS LOT--OF BASTARDS!
AND THERE SHALL COME A FRIGGIN' HERO!!
JEAN DE BATON!
LE PAN OU PAIN
FUH-FUH!

PTOOCCH
BRAVO, FLEMGEM, MON AMI! FIRST BLOOD TO US!
SMURD'S

PTOOOFF
FFFSSSS
SACRE CRAP!

YOU HAVE DISSOLVED MY COMRADE, CREATURE OF HELL! A BIENTOT! KNOW THE VENGEANCE OF JEAN DE BATON!
JEAN DE BATON!
JEAN DE BATON-BATON!

KRAK THRUST GRUNNCH
SNAP
KRENCH
POP
AAAAIIIIEEEE!!
AFE

JEAN--!
WHUMMP

THIS IS A FREAKIN' DISASTER!
WHERE THE HELL IS BUENO? HE'S USUALLY BRINGIN' UP THE REAR!

HEH, HEH, HEH...
EXCELLENTE...

ENOUGH OF THIS.

GAH--!
IT GOT DOGWELDER!

SHAKES AND THE DEFENESTRATOR ARE HIT TOO! IT'S ALL DOWN TO YOU, FRIENDLY FIRE!
BUT I--I--

I GOTTA DO IT! JUST THIS ONCE!
GOTTA HIT WHAT I'M AIMIN' AT! CAN'T LET MY BUDDIES DOWN!
MUST HOLD--THE POWER--!

FRZZAAP
CRAP!

FUH! FUH FUH FUH!
SHAKES, WHERE ARE YOU-- WAIT, DEFENESTRATOR! YOU'RE HEADING FOR THE CROWD! THEY'RE INNOCENT!
COME BACK!

WHAT THE--
KRESSH
JEEZ!

I KNOW NOW VY YOO CWY-- BUT IT ISS SOMETHING I CAN NEVAH DOO.

NO!
KRUMMPP

MY TEAM! MY WHOLE TEAM!
WELL, WELL.

ALL ALONE.

WE CAN'T LET IT GET HIM!
ALL WE GOT'S THE NINES--
MONAGHAN!

MONAGHAN, DON'T SHOOT THAT NAKED MADMAN! PROFESSOR HADDOCK HERE CONJURED SOME KIND OF ULTIMATE INTER-DIMENSIONAL EVIL INTO HIM, AND IF HE DIES, IT--
IT--

...NEVER MIND...

JACKSON, YOU SLIMY LITTLE NOSEPICK! YOU SENT US OUT AFTER THAT THING AN' YOU NEVER SAID JACK ABOUT ULTIMATE FREAKIN' EVIL!
WELL I DIDN'T KNOW, DID I? IT'S THIS STUPID OLD FART'S FAULT!
SO ASK HIM HOW TO *STOP IT!*

WE DOESN'T KNOW.
YOU SET US LOOSE, IGNATIUS HADDOCK. WE HAVE SOMETHING FOR YOU.
HEM HUM?

OUR GRATITUDE.
SHLATCH

AND THAT WAS JUST A *FRACTION.*

WE WHO WERE BORN OF HELL SHALL MAKE OF THIS WORLD A MONSTROUS HEAVEN.
WE SHALL GO ON FROM THIS PLACE, UNSTOPPABLE, A CONTINENT FOR EACH OF US. A BILLION SOULS TO SUCK AND SWALLOW, A BILLION MORE TO WASH THEM DOWN.
AN EARTH OF SCREAMING DEAD SHALL WE CREATE, A PLANET WREATHED IN TORMENT, RINGED BY DESPAIR.
AND WE SHALL RULE IN GLORY.
YOU HAVE NO HOPE. YOUR ARMIES WILL BE NOTHING TO US, YOUR RULERS BUT A JOKE.

YOUR SUPER-HUMANS?

HEH... HEH... HEH...

WELL THAT'D SUCK.
FFSSSSSS
JACKSON, HOW DO WE FIGHT THIS--
JACKSON?

SCREW THIS!
YOU FRIGGIN' YELLOW MAGGOT, JACKSON!
INJUN PEAK
MULLIS DNA

F-F-FELLAS? YOU GOT ANY IDEAS AT ALL?

JUST A REALLY LAME ONE, SIXPACK.

WHAT NEW STUPIDITY IS THIS?
WE GOTTA TRY IT, MAN! MAYBE IT'LL CAUSE A RIFT OR SOMETHIN' LIKE THAT!
A RIFT?

YOU BEEN WATCHIN' THE SCI-FI CHANNEL AGAIN WHEN YOU SHOULDA BEEN OUT MEETIN' GIRLS AN' HAVIN' SEX, AM I RIGHT?
BITE ME--

NO!!
FUH FUH FUHH!

GAS
SHAKES, NO! COME BACK, BUDDY!
I DON'T BELIEVE THIS! IT CAN'T BE HAPPENIN'!
WASH 'N' WAX
58¢
FUH FUH FUH FUH FUHH!

YOU PEOPLE GET OUTTA HERE! GO!
RUN, FOOLS!
OH MY GOD, IT'S GONNA BLOW--

GAS
SHAKES, STOP! THROW IT AWAY! SHAKES!
WAX
FUH! FUH FUH FUH!
58¢ GALLON

FFFUUUUU--

ARCUDI'S ARC
DELI
BURGERS
24hr open
LAUNDRY
For the Word OF GOD is quick, and powerful..."
TRINITY CHURCH
NEW CHURCH
JOHN GOURLEY PHARMACIST

LITTLE THING?
WHAT ARE YOU, LITTLE THING?

THE FLAMES WILL NOT TOUCH YOU.
WHAT ARE YOU?

I...I...
SIX PAC

I'M A SUPERHERO.

HAHAHA
HAHAHA
A SUPER-HERO...!

AND YOU WOULD STAND AGAINST US, SUPERHERO? YOU WOULD FIGHT US, THOUGH THE ODDS ARE HOPELESS AND YOUR DOOM BEYOND DOUBT?
YOU WOULD SACRIFICE YOURSELF...?
YEAH!

BUT... WHY?
'CAUSE THAT'S WHAT SUPERHEROES DO.

THEN WE HAVE A BARGAIN FOR YOU...
SUPERHERO...!

COME BACK WITH US. ENTER OUR REALM. TRY YOUR STRENGTH AGAINST US IN A BATTLE FOR YOUR OWN SOUL.
WIN YOUR SALVATION... OR MEET YOUR DAMNATION.
DO THIS NOW, AND WE SHALL SPARE THIS WORLD.

DONE.

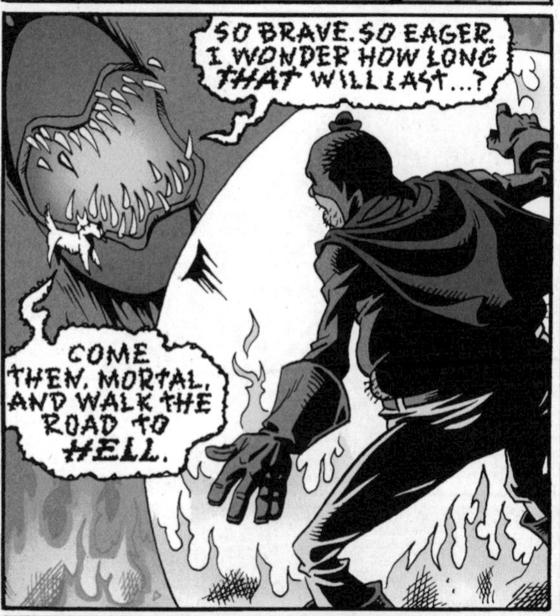
SO BRAVE. SO EAGER. I WONDER HOW LONG THAT WILL LAST...?
COME THEN, MORTAL, AND WALK THE ROAD TO HELL.

S... SIXPACK?

WELL, I... I GUESS THIS IS IT...

BUT ALL GOOD THINGS, HUH, FOLKS?

SIXPAAACKK!!!

THEY... THEY TOOK HIM.
HE JUST *GONE*...
HIS--

HIS LITTLE HAT...!

AAAAAIIIIIEEEEEEEEE

SIXPACK WAS NEVER SEEN IN THE CAULDRON AGAIN.
WEAZLE
NOONAN'S
OCCASIONALLY WORD WOULD REACH NOONAN'S OF A DRUNK PASSED OUT IN THE GUTTER, OR AN ESCAPED MENTAL PATIENT LIVING IN A TRASH CAN, AND THE BOYS WOULD GET THEIR HOPES UP...
BUT IT WOULD ALWAYS TURN OUT TO BE JUST A DRUNK PASSED OUT IN THE GUTTER, OR AN ESCAPED MENTAL PATIENT LIVING IN A TRASH CAN-- AND GRADUALLY THEY REALIZED THAT HE WASN'T COMING BACK.
Gotham Gazette
"GHASTLY INTERNAL INJURIES" CLAIM LIFE OF TOP RESEARCHER
EW BATGIRL SIGHTI
NO MANS LAND BAN LIFTED
HI! I'M BAYTOR!
PERHAPS SIDNEY SPECK, NOW ATTENDING A.A. MEETINGS IN NEW YORK CITY, MIGHT KNOW A THING OR TWO...
MY NAME'S SID, AND I'M AN ALCOHOLIC...
HI, SID!
SID
BUT IF HE DOES, HE ISN'T SAYING.
WHATEVER HIS FATE, THE PEOPLE OF GOTHAM CITY WOULD NEVER FORGET SIXPACK...

HIS BUDDIES SAW TO THAT.
SIXPACK
SUPERHERO AND SAVIOR OF THE WORLD

OF COURSE SHE RAN TO TOMMY.
JUST LIKE SHE ALWAYS DID.
McKIN
CONSTR
Closing Time: 1
GARTH ENNIS WRITER
JOHN McCREA PENCILLER
GARRY LEACH INKER
PAT PRENTICE LETTERER
CARLA FEENY COLORIST
HEROIC AGE SEPARATOR
L.A. WILLIAMS ASST. EDITOR
PETER TOMASI EDITOR
HITMAN CREATED BY ENNIS & McCREA

EVER SINCE THAT BLACK, BLACK NIGHT THE YEAR BEFORE, WHEN HE'D COME TO TELL HER THAT HER SON WAS DEAD, TOMMY'D BEEN MAGGIE'S GUARDIAN ANGEL.

IT HADN'T BEEN HIS FAULT.
IT HAPPENED IN THE BAD DAYS WHEN THE LAW ABANDONED GOTHAM, AND SOME AWFUL THING FROM THE SHADOWS CAME AND CLAIMED LITTLE MICHAEL FOR ITS OWN.
IT WAS PURE BAD LUCK THAT TOMMY'D BEEN TOO LATE...
CONS

BUT TOMMY, BEING TOMMY, FELT RESPONSIBLE.
FOR CRYING OUT LOUD! GET HER!

OH GOD--!
CAB

GO! GO!
JEEZ--!

AW NO, GOD, TELL ME THIS ISN'T HAPPENING...!
3K24

WHEN I CALL THIS IN?
I'M DEAD.

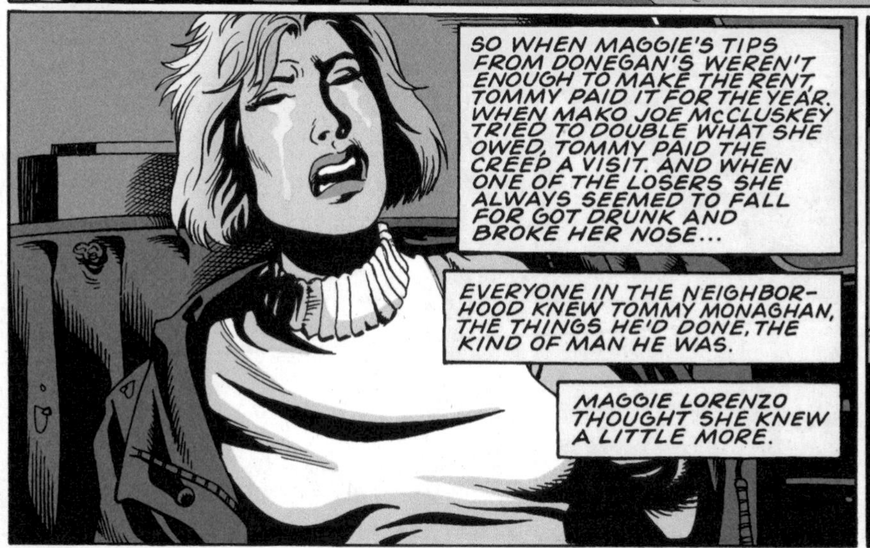
SO WHEN MAGGIE'S TIPS FROM DONEGAN'S WEREN'T ENOUGH TO MAKE THE RENT, TOMMY PAID IT FOR THE YEAR. WHEN MAKO JOE McCLUSKEY TRIED TO DOUBLE WHAT SHE OWED, TOMMY PAID THE CREEP A VISIT. AND WHEN ONE OF THE LOSERS SHE ALWAYS SEEMED TO FALL FOR GOT DRUNK AND BROKE HER NOSE...
EVERYONE IN THE NEIGHBORHOOD KNEW TOMMY MONAGHAN, THE THINGS HE'D DONE, THE KIND OF MAN HE WAS.
MAGGIE LORENZO THOUGHT SHE KNEW A LITTLE MORE.

OF COURSE SHE RAN TO TOMMY.
SHE'D NOWHERE ELSE TO GO.

THE CAR HOLE
SHAKE DOWN
NEW WORLD ORDER
STREET
I HAD THE STRANGEST DAMN DREAM LAST NIGHT...

YOU AN' ME WERE WALKIN' INTO NOONAN'S--
YEAH, LIKE I GOT NOTHIN' BETTER TO DO'N SHOW UP IN YO' STOOPID DREAMS.

NOONANS
HARD HAT AREA
NO TRESPASS
DUE TO MINOR STRUCTURAL WORK NOONANS
OPEN FOR BUSINESS
WELL THAT'S HOW I KNEW IT WAS A DREAM, 'CAUSE YOUR ASS ACTUALLY FIT THROUGH THE DOOR.
SO WE WALK IN, JUST LIKE ALWAYS--

AN' *EVERYONE'S THERE.*
THERE'S A BIG CROWD IN, WHOLE PLACE IS JUMPIN', THEY'RE HAVIN' A REALLY GREAT TIME. THE AIR'S FULLA SMOKE, YOU GOTTA SHOUT TO MAKE YOURSELF HEARD...
SEAN'S BEHIND THE BAR, DOIN' THE WORK OF TEN MEN LIKE HE ALWAYS DID, AN' PAT'S THERE, AN' RINGO--HE LOOKS HAPPY, I MEAN IT'S A TRULY *CLASSIC* NIGHT. AN' BOB MITCHELL, THE BRITISH AIRBORNE GUY, AN' EVEN MY SISTER, FRANCES...

THEY TURN ROUND AN' IT ALL GOES QUIET. AN' THEY'RE SMILIN', PLEASED TO SEE US, AN' SEAN SAYS --
DRINKS ONNA HOUSE, FELLAS. THERE AIN'T NO CLOSIN' TIME.

BUT YOU GOTTA LEAVE YOUR GUNS AT THE DOOR.

TUBORG
HEY, BAYTOR...
I AM BAYTOR...
7 BUSINE
"SINK IT ALL IN PORK BELLIES"
TOP MARK
BY KNOB

HADDA ICE A DUDE LAST NIGHT. SOME FOOL COME AT ME WIT' A UZI.
THERE'S A COINCIDENCE.
ITALIANS AIN'T GONNA LET THIS ONE GO. 'LEAST NOT ANY TIME SOON.

WOULD YOU?
MM. I GUESS I KINDA SHUT THE DOOR BEHIND US THERE, WHAT WITH THE FERETTI WEDDIN'...

NAW, MAN. THERE WAS BENITO, AN' EVEN WIT' OUT HIM THERE WAS MEN'S ROOM LOUIE. DOOR WAS SHUT AN' BOLTED A LONG TIME BACK.
HELL WIT' IT. WHAT YOU DOIN' TODAY, ANYHOW?

GOIN' TO A FUNERAL.
IT'S BEEN A WHILE SINCE THE LAST ONE. I DON'T WANNA GET OUTTA PRACTICE.

OB'S STURMT ODER SCHNEIT, OB DIE SONNE UNS LACHT...
SAINT JACKS

DER TAG GLUHEND HEIB, ODER EISKALT DIE NACHT!
BESTAUBT SIND DIE GESICHTER, DOCH FRO IS UNSER SIEG--JA, UNSER SIEG!!

SO...UH...
GRAMPS' OLD ARMY BUDDIES. THEY FLEW IN FROM SOUTH AMERICA YESTERDAY.
ES RAUSCHT UNSER PANZER, IM STURMWIND DAHIN!!

AUF WIEDERSEHEN, RUDI.
JA, MEIN FREUND. ALL... ALL IST GUT.
UM... THANK YOU FOR COMING TODAY, TOMMY...

'LEAST I COULD DO, MRS. TIEGEL. HE WAS A GOOD OLD GUY.
...WILL YOU EXCUSE ME FOR A MINUTE?

NICE OF HIM TO TAKE TIME OFF FROM A DAY'S MAYHEM, HUH?
SUSAN...

OKAY, RELAX. LITTLE SISTERS DON'T GET TO GIVE LECTURES.
HEY, HOW'S THE ZOO GOING?
IT'S GOOD. I'M ENJOYING IT A LOT.

BUT... YOU'D STILL RATHER BE A COP?

OF COURSE I WOULD.
IT'S BEEN THREE YEARS AND I STILL CAN'T QUITE BELIEVE I'M OFF THE FORCE. I WAKE UP EVERY MORNING AND I REMEMBER--AND THE DAY JUST GOES DOWNHILL FROM THERE. I NEVER HAD *ANYTHING* ELSE IN MY LIFE.
I STILL DON'T.

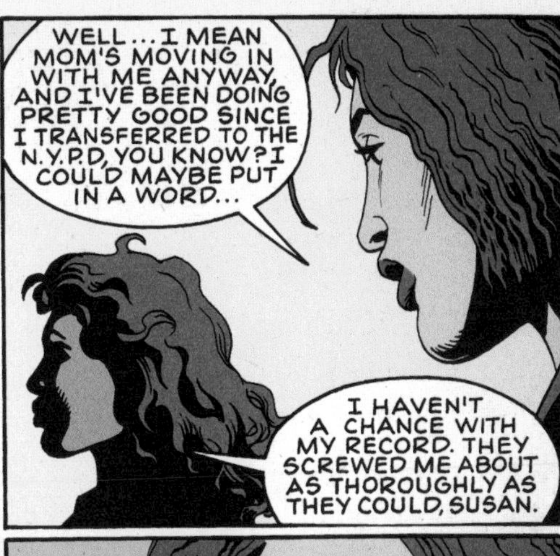
WELL... I MEAN MOM'S MOVING IN WITH ME ANYWAY, AND I'VE BEEN DOING PRETTY GOOD SINCE I TRANSFERRED TO THE N.Y.P.D, YOU KNOW? I COULD MAYBE PUT IN A WORD...
I HAVEN'T A CHANCE WITH MY RECORD. THEY SCREWED ME ABOUT AS THOROUGHLY AS THEY COULD, SUSAN.

I, UH, READ YOUR BOYFRIEND'S FILE BEFORE I CAME UP HERE. I KNOW THE STUFF HE'S INTO, SOME OF THE CONNECTIONS HE'S GOT -- EVEN HOW MANY PEOPLE HE'S --
YOU *SAID* NO LECTURES...
I KNOW I DID.

BUT DID YOU EVER CONSIDER THAT IF YOU TURNED HIM IN, THEY MIGHT JUST GIVE YOU YOUR JOB BACK?

RT NOONAN
-2000
FATHER
HELLO, SISTER CONCEPTA.
OUR SON

HELLO, TOMMY.
I THOUGHT IT WAS YOU.

I DON'T KNOW WHAT I'M BRINGING HIM FLOWERS FOR. DID YOU EVER KNOW HIM TO LOOK AT A FLOWER IN HIS WHOLE LIFE ?
HMH.
'LEAST YOU CAME. I'VE BEEN A JERK ABOUT IT, YOU KNOW, BUSY WITH STUPID STUFF...

SO I'VE BEEN READING.
THAT WAS A BAD BUSINESS AT THAT WEDDING. AN AWFUL, TERRIBLE BUSINESS.

HE WAS THE GREATEST GUY I EVER KNEW IN MY WHOLE LIFE, CONNIE. HE DIED TRYNNA SAVE ME FROM THOSE ANIMALS.
I SET THINGS RIGHT THE ONLY WAY I KNEW HOW.

YOU SET THINGS RIGHT.

THERE WERE *CHILDREN* IN THAT CHURCH, TOMMY.
THEY SAW THEIR FATHERS DIE IN A HAIL OF BULLETS. THEY'LL GROW UP THINKING THAT'S THE WAY THE WORLD WORKS.

THAT'S THE LESSON YOU'RE TEACHING, EVERY TIME YOU SOLVE YOUR PROBLEMS WITH GUNS.

HE WAS A GREAT MAN, WASN'T HE, CONNIE?

HE WAS JUST A *MAN*, TOMMY.
Saint Jack

HE WASN'T A GREAT MAN, OR A GOOD MAN, OR SOME KIND OF A SAINT. HE DID SOME DECENT THINGS AND HE DID SOME EVIL THINGS.

HE KILLED PEOPLE.
SOME-TIMES FOR HIS COUNTRY, SOMETIMES FOR MONEY. ONCE OR TWICE JUST TO HELP HIS FRIENDS.
HE DID WHAT HE THOUGHT HE HAD TO. HE WAS NO BETTER AND NO WORSE THAN A LOT OF PEOPLE WHO'VE WALKED THIS EARTH.

HE WAS JUST A MAN.

AND I LOVED HIM MORE THAN GOD ALMIGHTY.

WHO'S LAUGHING NOW
MENU

TOMMY ?

IT WAS *HUMAN*, TOMMY.
MAGGIE...?
IT WAS A HUMAN BEING BUT IT TORE HIS THROAT OUT WITH ITS *TEETH*--

PETERSON ? COLLINS. WE'RE AT THE CORNER OF SAINT AND PECKINPAH AND I THINK WE'VE GOT LORENZO, SHE'S JUST GONE INTO A BAR...
OUT-STANDING!
WANT US TO TAKE HER ?

NO, JUST MAKE SURE SHE STAYS THERE. THE REST OF US ARE ON OUR WAY.
ANOTHER FIASCO LIKE LAST NIGHT AND I AM DEFINITELY DEAD...

I RAN, I-I'M SORRY, I DIDN'T MEAN TO-- I MEAN I HID IN THE PARK ALL DAY, I DIDN'T WANT TO MOVE AROUND 'TIL DARK--
EASY, KID. GET SOME OF THIS INSIDE YOU.

SO... WHO GOT THEIR THROAT TORN OUT, EXACTLY?

OLD MAN DONEGAN.
ON THE FLOOR OF HIS OWN BAR.

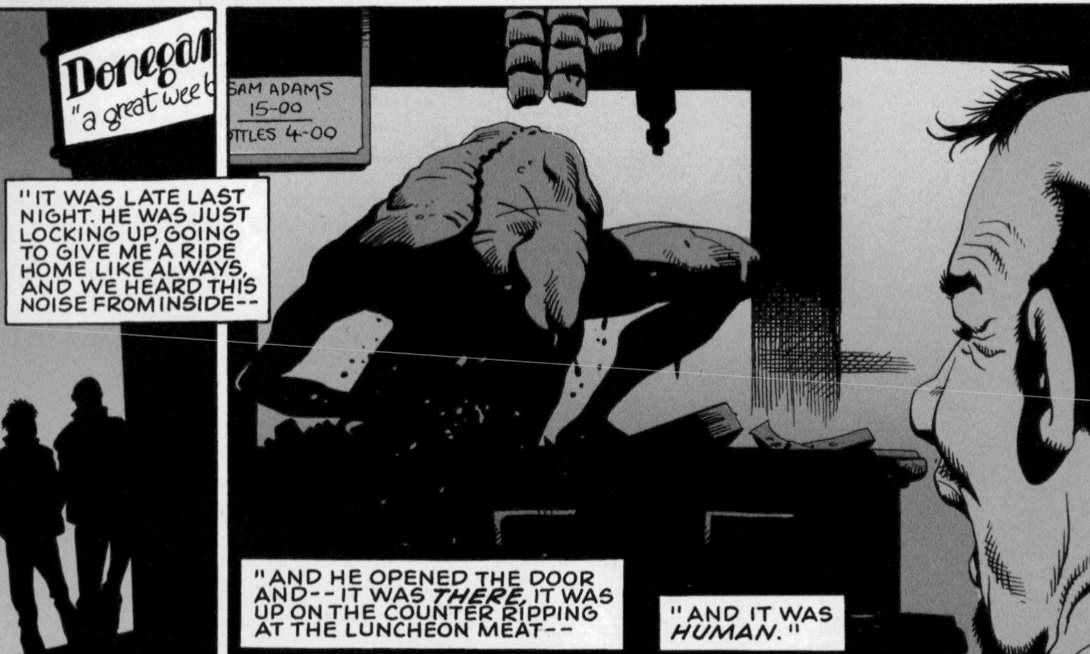
SAM ADAMS
15-00
TTLES 4-00
"IT WAS LATE LAST NIGHT. HE WAS JUST LOCKING UP, GOING TO GIVE ME A RIDE HOME LIKE ALWAYS, AND WE HEARD THIS NOISE FROM INSIDE--
"AND HE OPENED THE DOOR AND-- IT WAS *THERE*, IT WAS UP ON THE COUNTER RIPPING AT THE LUNCHEON MEAT--
"AND IT WAS *HUMAN*."

AAAARRRR
WAAAH--!

HKKK
GRRONCH
SHRRRRRP
RRTTTCHH
AAAIIIEEEE!

...OH GOD.
OH NO. OH PLEASE NO.
RRRRRRR

BADAMM

THEY BLEW ITS BRAINS OUT, TOMMY. THERE WAS GREY STUFF AND BITS OF SKULL EVERYWHERE, THE SIDE OF ITS HEAD WAS GONE--I'M TELLING YOU, I SAW IT--
THEN THEY WERE ALL AROUND ME.

BAR
...SAY AGAIN, SIR, OUR RUNNER IS DOWN. EMERGENCY OVER, WE'RE PREPARING TO CLEAN UP AND CLEAR OUT...
OLD MAN'S DEAD.
WHAT ABOUT THE WOMAN?

SHE'S SEEN IT, HASN'T SHE?

POINT.

RRRAAAARRRR

FOR GOD'S SAKE GET IT--
BLAM BLAM
BADAMM BLAM

BLOW IT APART! FINISH THE BASTARD!!

OH GOD! AFTER HER! NOW!
"BUT I WAS GONE."

I AM SO SORRY, I DIDN'T KNOW WHAT ELSE TO DO OR WHERE ELSE TO GO OR--
WHOA, MAGGIE, SLOW DOWN...

TOMMY, PLEASE DON'T *LEAVE ME*--!
LEAVE HER.

THE STUPID BITCH IS COMING WITH US.

WE DON'T GIVE A CRAP ABOUT YOU BOZOS. YOU STAY BACK AND SHUT UP AND WE'LL BE OUT OF HERE BEFORE YOU KNOW IT, AND YOU CAN ALL GO BACK TO SWILLING YOUR HORSEPISS.
JUST THINK OF THIS AS YOUR LUCKY NIGHT.

TALK ABOUT THE *WRONG* BAR...!

I AM BAYTOR!!
YOU CAN SAY THAT AGAIN.
GIMME A SECOND HERE...
CIGARS
BEEBEEP BEEBEEP BEEBEEP

SO WHO THESE FOOLS S'POSED TO BE, ANYHOW?
LET'S JUST SEE--
BEEBEEP KLIK

YEAH?
PETERSON?
YEAH.

THIS IS MR. TRUMAN, GROWING LESS PATIENT BY THE MINUTE. I TAKE IT YOU'VE SECURED THE LORENZO WOMAN?
CENTRAL... INTELLIGENCE... AGENCY.

COULD THAT BE THE C.I.A.?

PETERSON?
PETERSON...

THIS IS TOMMY MONAGHAN.
AGENT TRUMAN.

...MR. MONAGHAN. WELL, WELL.
AND PETERSON?
GUESS.

OH DEAR. SO, TO WHAT DO I OWE THE--
DROP DEAD, TRUMAN. GET YOUR IDIOTS OUT OF THE CAULDRON. CRAWL BACK IN YOUR HOLE.
EVEN ONE OF YOUR MAGGOTS COMES NEAR MAGGIE LORENZO--

I SWEAR TO GOD I'LL FEED YOUR ASS TO THE WOLVES.

IT'S GOING TO BE A BOY.

MISS BUNKER, WOULD YOU CALL OUR YOUNG FRIEND IN MIAMI FOR ME, PLEASE?
YES, MR. TRUMAN.
THANK YOU.

MR. MONAGHAN.
YES.

BLOODLINES
[MOST SECRET]
I'VE BEEN MEANING TO KILL YOU FOR SOME TIME.

TOMMY MONAGHAN? I'M KATHRYN McALLISTER.
NOONAN'S SLEAZY BAR

I ONCE SICCED A SUPERHERO ON YOU.
I HOPE THERE'S NO HARD FEELINGS.
Closing Time:2
GARTH ENNIS - writer
JOHN McCREA - penciller
GARRY LEACH - inker
CARLA FEENY - colorist
HEROIC AGE - separation
LA WILLIAMS - asst. editor
PETER TOMASI - editor
HITMAN created by ENNIS/McCREA

...COME AGAIN?

NO, WAIT, I REMEMBER. YOU'RE ONE OF TRUMAN'S PEOPLE. YOU'RE HARDCORE C.I.A.
NO HARD FEELINGS.
KLIK

YOU KEEP POINTING THAT THING IF IT MAKES YOU FEEL COMFORTABLE. BUT WE NEED TO TALK.
WE DO?
I *WAS* ONE OF TRUMAN'S OUTFIT. BUT I HAVE MY LIMITS.

AND KILLING AN INNOCENT LIKE MAGGIE LORENZO-- MAYBE STARTING SOME-THING A THOUSAND TIMES WORSE-- GOES WAY, WAY BEYOND THEM.

GOT A LIGHT?

I'M SUPPOSED TO BELIEVE YOU QUIT THE COMPANY?
THANK YOU.
MM-HMM.

IS THERE SOMEWHERE ELSE WE CAN TALK, OUT OF SIGHT OF THE STREET?
HOLD ON A SECOND--
THE BACK ROOM'LL DO. AND BRING MAGGIE.

IT'S ONLY FAIR SHE SHOULD BE THERE.
IT'S HER LIFE WE'RE TRYING TO SAVE.

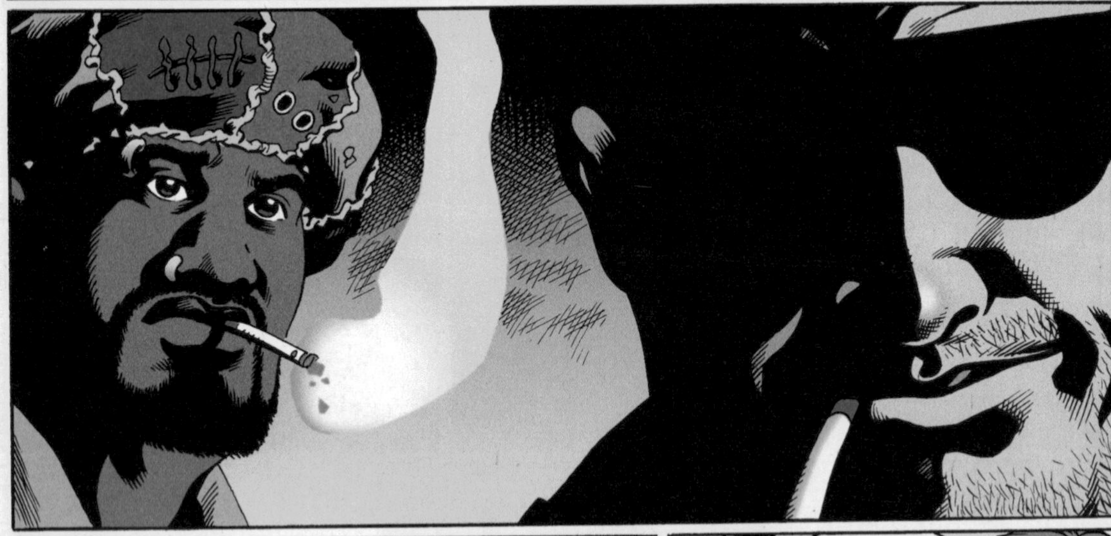

SO THAT WAS YOU SET THE GREEN SUPERGOOF ON ME?
NOTHING PERSONAL.
AN' YOU *REALLY TOLD HIM*--I ALWAYS THOUGHT YOU WERE THE SUPEREST HERO?

COULDN'T RESIST.

BLAM
BLAM
BLAM
BLAM

BLAM
BLAM
BLAM
BLAM

BLAM
BLAM
BLAM
BLAM

BLAM
BLAM
BLAM
BLAM

BLAM
BLAM
BLAM
KLIK
KLAK
HE DOESN'T EVEN *LOOK?*
BLAM
BLAM
BLAM
BLAM
JUST ONCE.
AFTER THAT HE REMEMBERS.
BLAM BLAM
BLAM BLAM
HELLO, MR. TRUMAN.

HELLO, MARC. GOOD FLIGHT?
YES, THANK YOU.
AND KEEPING YOUR HAND IN, I SEE.

JUST WARMING UP.
I'M ANXIOUS TO BEGIN WORK, SIR. THE KIND OF ASSIGNMENTS YOU'VE TALKED ABOUT ARE JUST WHAT I'VE BEEN WAITING FOR.
OF COURSE, MY BOY. BUT FIRST WE'D LIKE TO CONTINUE OBSERVING YOUR PRACTICE.

AND... IF IT'S NOT TOO MUCH OF AN IMPOSITION...?

BE MY GUEST.

TRUMAN'S INITIAL BRIEF...
WHICH I PERSONALLY BELIEVE HAS BECOME HIS OBSESSION, WAS THE MANIPULATION AND CONTROL OF METAHUMAN LIFE ON EARTH.
LAST YEAR, WHEN GOTHAM WENT TO PIECES, HE BEGAN MOVING MASSIVE RESOURCES INTO A HIDDEN LOCATION IN THE CITY. NO MAN'S LAND WAS THE PERFECT COVER FOR HIM.
HE'S ATTEMPTING TO REOPEN A FILE THE AGENCY ITSELF OFFICIALLY TERMINATED. FOR THEM TO DO THAT, A FILE MUST BE EITHER USELESS OR SO UTTERLY LETHAL THAT EVEN *THEY* DAREN'T RISK ITS APPLICATION.
THIS ONE IS THE LATTER.
IT'S REFERRED TO ONLY AS *BLOOD-LINES*.
SOME YEARS AGO A RACE OF ALIEN PARASITES ARRIVED ON EARTH AND ATTEMPTED TO ERADICATE ALL INDIGENOUS LIFE AS A PRELUDE TO COLONIZATION. IN THIS THEY WERE DULY DEFEATED.
MOST OF THEIR VICTIMS DIED. FOR ABOUT ONE IN A THOUSAND, HOWEVER, THE ALIENS' BODILY ASSAULT TRIGGERED A REACTION ON A BASIC GENETIC--
I *KNOW*.

WELL, ANYWAY. THE RESULT WAS A COMPLETELY NEW GENERATION OF SUPERPOWERED HUMAN BEINGS...
YOU MEAN LIKE WHATSIZNAME? AN' THAT OTHER GUY?
THAT'S THEM.

HIM TOO.
WHAT?
WHAT'S NOT GENERALLY KNOWN IS THAT TISSUE SAMPLES WERE TAKEN FROM THE ALIENS' INERT BODIES...

AND THE RESULTING RESEARCH INTO THE POSSIBILITY OF GROW-YOUR-OWN SUPERHEROES BECAME THE BLOODLINES FILE.
THE OBVIOUS DANGER OF SPARKING A SECOND, EVEN MORE VIRULENT PARASITE ATTACK WAS ENOUGH TO RENDER THE FILE INACTIVE. BUT THEN, OF COURSE, TRUMAN GOT HIS HANDS ON IT.

THE MAN WHO KILLED YOUR BOSS, MAGGIE--THE MAN YOU THEN SAW EXECUTED BY A C.I.A. HIT-TEAM--WAS PART OF TRUMAN'S CURRENT WORK ON THE PROJECT.
BUT IT... HE WAS LIKE SOME KIND OF WILD ANIMAL, NOT A SUPER-HERO...!
OUT OF ORDER

NO.
BUT HE MIGHT'VE BEEN TRUMAN'S FIRST GO AT ONE.

AW, I DUNNO 'BOUT THIS...!
THIS ALIEN CRAP WORKS ON PEOPLE, NATT. I'M LIVIN' PROOF.
SO YOU THINK TRUMAN'S TRYNNA... WHAT, MAKE THE PARASITE THING WORK IN A LAB?
I'M NOT SURE OF THE EXACT PROCESS. BUT HE'S TRYING IT.

SO WHY DIDN'T SOMEBODY STOP HIM?
TAKING TRUMAN DOWN INTERNALLY WOULD'VE BEEN NEXT TO IMPOSSIBLE. HE'S OLD-SCHOOL C.I.A.; HE'S BEEN PLAYING THE GAME FOR FORTY YEARS.

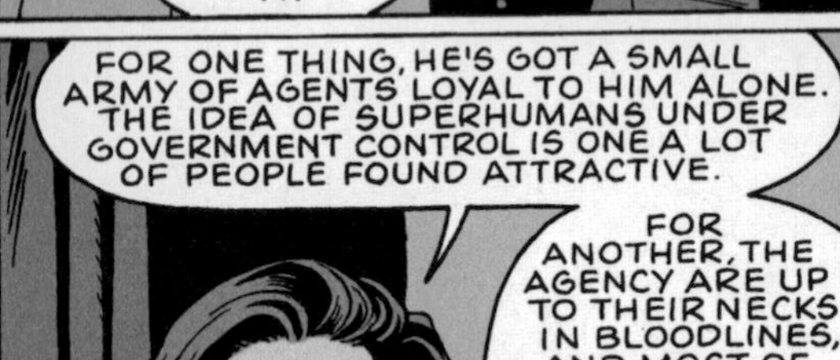
FOR ONE THING, HE'S GOT A SMALL ARMY OF AGENTS LOYAL TO HIM ALONE. THE IDEA OF SUPERHUMANS UNDER GOVERNMENT CONTROL IS ONE A LOT OF PEOPLE FOUND ATTRACTIVE.
FOR ANOTHER, THE AGENCY ARE UP TO THEIR NECKS IN BLOODLINES, AND MOST OF TRUMAN'S OTHER LITTLE ENDEAVORS INTO THE BARGAIN. THEY CAN'T RISK ANY OF IT COMING OUT IN THE WASH.

AND NOT JUST THE AGENCY. SOME OF THE SIGNATURES I'VE SEEN IN THOSE FILES... WELL.
MONICA-GATE WOULD BE A JOKE.

THEY WERE TOO SCARED TO STOP HIM, MAGGIE. AND IT'S TOO LATE NOW, ANYWAY.
TRUMAN IS SAFELY ENSCONCED IN A SECRET LOCATION IN GOTHAM, SURROUNDED BY GUNS, NEXT TO UNTOUCHABLE, MESSING AROUND WITH A BIOLOGICAL PROCESS THAT COULD WIPE OUT LIFE ON THIS PLANET.
IN THE MEANTIME, HE'S MAKING A START WITH YOU.

AN' WHAT'S YO' STORY, EXACTLY?
I'VE BEEN ON OVERSEAS OPS THE LAST YEAR OR SO. WHEN I RETURNED TO D.C. I FOUND TRUMAN HAD LEFT ME OUT OF THE LOOP.

I WAS QUIETLY HACKING MY WAY BACK IN YESTERDAY, FINDING OUT THE STUFF I'VE BEEN TELLING YOU, AND I WAS JUST PICKING MY JAW OFF THE FLOOR WHEN I FOUND THREE CROSSLINKED NOTES IN TRUMAN'S PRIVATE FILES:
THE BREACH IN BLOODLINES SECURITY FROM THE NIGHT BEFORE... A CALL FROM ONE TOMMY MONAGHAN... AND A LOOSE END CALLED MAGGIE LORENZO.

THEN I REALIZED I'D TRIPPED AN ALARM IN THE SYSTEM, AND I HAD TO SHOOT MY WAY OUT OF THE PENTAGON.

YOU SAW TOO MUCH, MAGGIE. MORE THAN ENOUGH FOR TRUMAN TO HAVE YOU TERMINATED.

BUT TO ME THAT'S COMPLETELY UNACCEPTABLE.

TWO QUESTIONS. ONE: WHERE DO WE GO FROM HERE?

WELL, THE LOCAL COPS ARE NO GOOD, TRUMAN'LL HAVE THEM IN HIS POCKET BY NOW. EITHER THAT, OR THE AGENCY'LL PUT ENOUGH PRESSURE ON THEM TO STAY WELL CLEAR. YOU CAN'T UNDERESTIMATE HOW HIGH THIS GOES, THE KIND OF PEOPLE WHO CAN'T AFFORD TO HAVE IT COME OUT...
BUT I HAVE SOME MEDIA CONTACTS, AND I KNOW SOME PEOPLE AT THE F.B.I. WOULD *LOVE* TO SCREW THEIR PENTAGON PALS WITH THIS. I'LL NEED SOME TIME TO SEE WHAT I CAN PUT TOGETHER.

AS I REMEMBER, YOU HAVE SOME DIRT ON TRUMAN FROM LAST TIME, DON'T YOU? TAPES AND PICTURES, RIGHT?

QUESTION TWO: WHY THE HELL SHOULD WE TRUST YOU, ANYWAY?

I ALREADY KINDA WARNED HIM...
I'LL TAKE A LOOK AT IT. MAYBE IT'LL BUY US SOME BREATHING SPACE.

BUY ME LUNCH.
Duff Be
IN ALL ITS G

CONEY'S BAR
YOU REALLY KNOW HOW TO SHOW A GIRL A GOOD TIME, DON'T YOU?

HEY, CORNED BEEF HOT PLATE FOR A BUCK FIFTY. YOU DON'T TURN YOUR NOSE UP AT THAT.
YOU WANT YOUR CABBAGE?
KNOCK YOURSELF OUT.

YOU KNOW, THIS IS SOME PRETTY GOOD STUFF YOU'VE GOT HERE. ASSOCIATING WITH A KNOWN KILLER, THREATS OF TORTURE... AT ONE POINT HE EVEN TALKS ABOUT ASSASSINATING SUPERMAN...
AT ANY OTHER TIME WE COULD PROBABLY BURY HIM WITH THIS.

BUT...?
THE WAY HE'S SET UP NOW, THE LITTLE CREEP'S ALL BUT BULLETPROOF. THE AGENCY WOULD CRAP THEMSELVES OVER A SCANDAL LIKE THIS ONE.

I DOUBT TRUMAN WOULD EVEN BLINK.

YOU'RE QUITE A CHARACTER, AIN'T YOU? HERE I AM LETTIN' YOU IN ON ALLA THIS, AN' YOU STILL AIN'T GIVEN ME JACK...
I HAVE MY MOMENTS.

WHAT DO YOU WANT TO KNOW, ANYWAY? THAT I'M HEARTILY SICK OF COMPANY WORK? THAT KILLING FOR MY COUNTRY HAS SOMEHOW LOST ITS SPARKLE, AND TRUMAN'S LEFT ME OUT IN THE COLD BECAUSE HE THINKS I'M ALL USED UP?
COME ON, THERE'S NOTHING I CAN SAY THAT'LL *MAKE YOU* TRUST ME...

POINT.
I MIGHT KNOW A LITTLE BIT ABOUT WHAT YOU MEAN THOUGH.
I'D BE PRETTY SURPRISED IF YOU DIDN'T. I'VE READ YOUR FILE, REMEMBER?

OH, THERE'S STUFF THAT'S NOT IN THE FILE...

WELL, WELL, ***WELL***.

YOU TWO MAGGOTS SHOULD NEVERA LEFT THAT OTHER DUMP. I PICKED YOU UP STRAIGHTAWAY.
TRUMAN SAYS YOU'RE *MINE,* McALLISTER. OH, I AM LOOKIN' FORWARD TO SPENDIN' SOME TIME ALONE WITH YOU...
C.I.A. AGENT BOLD

OKAY, LET'S GO. HE'S WAITIN' FOR US.
LET'S *GO,* I SAID...!
C.I.A. AGENT BOLD

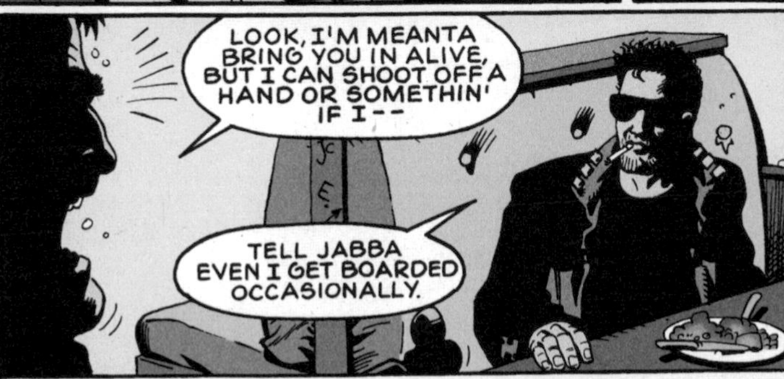
LOOK, I'M MEANTA BRING YOU IN ALIVE, BUT I CAN SHOOT OFF A HAND OR SOMETHIN' IF I--
TELL JABBA EVEN I GET BOARDED OCCASIONALLY.

WHAT?

BADAMM

HEY, MEL, SORRY ABOUT--
THE MESS, YEAH. I KNOW, TOMMY.
'FRAID I AIN'T GOT TIME TO CLEAN IT UP...
ONNA HOUSE.
the front page
Department of Corrections
Baldy Award fever!
BEEBEEP BEEBEEP BEEBEEP

I SEE THAT.
I GOT A WEIRD FEELIN' THIS MIGHT BE FOR ME...
Joey Connie
BEEBEEP BEEBEEP BEEBEEP

TRUMAN, YOU NOSEPICK. ASK ME HOW I GUESSED.

MR. MONAGHAN.
YOU GOTTA START HIRIN' SOME BETTER HELP...
OH, I CAN SPARE THE OCCASIONAL OAF, IF ONLY TO MAKE A POINT.

MY RESOURCES ARE UTTERLY LIMITLESS. I HOPE YOU'RE AWARE OF THAT. AND I'M IGNORING YOUR THREAT OF BLACK-MAIL; MY CURRENT CIRCUMSTANCES HAVE RENDERED IT MEANINGLESS.
THERE'S A VIDEOTAPE IN THE CRETIN'S POCKET.

GOODBYE, MR. MONAGHAN.
WE WON'T SPEAK AGAIN.

ALL THOSE WASTED YEARS FIGHTING FOR LAW AND ORDER, WHEN I COULD'VE BEEN LUXURIATING IN AN ILL-GOTTEN PALACE LIKE THIS ONE...

IT USETA BELONG TO A FRIENDA MINE. I AIN'T HERE THAT OFTEN.
ANYWAY, WHAT WERE YOU EXPECTIN'? MAYBE SOME ROOM SERVICE AN' A HOT TUB?
YOU WISH.
PETE'S PIZZA
DELIVERED HOT
5 MUSIC VIDEOS FOR $1

WHAT HAVE WE GOT HERE...?
BLAM BLAM BLAM BLAM

BLAM BLAM BLAM BLAM

BLAM BLAM BLAM BLAM
?

THIS MEAN ANYTHING TO YOU?
I DUNNO, I...
BLAM BLAM BLAM BLAM

DO I KNOW HIM?
VERY GOOD, MARC. CAN WE GET A LOOK AT YOUR TARGET, PLEASE?

THAT'S TRUMAN SPEAKING.
THANK YOU.

WOULD YOU INDULGE ME FOR A MOMENT, MARC? WOULD YOU TURN TO CAMERA AND CLEARLY STATE YOUR FATHER'S NAME?
JOHNNY NAVARONE.

THANK YOU.
WE WON'T DISTURB YOUR PRACTICE ANY LONGER.

OH... CHRIST...
WHAT'S WRONG? DO YOU KNOW HIM?

I KNEW HIS OLD MAN. I FRIGGIN' KILLED HIS OLD MAN.
JOHNNY NAVARONE WAS GREASED WHITE LIGHTNIN', BUT THIS LITTLE BASTARD LOOKS LIKE HE'S EVEN BETTER-- HOLY CRAP, ARE WE IN TROUBLE NOW...!

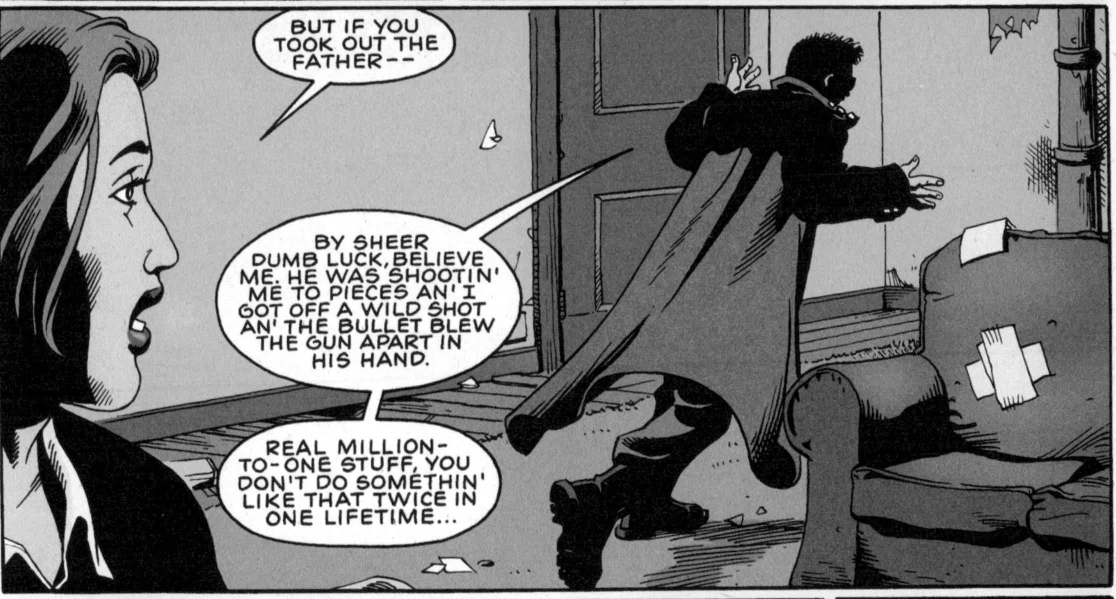
BUT IF YOU TOOK OUT THE FATHER--
BY SHEER DUMB LUCK, BELIEVE ME. HE WAS SHOOTIN' ME TO PIECES AN' I GOT OFF A WILD SHOT AN' THE BULLET BLEW THE GUN APART IN HIS HAND.
REAL MILLION-TO-ONE STUFF, YOU DON'T DO SOMETHIN' LIKE THAT TWICE IN ONE LIFETIME...

WELL THAT'S JUST WONDERFUL, DAMN IT ALL TO HELL, THAT IS JUST WHAT I FREAKIN' NEED--!
WAIT A SECOND--

THERMITE!

SON OF A BITCH, IT'S IN THE TAPE!
MOVE!!

MOVE, YOU IDIOT!!

HOLY CRAP!!

DAMMIT--!

AAAAH--!
HNNGGHH!

SO HEY.

DO YOU TRUST ME?

NNNGGHHH

GAHHH--!

JESUS--
HOLY--
JESUS--

YOU DO THINGS LIKE THIS WHEN YOU'RE INCHES FROM DEATH.

ACTUALLY--
THERE'S NO BETTER TIME.

McCREA
2000

Closing Time: 3

GARTH ENNIS WRITER	JOHN McCREA PENCILLER	GARRY LEACH INKER	PAT PRENTICE LETTERER	CARLA FEENY COLORIST	HEROIC AGE COLOR SEPS	PETER TOMASI EDITOR	HITMAN CREATED BY ENNIS & McCREA

I WAS THE KID IN SCHOOL WHO WAS SMART BUT NEVER TRIED, WHO WAS TOUGH BUT NEVER FOUGHT, WHO SURVIVED BECAUSE THE BIG KIDS LIKED HIS JOKES AN' THE LITTLE KIDS WERE EASIER MEAT THAN HE WAS.
I WAS IN YOUR CLASS. YOU REMEMBER ME.
GIGS

I WAS A NIGHTMARE TO THE TEACHERS.
--MONAGHAN YOU'RE BRIGHT YOU'VE GOT IMAGINATION IF YOU'D SPEND HALF THE EFFORT WORKING THAT YOU DO GOOFING OFF AND DAYDREAMING YOU COULD MAKE SOMETHING OF YOURSELF ONE DAY--

AN' I WOULDN'T...

AN' I DIDN'T.

AN' NEITHER DID STEVIE KELLY, WHO I SAT BESIDE IN MATH CLASS, WHO'S BEEN TRYNNA BLOW MY HEAD OFF SINCE I WANDERED IN HERE A MINUTE AGO FOR A DRINK AN' A THINK--
SLOW, TOMMY!

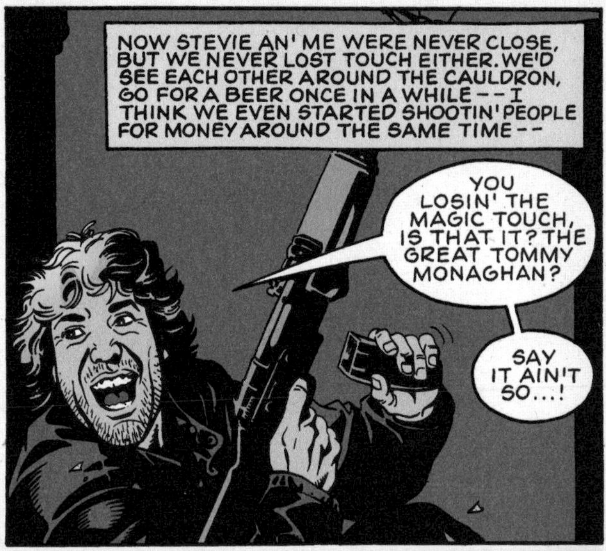
NOW STEVIE AN' ME WERE NEVER CLOSE, BUT WE NEVER LOST TOUCH EITHER. WE'D SEE EACH OTHER AROUND THE CAULDRON, GO FOR A BEER ONCE IN A WHILE--I THINK WE EVEN STARTED SHOOTIN' PEOPLE FOR MONEY AROUND THE SAME TIME--
YOU LOSIN' THE MAGIC TOUCH, IS THAT IT? THE GREAT TOMMY MONAGHAN?
SAY IT AIN'T SO...!

AN' I GOTTA TELL YOU, I NEVER FIGURED STEVIE FOR A GUY WOULD TURN ON A FRIEND, WOULD DO IT IN A CROWDED BAR WITH AN A.K. SET ON FULL AUTO--
BUT THE MOB'S GOT A TWO MIL OPEN CONTRACT ON MY HEAD, AN' I GUESS THAT DID THE TRICK.
IT MAKES ME SAD, THAT KINDA THING. NOT PISSED.

WHAT MAKES ME PISSED IS THE SADIST WHO PUT BRITNEY SPEARS ON THE MOTHERLOVIN' JUKEBOX--

OH, WELL DON'T EVERYBODY THANK ME AT ONCE!
HA!!

YOU ALWAYS WAS A COMEDIAN, TOMMY! I'M GONNA MISS YOU!

I KNOW YOU ARE, STEVIE.

I KNOW YOU ARE.

SOME OF THEM STARTED CHEWING THROUGH THEIR TONGUES LAST NIGHT. I HAD TO HAVE THEM FITTED WITH BITS.
HOW CHARMING...

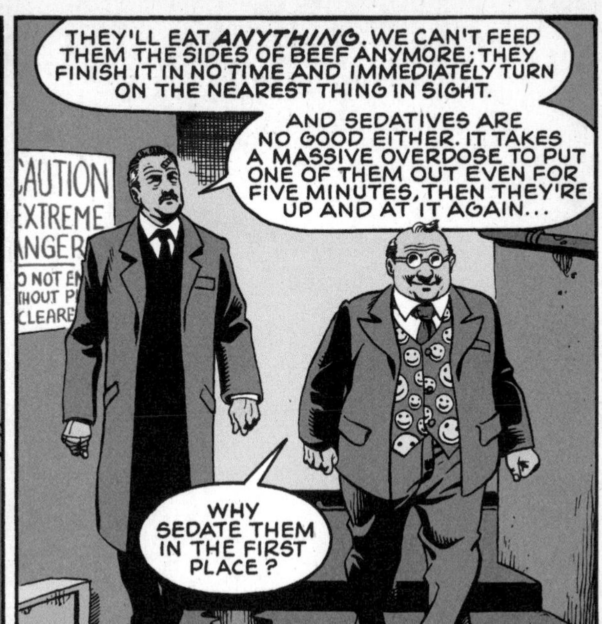
THEY'LL EAT ANYTHING. WE CAN'T FEED THEM THE SIDES OF BEEF ANYMORE; THEY FINISH IT IN NO TIME AND IMMEDIATELY TURN ON THE NEAREST THING IN SIGHT.
AND SEDATIVES ARE NO GOOD EITHER. IT TAKES A MASSIVE OVERDOSE TO PUT ONE OF THEM OUT EVEN FOR FIVE MINUTES, THEN THEY'RE UP AND AT IT AGAIN...
WHY SEDATE THEM IN THE FIRST PLACE?
CAUTION
EXTREME
ANGER

TO FIT THE BITS.

IS THERE ANYTHING LEFT OF THEM? MENTALLY SPEAKING, I MEAN?
OH YES. DON'T FORGET THAT OUR ESCAPEE UNSCREWED THE BOLTS IN ITS SHACKLES, STOLE KEYS, USED THE DEAD GUARD'S SECURITY SWIPECARD. IF THEY WEREN'T BURNING WITH INHUMAN LEVELS OF HUNGER THEY'D STILL BE MORE OR LESS RATIONAL.
SOME OF THEM WERE STILL VERBALIZING, AT LEAST BEFORE YESTERDAY'S INCIDENT...
KEEP OUT!
DANGER.

SAYING WHAT?
SCREAMING OBSCENITIES. ONE BEGGED ME TO KILL IT.
THAT'S THE WORST THING, MR. TRUMAN.

THEY KNOW.

SO WHAT'S YOUR RECOMMENDATION?
TERMINATE.
SMAS

WE CAN'T FEED THEM, WE CAN'T SEDATE THEM. THEY'RE NO USE TO US WHATSOEVER. AND AT THE RATE THEIR BODIES BURN ENERGY THEY'LL EXPIRE ANYWAY, IN TWENTY-FOUR HOURS AT THE MOST.
SEEMS RATHER A WASTE TO JUST KILL THEM.
WHAT IF WE REMOVED THEIR RESTRAINTS AND LEFT THEM TO IT?

WELL--THEY'D TEAR EACH OTHER APART, THEY'D TEAR *THEMSELVES* APART...
WHAT THE HELL WOULD THE POINT OF THAT BE?
I THOUGHT IT MIGHT BE INTERESTING. AS A SORT OF... CONTROLLED EXPERIMENT, ISN'T THAT WHAT YOU CALL IT?

I'D CALL IT *ANYTHING BUT*--
DO IT.
FILM IT.

I MUST SAY, DOCTOR, FOR A RESEARCH SCIENTIST YOU DON'T HAVE MUCH OF AN ENQUIRING MIND...
MR. TRUMAN--!

LET'S FACE FACTS : PROJECT BLOODLINES IS AN UNQUALIFIED DISASTER. OUR SUCCESS RATE IS ZERO, WE'VE HAD A SERIOUS SECURITY BREACH--
SECURITY IS MY CONCERN, NOT YOURS.
SO THE FACT THAT ONE OF THE SUBJECTS WAS SEEN, IS THAT ENOUGH TO CONCERN YOU ?

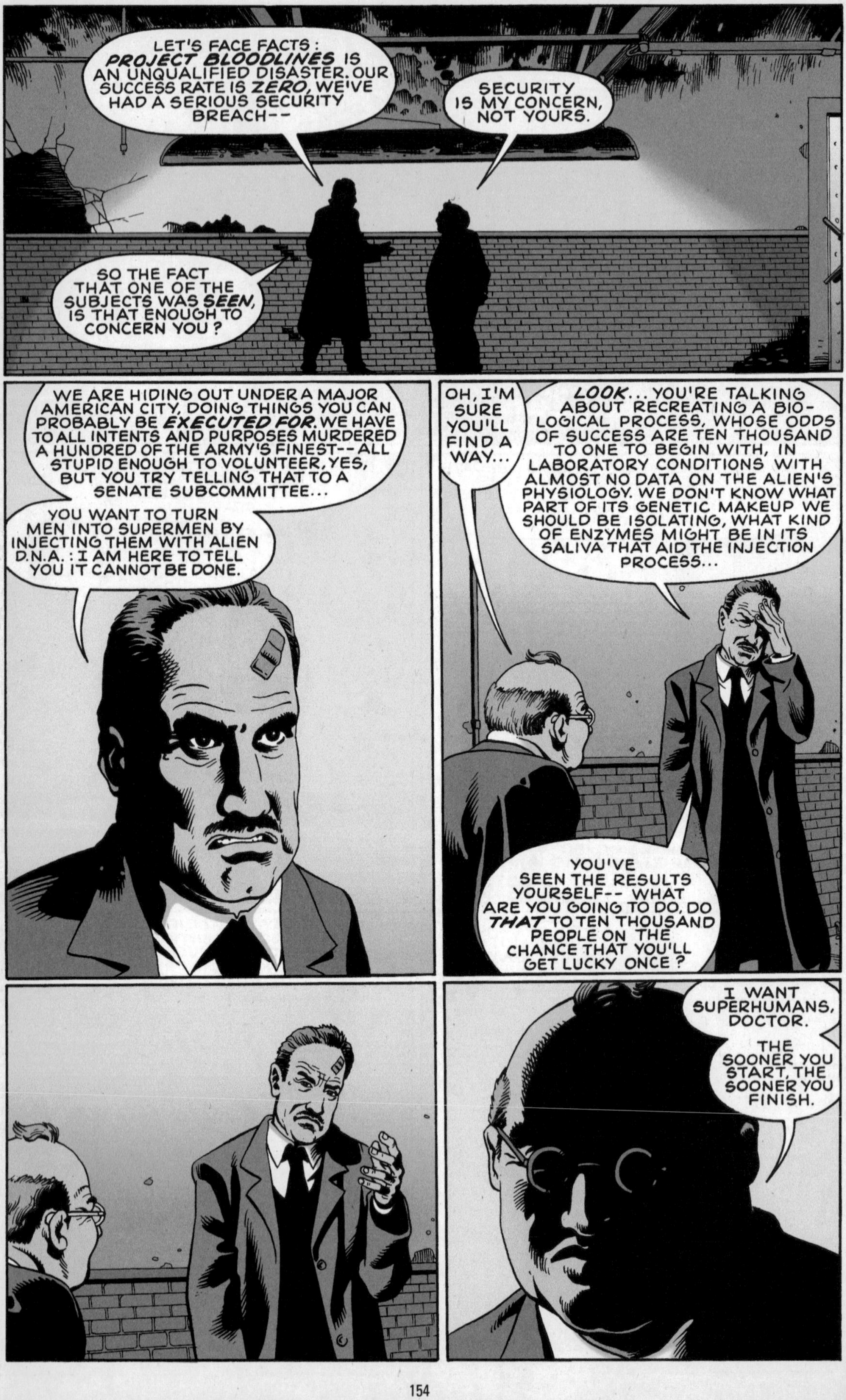

WE ARE HIDING OUT UNDER A MAJOR AMERICAN CITY, DOING THINGS YOU CAN PROBABLY BE EXECUTED FOR. WE HAVE TO ALL INTENTS AND PURPOSES MURDERED A HUNDRED OF THE ARMY'S FINEST--ALL STUPID ENOUGH TO VOLUNTEER, YES, BUT YOU TRY TELLING THAT TO A SENATE SUBCOMMITTEE...
YOU WANT TO TURN MEN INTO SUPERMEN BY INJECTING THEM WITH ALIEN D.N.A. : I AM HERE TO TELL YOU IT CANNOT BE DONE.
OH, I'M SURE YOU'LL FIND A WAY...
LOOK... YOU'RE TALKING ABOUT RECREATING A BIO-LOGICAL PROCESS, WHOSE ODDS OF SUCCESS ARE TEN THOUSAND TO ONE TO BEGIN WITH, IN LABORATORY CONDITIONS WITH ALMOST NO DATA ON THE ALIEN'S PHYSIOLOGY. WE DON'T KNOW WHAT PART OF ITS GENETIC MAKEUP WE SHOULD BE ISOLATING, WHAT KIND OF ENZYMES MIGHT BE IN ITS SALIVA THAT AID THE INJECTION PROCESS...
YOU'VE SEEN THE RESULTS YOURSELF-- WHAT ARE YOU GOING TO DO, DO THAT TO TEN THOUSAND PEOPLE ON THE CHANCE THAT YOU'LL GET LUCKY ONCE ?

I WANT SUPERHUMANS, DOCTOR.
THE SOONER YOU START, THE SOONER YOU FINISH.

WHAT I WAS GONNA HAVE MY DRINK AN' THINK ABOUT-- BEFORE STEVIE RUINED MY DAY-- GOES MORE OR LESS LIKE THIS:

THIS MORNIN' I WOKE UP IN A HOTEL ROOM WITH A WOMAN I KNOW IS GONNA BE BAD FOR ME, AN' WHEN WE EVENTUALLY GOT ROUND TO EATIN' BREAKFAST SHE ASKED ME IF I WAS SEEIN' ANY-ONE. AN' I SAID SORT OF.
AN' SHE GAVE ME THIS LOOK AN' I SAID NO, WITH THIS SOMEONE IT'S ALWAYS SORT OF, AN' I THOUGHT ABOUT THAT FOR A WHILE --

AN' I GUESS THAT'S WHY I'M HERE.

I'M GOING TO DO THIS.
AREN'T I?

I'M GOING TO DO THIS.
I'M GOING TO TAKE HIS GUNS AND PUT THE CUFFS ON HIM AND HAUL HIM DOWN TO THE PRECINCT AND SAY BOOK HIS ASS--
BECAUSE HE'S GOING TO WALK IN HERE AND FEED ME THE SAME OLD LINE OF GARBAGE, BECAUSE HE'S BAD FOR ME, BECAUSE HE CHEATED ON ME, BECAUSE HE'S A MULTIPLE MURDERER, BECAUSE IF I BRING IN TOMMY MONAGHAN THEY'LL GIVE ME MY JOB BACK AND I CAN BE A COP AGAIN.
I AM GOING TO DO THIS.
RIGHT?
HEY.
YOU SAID ON THE PHONE YOU WANTED TO TALK, UM... I DO TOO...
ME FIRST.
OH, WELL HERE WE GO...

WELL... I DUNNO WHAT IT IS YOU THINK I'M GONNA SAY, BUT...
OKAY.
I'M BAD FOR YOU. I'M ALWAYS GONNA BE BAD FOR YOU. I'M GONNA LET YOU DOWN AGAIN AN' AGAIN AN' AGAIN, OR I'M GONNA GET YOU HURT, OR MAYBE EVEN KILLED.
SO WE OUGHTA STOP DOIN' THIS. WE OUGHTA DECIDE TO STAY AWAY FROM EACH OTHER AN' STICK TO IT FOR A CHANGE.
FOR BOTH OUR SAKES.
GO ON.
THIS IS ALL THE MONEY I BEEN ABLE TO STASH AWAY. THERE'S NEARLY A HUNDRED GRAND HERE.
THAT OUGHTA BE ENOUGH TO GET YOU SET UP IN NEW YORK.
YOU'RE GIVING ME YOUR *BLOOD MONEY?*

YOU THINK I'M GOING TO TAKE MONEY YOU GOT FOR--
CAN WE NOT DO THE SCREAMIN'-AT-EACH-OTHER THING FOR ONCE?

ALL MONEY'S BLOOD MONEY. THERE AIN'T A BANKNOTE IN THIS COUNTRY WON'T TEST POSITIVE FOR COCAINE RESIDUE. AN' YOU DON'T EVEN WANNA THINK ABOUT WHAT THE GOVERNMENT GETS UP TO IN AFRICA AN' CENTRAL AMERICA AN' PLACES, IN YOUR NAME, WITH YOUR TAX DOLLARS.
THIS IS A BAD, BAD WORLD, TIEGEL. MONEY'S JUST A TOOL TO GET YOU THROUGH IT.

SO TAKE THIS AN' GO TO NEW YORK. GO BE WITH YOUR MOM AN' YOUR SISTER.
IF YOU WANNA DO SOMETHIN' FOR ME, YOU COULD GET A BOTTLE OF BLACK BUSH AN' GO TO BATTERY PARK, AN' WATCH THE SUN COME UP OVER THE STATUE OF LIBERTY.

IT'S SOMETHIN' A FRIEND AN' ME WERE GONNA DO, A LONG, LONG TIME AGO.

MONAGHAN...
WHY ARE YOU DOING THIS?

BECAUSE THIS IS A BAD WORLD, BUT THIS CITY'S *HELL*, TIEGEL. YOU STAY HERE AN' IT'LL GET YOU EVENTUALLY, ONE WAY OR THE OTHER.
YOU SHOULD GO AN' BE WITH GOOD PEOPLE AN' HAVE A GOOD LIFE...

BECAUSE YOU ARE GOOD PEOPLE,
AN' IT'S WHAT YOU DESERVE.

I'M GONNA GO NOW.

I GUESS I'M NOT GOING TO DO THIS.

OH, HEY.
NATT CALLED. I SAID WE'D BE AT NOONAN'S AT SEVEN, SPELL HIM WATCHING MAGGIE.
FINE.
BEEN TO SEE YOUR SORT-OF SOMEONE?
YEP.
I HAD A JOB GO BAD ON ME A WHILE BACK. IN KAZAKHSTAN. ORDERS WERE TO KILL THE LOCAL TEAM BEFORE I MADE THE EXFIL, FOR SECURITY.
WHEN I GOT HOME I BROKE UP WITH MY FIANCÉ, BECAUSE I FIGURED IT WAS ONLY A MATTER OF TIME BEFORE I GOT KILLED MYSELF--
BUT MAINLY BECAUSE I DIDN'T WANT TO INFLICT MYSELF ON ANYBODY DECENT.

YOU THINK WE'RE DAMNED, PEOPLE LIKE US ?
I THINK ABOUT IT ALL THE TIME.
BUT, WELL, I CAN SEE SOMETHIN' BAD'S COMIN' DOWN THE LINE. I'M PRETTY SURE I FINALLY BIT OFF MORE'N I CAN CHEW.
THIS WAS AS GOOD A TIME AS ANY TO SET THINGS STRAIGHT.
I SOMETIMES IMAGINE A PLACE IN THE SUN.
SOMEWHERE KILLERS CAN GO WHEN THEY THROW THEIR GUNS AWAY.
JUST LIE ON YOUR ASS ALL DAY AND DRINK GOOD BOURBON, AND SWIM IN THE OCEAN, AND WALK IN THE COOL PLACES UNDER THE TREES, AND NOT DO TERRIBLE THINGS TO PEOPLE.
YOU THINK THERE MIGHT BE A PLACE LIKE THAT, SOMEWHERE?

HEH.
WELL.
IT SURE SOUNDS LIKE A NICE IDEA.

...YEAH.

YOU GOT ANYTHING PLANNED FOR THE NEXT HOUR OR TWO?

NO.
YOU GOT ANYTHING IN MIND?

THE REAL TRICK'S GOING TO BE GETTING MAGGIE OUT OF GOTHAM.
NOONA

I CALLED MY FRIEND IN THE BUREAU. IT SEEMS TRUMAN'S HOLD ON THE LOCAL POLICE IS STRONGER THAN WE THOUGHT; ALL HE HAD TO SAY WAS *C.I.A.* AND THEY BENT OVER ON THE SPOT.
SO WHY DON'T THE REAL C.I.A. GUYS CALL THE COPS, TELL 'EM TRUMAN'S GONE ROGUE?

BECAUSE IT'D BE THE WORST LOSS OF FACE THEY'D EVER HAVE SUFFERED. THEY SIMPLY CAN'T AFFORD TO ADMIT A THING LIKE THIS.
MY FED GUY'S TRYING TO INTEREST HIS BOSSES IN A RESCUE MISSION-- THEY'LL COME IN AND BRING US OUT, TAKE MAGGIE TO A SAFEHOUSE. ONCE HER TESTIMONY'S ON RECORD AND TRUMAN'S BLOODLINES PROJECT GOES PUBLIC, HIS LITTLE EMPIRE SHOULD COLLAPSE LIKE A PACK OF CARDS.
ALL WE CAN DO NOW IS SIT TIGHT 'TIL I GET THE WORD.

AN' THAT'S THE BEST YOU CAN COME UP WIT'?
YEAH, THAT'S ABOUT IT. I'D BE FASCINATED TO SEE IF YOU CAN DO ANY BETTER, CONSIDERING THE SUM TOTAL OF YOUR ACHIEVEMENTS IS HAVING A MAFIA CONTRACT PUT ON YOUR HEAD.

LISTEN, YOU--
OH MY GOD, I AM SO SCREWED...

I'M NEVER GOING TO GET OUT OF THIS. I'VE GOT THE C.I.A. TRYING TO KILL ME-- I MEAN I'M JUST ONE PERSON, WHAT CAN I HOPE TO DO?
THEY'RE GOING TO KILL ME AND IT'LL BE LIKE I NEVER EXISTED, I'LL NEVER HAVE MY BABY, I'M JUST TOTALLY AND COMPLETELY *SCREWED...!*

C'MON, KID. YOU AIN'T SCREWED.
WHY?

BECAUSE WE SAY SO.

I'M GONNA GO GET SOME SLEEP.
I'LL WALK OUT WITH YOU.

COME ON THEN, LET'S HEAR IT...
OH YEAH, LIKE I'M THE ONE CAUSIN' THE MOTHER-LOVIN' PROBLEM! LIKE I'M THE ONE MESSIN' AROUND WIT' THE GOVERNMENT BITCH!
Madame Xanadu

I MEAN YOU DON'T EVEN KNOW HER, MAN! WE GOIN' UP AGAINST THE COMPANY HERE, AN' YOU PUTTIN' OUR LIVES IN HER HANDS! HOW THE HELL YOU SO SURE YOU CAN TRUST THIS--
HEY.
HEY.

ENOUGH WITH THE BITCH, OKAY?

OH... GREAT.
YOU STARTED FALLIN' FOR HER ALREADY, AIN'T YOU?
LOOK: THE REASON I TRUST HER--

FAKOOM

UH...?
HEY, TOMMY.

...PHIL KELLY.
GUESS THIS IS FOR STEVIE, HUH ?
ACTUALLY, I WAS THINKIN' MORE ABOUT THE TWO MILLION THE ITALIANS'RE OFFERIN', TOMMY. BUT YEAH, SURE, IF IT MAKES YOU FEEL ANY BETTER.

YOU DIRTY RAT, YOU KILLED MY BROTHER.
OKAY ?

WHAT THE HELL--?!

I'M YOUR GUARDIAN ANGEL.

SEAN NOONAN SENT ME.

WHUNKK
UNNH!!

I'M GONNA SAVE YOUR LIFE WHETHER YOU LIKE IT OR NOT.

THERE'S THREE HUNDRED THIRTY-SEVEN SINGLE AN' MULTIPLE MURDERS IN HERE.
THERE'S ALSO A REPORT FROM A TASK FORCE GUY, SAYS YOUR REAL TALLY'S PROBABLY TWICE THAT.
THE ART OF WAR
THE ROMAN ARMY
BATTLE OF THE BU
MONAGHAN.T
GOTHAM CITY POLICE DEPT.

YOU'RE QUITE A PIECE OF WORK, AREN'T YOU, PUNK?
Closing Time: 4
GARTH ENNIS WRITER
JOHN McCREA PENCILLER
GARRY LEACH INKER
PAT PRENTICE LETTERER
CARLA FEENY COLORIST
HEROIC AGE SEPARATOR
PETER TOMASI EDITOR
HITMAN CREATED BY ENNIS & McCREA

WHO THE HELL ARE YOU...?
NAME'S CONNOLLY.
RANK'S LIEUTENANT.
WELCOME

SO WHAT KINDA CELL IS THIS SUPPOSED TO BE?
IT AIN'T. IT'S MY PLACE. THIS AIN'T OFFICIAL BUSINESS.
IT'S SOMETHIN' I'M DOIN' FOR YOUR FRIEND SEAN NOONAN.

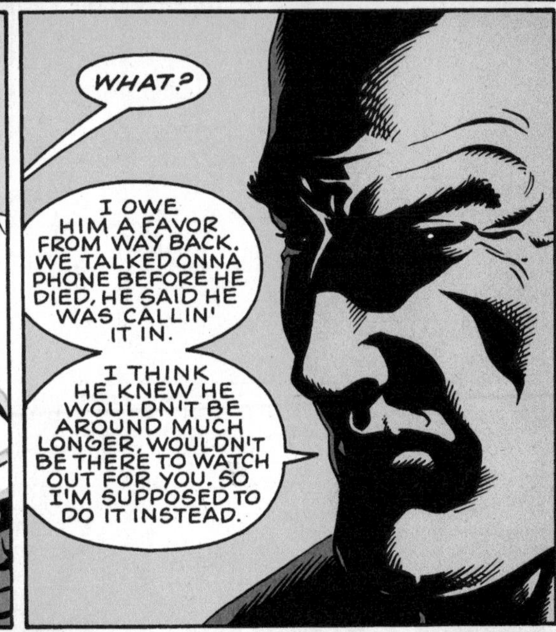
WHAT?
I OWE HIM A FAVOR FROM WAY BACK. WE TALKED ONNA PHONE BEFORE HE DIED, HE SAID HE WAS CALLIN' IT IN.
I THINK HE KNEW HE WOULDN'T BE AROUND MUCH LONGER, WOULDN'T BE THERE TO WATCH OUT FOR YOU. SO I'M SUPPOSED TO DO IT INSTEAD.

YOU GOTTA BE KIDDIN'--!
WAIT A MINUTE, THIS IS CRAZY! SEAN NEVER MENTIONED KNOWIN' A COP!

NO, AN' I NEVER TOLD THE BOYS AT THE PRECINCT I KNEW A RETIRED HITMAN RAN A BAR INNA CAULDRON.
READIN' THIS, I WISH I NEVER HEARDA EITHER OF YOU.

THEN AGAIN, IF HE RAISED YOU, WHY WOULD I BE SURPRISED...
WHAT KINDA FRIGGIN' LUNATIC ARE YOU? HOW DOES SMASHIN' MY HEAD IN AN' TYIN' ME TO A CHAIR COUNT AS WATCHIN' OUT FOR ME?

MY CAPTAIN GOT A CALL FROM THE COMMISSIONER'S OFFICE YESTERDAY. THERE'S SOME KINDA GOVERNMENT OUTFIT OPERATIN' IN GOTHAM. YOUR NAME WAS MEN-TIONED, AN' NOT IN A GOOD WAY.
SO WE BEEN ORDERED TO REDUCE OUR PRESENCE INNA CAULDRON, STAY WELL CLEARA A CERTAIN BAR AT THE CORNER OF SAINT AN' PECKINPAH. SOON AS I HEARD THAT I KNEW THEY'D BE COMIN' FOR YOU.
I FIGURED I'D GET TO YOU FIRST.

OH JESUS, YOU STUPID SON OF A BITCH! THOSE MAGGOTS ARE AFTER MAGGIE LORENZO! THEY'RE GONNA BUTCHER AN INNOCENT WOMAN!
NATT! MY BUDDY NATT WHO WAS WITH ME--
HE WAS ALIVE WHEN I LEFT HIM.

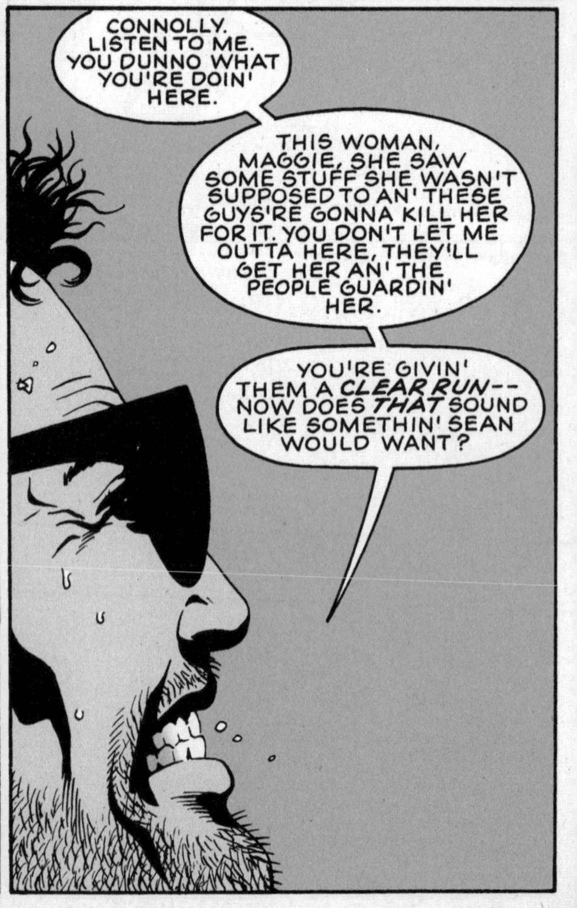
CONNOLLY. LISTEN TO ME. YOU DUNNO WHAT YOU'RE DOIN' HERE.
THIS WOMAN, MAGGIE, SHE SAW SOME STUFF SHE WASN'T SUPPOSED TO AN' THESE GUYS'RE GONNA KILL HER FOR IT. YOU DON'T LET ME OUTTA HERE, THEY'LL GET HER AN' THE PEOPLE GUARDIN' HER.
YOU'RE GIVIN' THEM A CLEAR RUN-- NOW DOES THAT SOUND LIKE SOMETHIN' SEAN WOULD WANT?

THE FAVOR WAS KEEPIN' YOU ALIVE, NOT CLEANIN' UP YOUR MESS.
UNTIL THIS THING BLOWS OVER, YOU STAY TIED TO THAT CHAIR AN' THIS ARSENAL OF YOURS STAYS RIGHT HERE. AN' THEN YOUR ASS IS ON THE NEXT FLIGHT TO MEXICO, PUNK.
CONNOLLY--!
FEEL FREE TO YELL YOUR HEAD OFF. PEOPLE SCREAM ALL THE TIME IN THIS NEIGHBORHOOD.
ONCE THIS IS OVER, NOONAN AN' ME ARE SQUARE. THE DEBT IS CANCELLED. I NEVER THOUGHT TOO MUCHA HIM, BUT I KNOW HE WAS A MAN OF HONOR.
SO AM I.

KINNER'S SLEAZY
PECKIN
HURRY UP, TOMMY! THE OLD CREEP'S GONNA CATCH US!
OKAY, OKAY!

SLEAZ
WHY YOU LITTLE--!
RUN PAT!

YOU LOUSY PAIR OF ANIMALS, I'LL HAVE YOU LOCKED AWAY! I'LL DAMN WELL SHOOT YOU IS WHAT I'LL DO!
CAN'T CATCH US, SKINNER!
WAH HA HA HA HA HA!
STARSKY AND HUTCH

... NOONAN, CAN'T YOU CONTROL THAT NEPHEW OF YOURS, AND HIS LITTLE BRAT PAL FROM THE ORPHANAGE?
AND GET THAT SIGN REPAINTED! TODAY!
THEY'RE JUST KIDS, MR. SKINNER.
I'LL GET RIGHT ON IT, MR. SKINNER.

HOW COME YOU TAKE SO MUCH CRAP OFF OLD MAN SKINNER, UNCLE SEAN?
YEAH, YOU'RE TEN TIMES TOUGHER'N HE IS!
WELL, FELLAS...

ONE OF THE THINGS ABOUT BEIN' A TOUGH GUY IS KNOWIN' WHEN TO BE TOUGH. AN' A WORM LIKE SKINNER, HE AIN'T WORTH GETTIN' UPSET OVER.
IF I DID IT'D GIVE HIM THE IDEA I THINK HE'S IMPORTANT, OR MAYBE EVEN DANGEROUS, WHEN REALLY HE JUST MAKES ME LAUGH.

I DON'T GET IT.
YOU WILL, TOMMY.
ANYHOW, IF I DON'T KEEP OLD MAN SKINNER SWEET, HE WON'T LET ME IN ON HIS POKER GAME TUESDAY NIGHT.

AN' OLD MAN SKINNER'S GOT SOMETHIN' I *WANT*.

CAN WE STAY UP AN' WATCH YOU PLAY, UNCLE SEAN?
TUESDAY'S A SCHOOL NIGHT, PAT. YOU THINK SISTER CONCEPTA'S GONNA LET TOMMY STAY OUT LATE TO SEE A POKER GAME?
YOU THINK I'M CRAZY ENOUGH TO ASK HER?

SKINNER'S
SLEAZY BAR
YOU TOOK YOUR TIME...
MORE NUNS ON GUARD THAN USUAL. WHAT'D I MISS?

UNCLE SEAN'S JUST ABOUT CLEANED SKINNER OUT. FRITZ THE KRAUT AN' JOE Q FOLDED ALREADY.
DAMMIT, NOONAN--!
THIS WAY UP
FRAGILE

WHAT D'YOU MEAN, YOU WON'T TAKE AN I.O.U.? YOU *KNOW* I'M GOOD FOR IT!
I'M JUST CAREFUL WHEN IT COMES TO DOIN' BUSINESS, MR. SKINNER. YOU WANNA SEE ME IT'LL COST YOU THREE GRAND.
SO WHAT AM I S'POSED TO DO, WALK TWENTY BLOCKS TO MY HOUSE TO GET IT?
THIS WAY UP
FRAGILE

YOU COULD DO THAT.
OR YOU COULD SAVE YOURSELF THE TRIP AN' USE THE DEEDS TO THIS PLACE INSTEAD.

THIS PLACE IS WORTH MORE THAN--
YOU GOT ANYTHING ELSE YOU CAN USE HERE ?

C'MON, SKINNER...! A MINUTE AGO YOU WERE SURE YOU HAD HIM BEAT!
JA! "ZIS VINNING STREAK OF YOURS CAN'T LAST FOREVER," ISN'T ZAT VAT YOU TOLD HIM ?

OKAY--
I MEAN YOU'RE GONNA LET HIM GET THIS FAR IN FRONT, DON'T BE SURPRISED IF HE UPS THE ANTE...
I SAID OKAY!

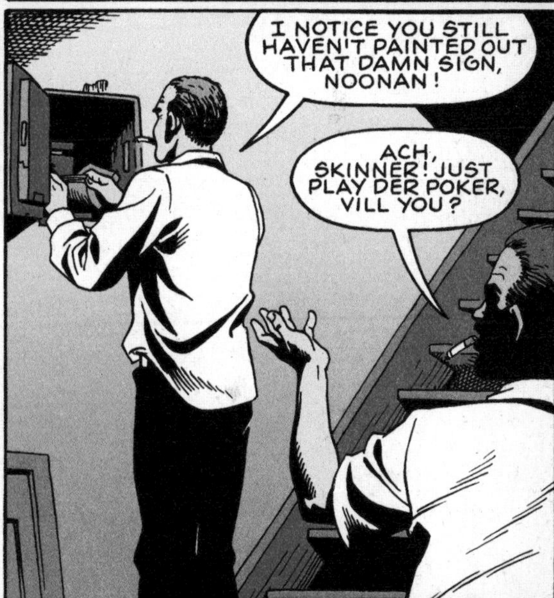
I NOTICE YOU STILL HAVEN'T PAINTED OUT THAT DAMN SIGN, NOONAN!
ACH, SKINNER! JUST PLAY DER POKER, VILL YOU ?

MOMENT OF TRUTH.
THREE JACKS...
AND, WAIT FOR IT...!

OVER TO YOU, *NOONAN*.

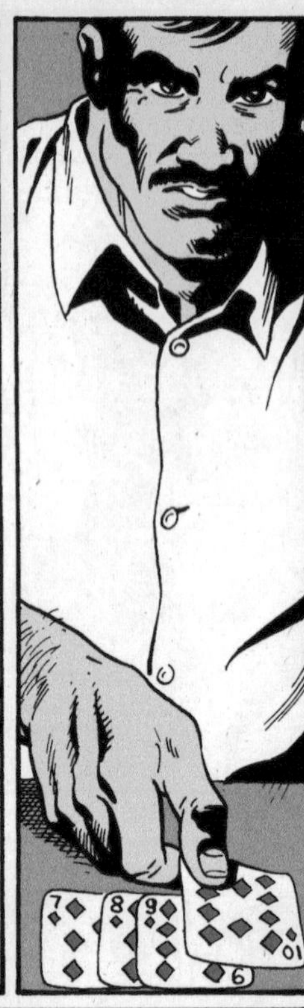

YOU AIN'T GOT THE JACK! YOU CAN'T HAVE IT!
YOU ARE *THROUGH*--

NO!!

YOU CHEATED. I DUNNO HOW BUT YOU CHEATED! YOU LOUSY FRIGGIN' BASTARD. I WANNA DAMN RE--
SKINNER.
DEED OF O

GET THE HELL OUTTA MY PLACE.

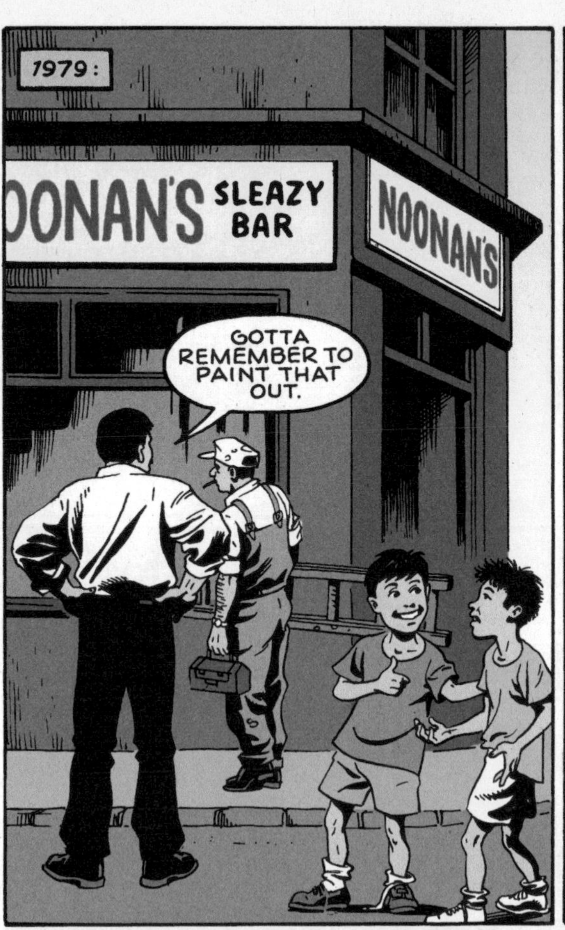
1979:
NOONAN'S SLEAZY BAR
NOONAN'S
GOTTA REMEMBER TO PAINT THAT OUT.

1982:
NOONAN'S SLEAZY BAR
NOONAN'S
GOTTA REMEMBER TO PAINT THAT OUT.

1985:
NOONAN'S SLEAZY BAR
NOONAN'S
GOTTA REMEMBER TO PAINT
GIRLS!GIRLS!GIRLS!

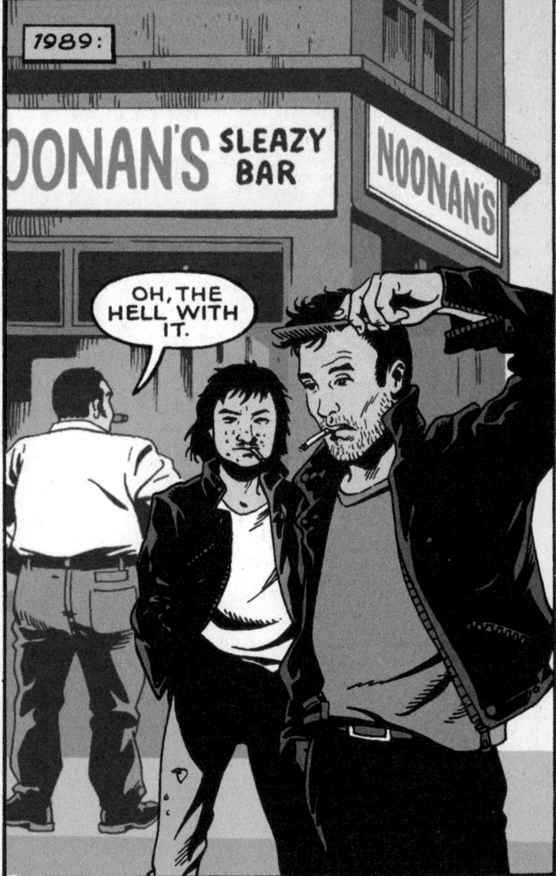
1989:
NOONAN'S SLEAZY BAR
NOONAN'S
OH, THE HELL WITH IT.

WHAT THE HELL ARE YOU DOIN' WITH *THAT?*
WB U HERE

BOUGHT IT OFF THAT GUY TIMMY THE FISH. FIGURED WE COULD USE A LITTLE INSURANCE.
TOMMY, WE'RE BUYIN' *POT* HERE! IT'S NOT LIKE WE'RE DOIN' BUSINESS WITH THE FRIGGIN' MEDELLIN CARTEL!

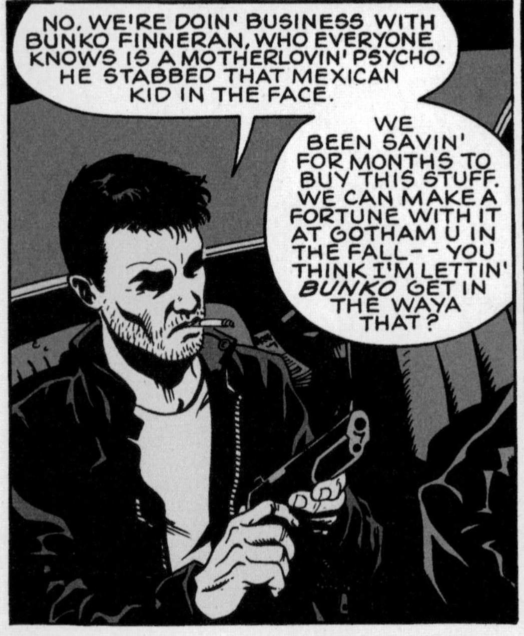
NO, WE'RE DOIN' BUSINESS WITH BUNKO FINNERAN, WHO EVERYONE KNOWS IS A MOTHERLOVIN' PSYCHO. HE STABBED THAT MEXICAN KID IN THE FACE.
WE BEEN SAVIN' FOR MONTHS TO BUY THIS STUFF. WE CAN MAKE A FORTUNE WITH IT AT GOTHAM U IN THE FALL-- YOU THINK I'M LETTIN' *BUNKO* GET IN THE WAYA THAT?

OH JESUS, WHAT WOULD UNCLE SEAN SAY...?
"TOMMY, WHAT THE HELL ARE YOU THINKIN', BRINGIN' A GUN TO MY NEPHEW'S DRUG DEAL?"
HEADS UP...

DO YOU EVEN KNOW HOW TO USE THAT THING?
GUESS HERE'S WHERE I FIND OUT.

TOMMY--!
KIDDING...

EVENIN', GIRLS.

YOU ON YOUR OWN TONIGHT, BUNKO?
I DON'T NEED BACKUP TO HANDLE YOU TWO FAIRIES.
HERE'S THE STUFF.

FINE...
THREE GRAND. CHECK IT.
OH, I THINK YOU MEAN FIVE.

YOU SAID THREE YESTERDAY.
TODAY I'M SAYIN' FIVE.

WHAT IS THIS, WHAT'RE YOU TALKIN' ABOUT?
LOOK, THIS IS CRAZY, ALL WE'RE DOIN'S BUYIN' A LITTLE WEED HERE...!
DEAL'S OFF, WE'RE OUTTA HERE. GIVE HIM THE MONEY BACK, BUNKO.

HERE.

MAGGOT!!

AAAAAH. NO! TOMMY! NO!!
YOU LISTENIN' TO ME, YOU LITTLE PISSBAG?

NO NO NOT ME WAAAHH--
LOOK AT ME. NOONAN! LOOK AT ME!
YOU TAKE YOUR BITCH PARTNER AN' YOU GO GET MY OTHER TWO GRAND, YOU HEAR ME?!

AN' YOU GET USED TO IT, YOU GET USED TO WORKIN' FOR BUNKO FINNERAN, 'CAUSE THAT'S HOW THINGS ARE GONNA BE AROUND--
BLAM

WELL--
WELL--

WELL SCREW YOU, BUNKO.

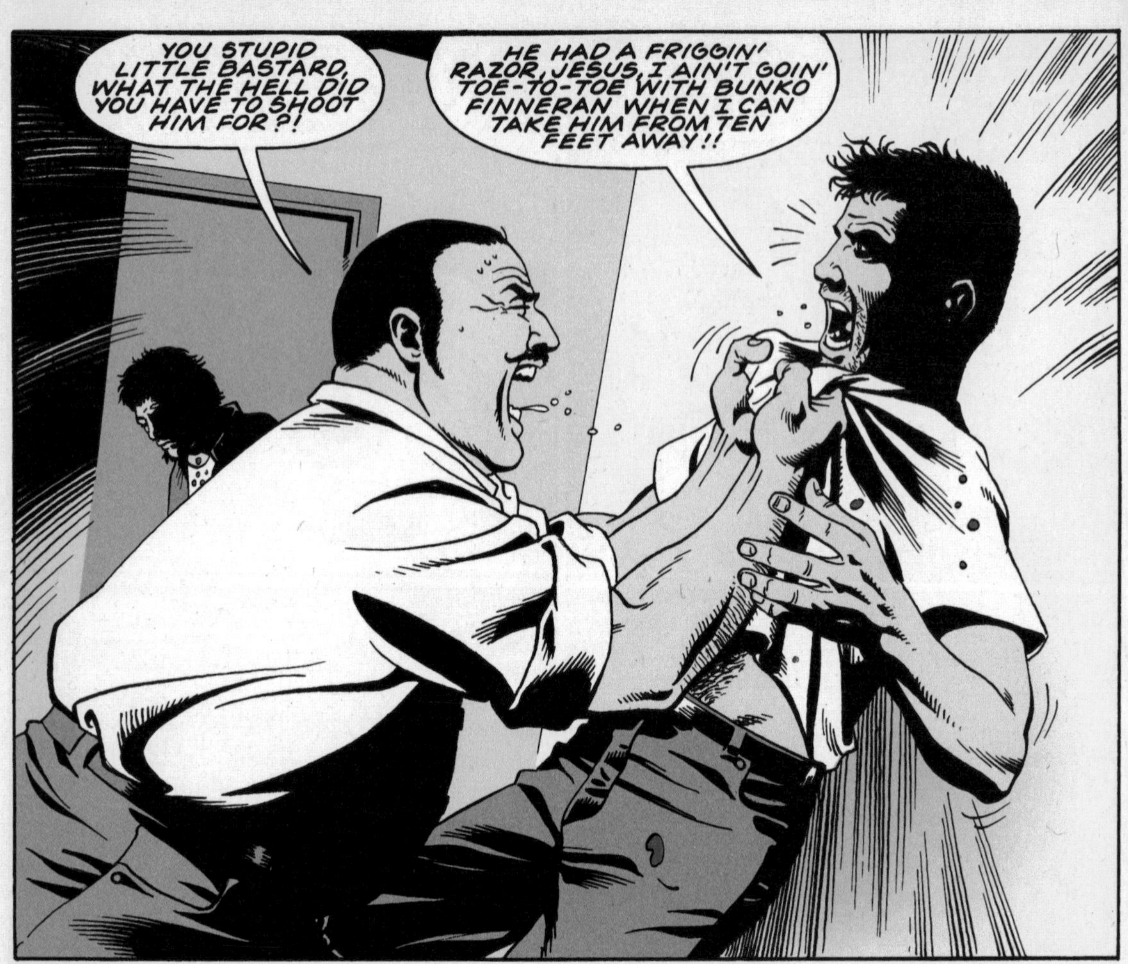
YOU STUPID LITTLE BASTARD, WHAT THE HELL DID YOU HAVE TO SHOOT HIM FOR?!
HE HAD A FRIGGIN' RAZOR, JESUS, I AIN'T GOIN' TOE-TO-TOE WITH BUNKO FINNERAN WHEN I CAN TAKE HIM FROM TEN FEET AWAY!!

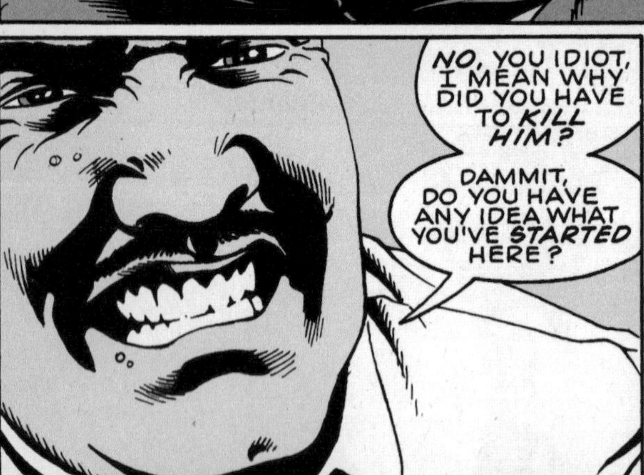
NO, YOU IDIOT, I MEAN WHY DID YOU HAVE TO *KILL HIM*?
DAMMIT, DO YOU HAVE ANY IDEA WHAT YOU'VE *STARTED* HERE?

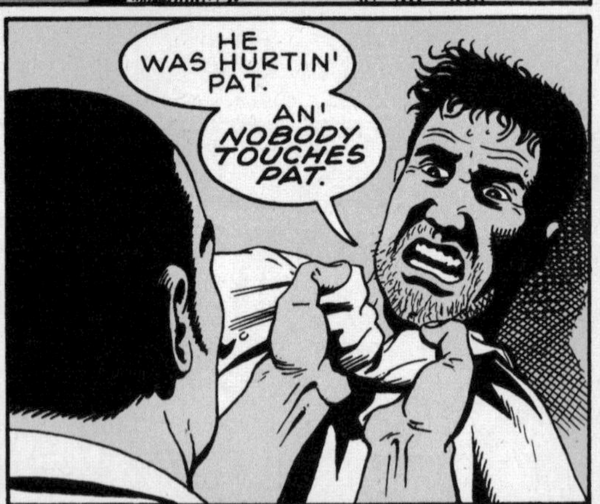
HE WAS HURTIN' PAT.
AN' *NOBODY TOUCHES PAT*.

STOP IT.

JUST STOP IT, WILL YOU?

IT'S ALL RIGHT, PAT.
WHY DON'T YOU GO GET MY MEDICAL BAG, OKAY? I NEED TO TAKE A LOOK AT TOMMY'S HAND.

YOU DID THE RIGHT THING TONIGHT.

NOT WITH DEALIN' DOPE AN' CARRYIN' A GUN, I DON'T MEAN THAT. I'D BREAK YOUR LOUSY LEGS FOR THAT, EXCEPT I'D BE A TOTAL HYPOCRITE AN' IT WOULDN'T MAKE ANY DIFFERENCE.
I MEAN WHAT YOU DID FOR PAT.

YOU ALWAYS STICK BY YOUR FRIENDS.
IF IT COMES TO IT, YOU GIVE YOUR LIFE FOR 'EM.

IT'S JUST THAT TONIGHT YOU TOOK YOUR FIRST STEP ON A PATH THAT'S ONLY GOT ONE POSSIBLE END, AN' BELIEVE ME, I SHOULD KNOW.
OKAY, THAT'S GONNA NEED STITCHES...

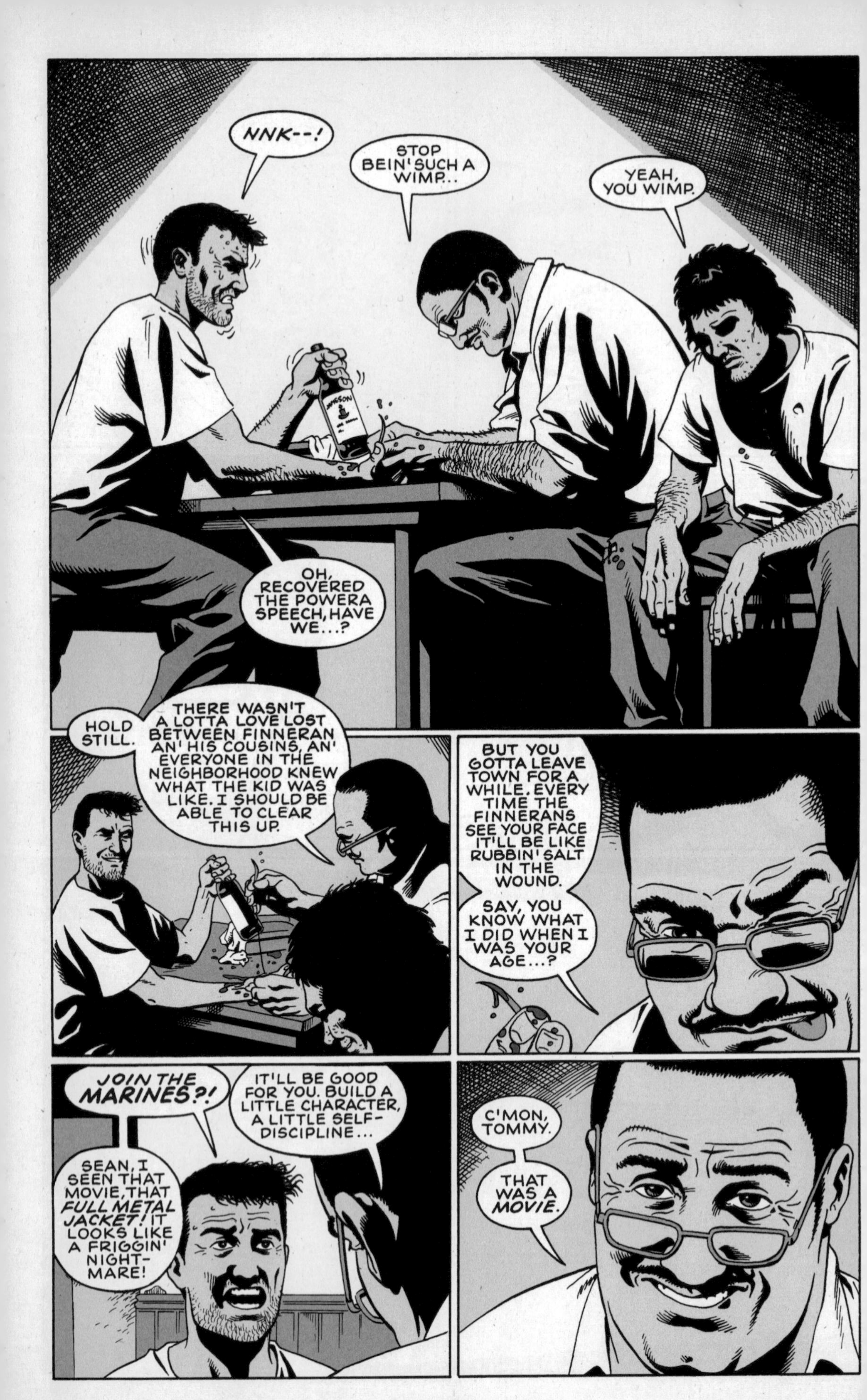
NNK--!
STOP BEIN' SUCH A WIMP...
YEAH, YOU WIMP.
OH, RECOVERED THE POWERA SPEECH, HAVE WE...?
HOLD STILL.
THERE WASN'T A LOTTA LOVE LOST BETWEEN FINNERAN AN' HIS COUSINS, AN' EVERYONE IN THE NEIGHBORHOOD KNEW WHAT THE KID WAS LIKE. I SHOULD BE ABLE TO CLEAR THIS UP.
BUT YOU GOTTA LEAVE TOWN FOR A WHILE. EVERY TIME THE FINNERANS SEE YOUR FACE IT'LL BE LIKE RUBBIN' SALT IN THE WOUND.
SAY, YOU KNOW WHAT I DID WHEN I WAS YOUR AGE...?
JOIN THE MARINES?!
IT'LL BE GOOD FOR YOU. BUILD A LITTLE CHARACTER, A LITTLE SELF-DISCIPLINE...
SEAN, I SEEN THAT MOVIE, THAT FULL METAL JACKET! IT LOOKS LIKE A FRIGGIN' NIGHT-MARE!
C'MON, TOMMY.
THAT WAS A MOVIE.

WHY YOU LITTLE PILES OF INVERTEBRATE , HOW DARE YOU EVEN THINK YOU ARE WORTHY TO SERVE AS RIFLEMEN IN MY BELOVED CORPS?!!*
*NOT EVEN IF THIS WAS VERTIGO

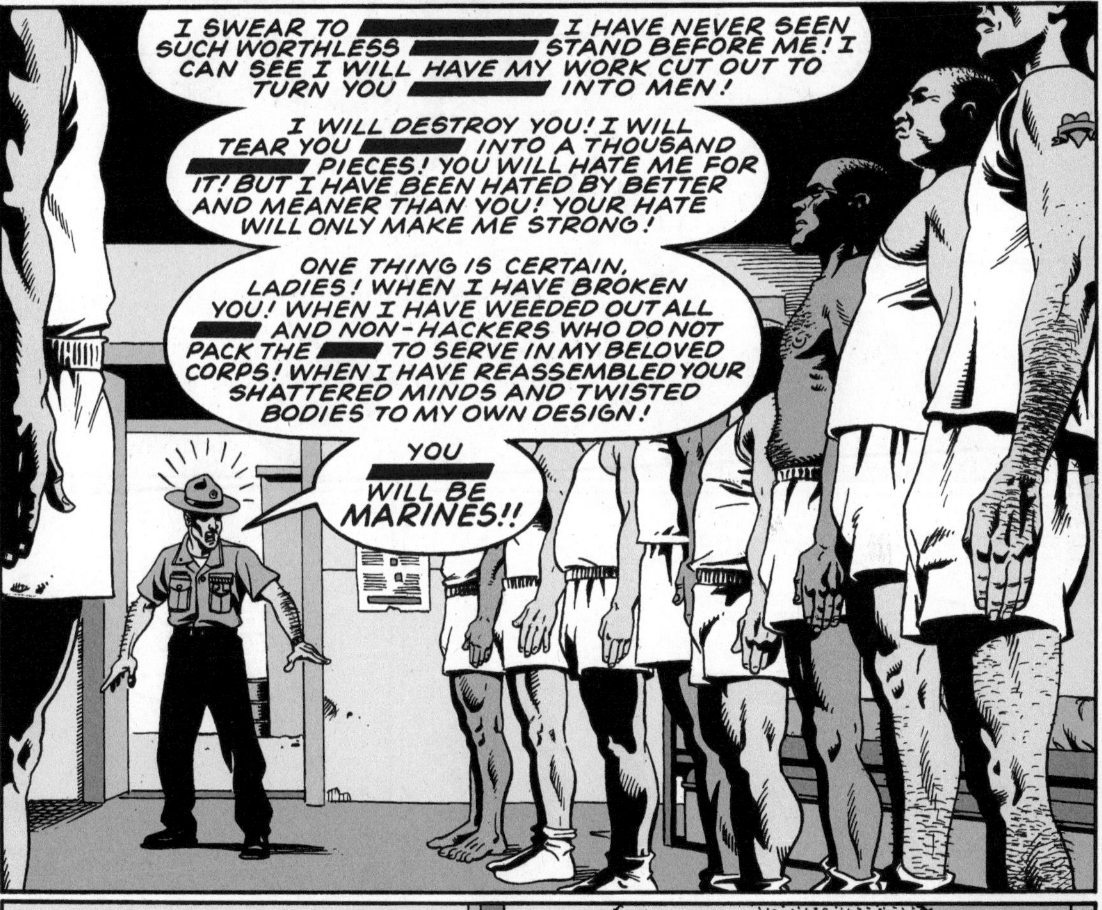
I SWEAR TO I HAVE NEVER SEEN SUCH WORTHLESS STAND BEFORE ME! I CAN SEE I WILL HAVE MY WORK CUT OUT TO TURN YOU INTO MEN!
I WILL DESTROY YOU! I WILL TEAR YOU INTO A THOUSAND PIECES! YOU WILL HATE ME FOR IT! BUT I HAVE BEEN HATED BY BETTER AND MEANER THAN YOU! YOUR HATE WILL ONLY MAKE ME STRONG!
ONE THING IS CERTAIN, LADIES! WHEN I HAVE BROKEN YOU! WHEN I HAVE WEEDED OUT ALL AND NON-HACKERS WHO DO NOT PACK THE TO SERVE IN MY BELOVED CORPS! WHEN I HAVE REASSEMBLED YOUR SHATTERED MINDS AND TWISTED BODIES TO MY OWN DESIGN!
YOU WILL BE MARINES!!

DAMN YOU, SEAN...

WHO THE ▬▬ SAID THAT?!

WHAT ▬▬ SAID THAT?
WHICH ONE OF YOU ▬▬ ▬▬ PIECES OF ▬▬ JUST SIGNED HIS OWN ▬▬ DEATH WARRANT?!

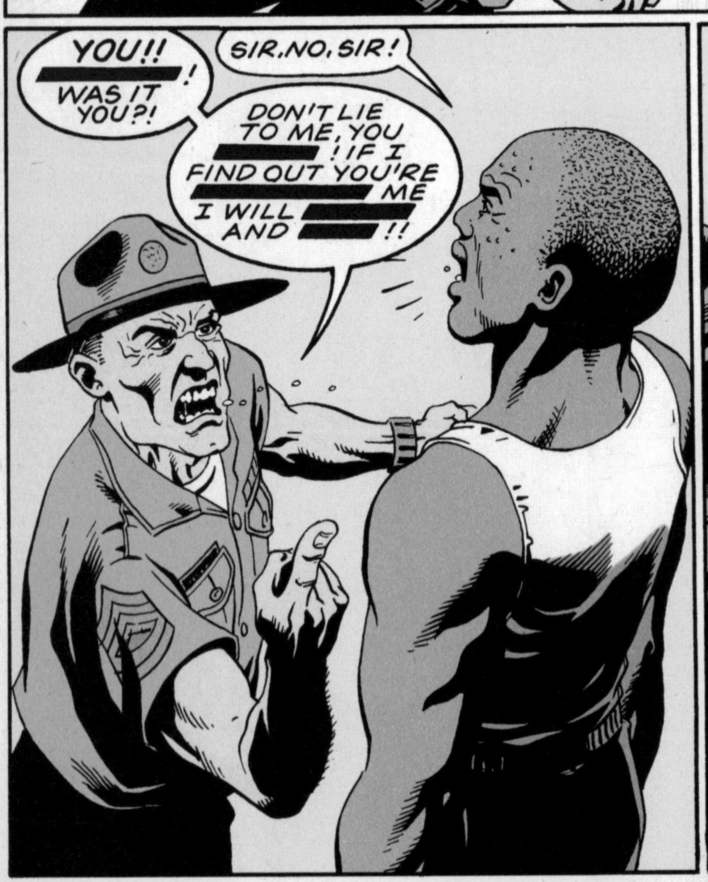
YOU!! ▬▬! WAS IT YOU?!
SIR, NO, SIR!
DON'T LIE TO ME, YOU ▬▬! IF I FIND OUT YOU'RE ▬▬ ME I WILL ▬▬ AND ▬▬!!

WHAT ABOUT YOU, ▬▬?!
SIR--

DON'T EVEN BOTHER TO ANSWER, YOU ! I KNEW IT WAS YOU!

! AND ! ! IN !!!
WALLS.N.
MONAGHAN.T

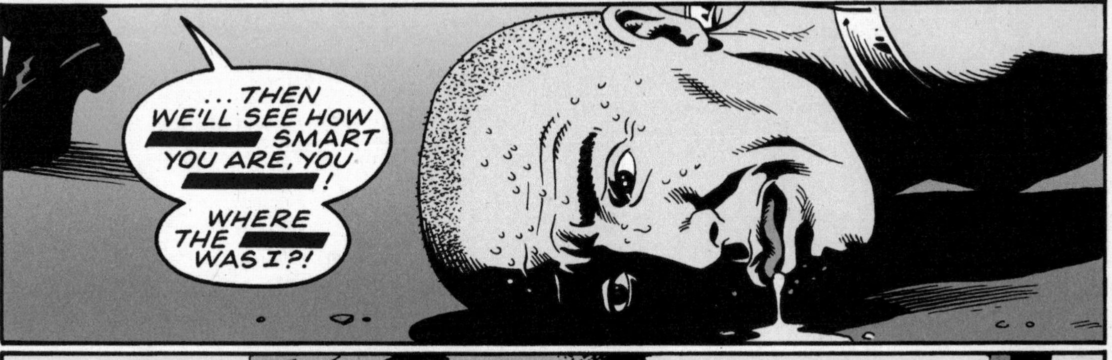
...THEN WE'LL SEE HOW SMART YOU ARE, YOU !
WHERE THE WAS I?!

DUMB.
YEP.

WHAT'S THIS?
HOW'M I S'POSED TO EAT IT?
SOUP.
WORLD ATLAS

NICE.
WHAT'S WITH ALL THE HISTORY BOOKS?
I READ 'EM. IT'S WHAT YOU DO WITH BOOKS.
SIX-DAY WARRIORS by DANIEL MATSUKA
by BROWNWYN R. CONNORS
WINGS OVER BERLIN by TRISTAN RODERICK
by JASON T. PETRIZZI
RUSSIA: HITLER'S FOLLY by DR. J.T. MASTERS
AGINCOURT
LIGHT BRIGADE by R. KENT
ALL THE WAY TO KHE SAN by B. KRAUSE

YEAH, I BEEN KNOWN TO READ A FEW MYSELF. THAT'S HOW I COULD TELL THEY WERE HISTORY BOOKS.

WHEN I WAS A KID MY HISTORY TEACHER WAS ALWAYS BANGIN' ON ABOUT THIS FAVORITE QUOTE HE HAD, *"HE WHO IGNORES THE PAST IS CONDEMNED TO REPEAT IT,"* OR SOMETHING LIKE THAT. AN' I PRETTY MUCH IGNORED IT AN' WENT BACK TO SLEEP.
BUT I GREW UP AN' BECAME A COP AN' SAW WHAT A MESS WE MADE OF THE WORLD, AN' I THOUGHT-- HEY, MAYBE HE HAD A POINT. THAT'S HOW I GOT INTERESTED IN READIN' THIS STUFF.

AN' AFTER FORTY YEARS OF IT I'D HAVETA SAY HE WHO *DON'T* IGNORE THE PAST'S GONNA END UP REPEATIN' IT ANYWAY. 'CAUSE PEOPLE NEVER TAKE MORE FROM HISTORY THAN EXACTLY WHAT SUITS THEM.
WHICH IS WHY YOU GOT IDIOTS SLAUGHTERIN' EACH OTHER FROM BELFAST TO CHECHNYA, JUST 'CAUSE THEY HOLD ONTO ENOUGH CRAP FROM THE PAST TO JUSTIFY IT...

YOU AN' NOONAN'RE A CASE IN POINT.
HEY, SCREW YOU, CONNOLLY! SEAN NEVER WANTED ME DOIN' THIS! IF ANYTHING, HE TRIED TO STOP ME!

TRIED REAL HARD, DIDN'T HE, PUNK?

DON'T BOTHER KIDDIN' YOURSELF. YOU'RE SCUM. YOU'LL ALWAYS BE SCUM.
SEAN NOONAN WASN'T A HELL OF A LOT BETTER.

USMC
Now you can race the same cars used in
McCrea Motoring Invitational
GIANT DC
64 PAGES
ARMY AT WAR
SGT ROCK's
PRIZE BATTLE TALES
ONLY 25¢
HERE ARE THE REASONS THAT MEN HAVE FOUGHT AN' BLED... AN' DIED!
BATTLE OF THE SERGEANTS
TIGER
TWO MEN...ONE HILL
SURRENDER TICKET
McCREA 00

MR. PRESIDENT, FIRING NUKES AT THAT THING WOULD BE LIKE SHOOTING A B.B. GUN AT A FREIGHT TRAIN! THE WORLD IS HOURS AWAY FROM DESTRUCTION! WE HAVE ONE CHANCE AND ONCE CHANCE ONLY TO SAVE THIS PLANET!!
SAY WHAT?!
BRUCE WILLIS IS AN ACTOR, MR. PRESIDENT!!
YOU HAVE TO LISTEN TO ME! THERE'S ONLY ONE MAN THAT CAN SAVE US!
I'M TALKING ABOUT--
NATT
AAH-AAAAAAAAAAHHHH

WHAT THE HELL--?

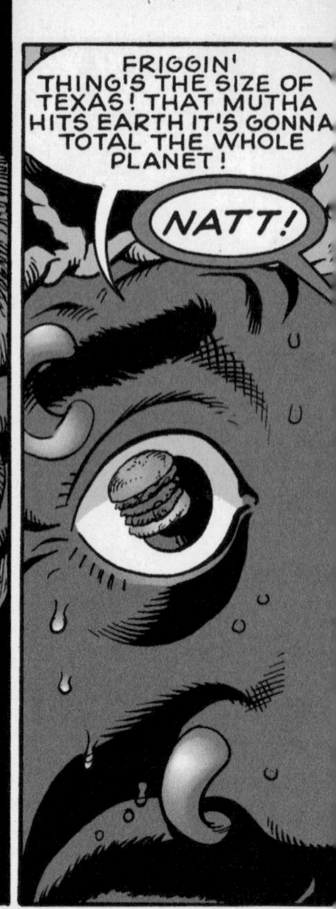
FRIGGIN' THING'S THE SIZE OF TEXAS! THAT MUTHA HITS EARTH IT'S GONNA TOTAL THE WHOLE PLANET!
NATT!

NATT, WE LOVE YOU! BUT YOU ONLY HAVE TWENTY-THREE HOURS AND SEVENTEEN MINUTES TO EAT THE BURGER!!

THEY'RE RIGHT! GOTTA EAT THE BURGER AN' SAVE THE WORLD!
WHY WON'T HE WAKE UP?

GRONCH CHOMP GARRONCH GRROMMFF
MAYBE HE'S HURT WORSE THAN HE LOOKS...

GRARRHH CHOMP CHOMP GRONNCCHH
THERE'S NOTHING WRONG WITH HIM. THROW A BUCKET OF WATER OVER HIS HEAD AND SNAP HIM OUT OF IT, FOR GOD'S SAKE.

YAAAAHH!

ENNIS WRITER McCREA PENCILLER LEACH INKER PRENTICE LETTERER FEENY COLORIST HEROICAGE SEPARATOR TOMASI EDITOR HITMAN CREATED BY ENNIS & McCREA

1972:
HAPPY BIRTHDAY TO YOU...
BLAM
AAAGGH!

1978:
HAPPY BIRTHDAY TO YOU...
BLAM
AAAGGH!

1985:
HAPPY BIRTHDAY, DEAR NAA-AATT...
BLAM
AAAGGH!

1989:
HAPPY BIRTHDAY TO YOU...
BLAM
AAAGGH!

THIS IS KIND OF A BAD AREA, AIN'T IT?
YOU THINK?

WHAT THE HELL YOU MEAN YOU JOININ' THE MARINES?!

YOU GONNA GO AN' GET YOURSELF KILLED FOR YOUR COUNTRY? WHAT YOUR COUNTRY EVER DONE FOR YOU, FOOL?
POPS, I AIN'T ABOUT TO GET KILLED! I'M'A GO IN FOR A COUPLE YEARS, LEARN SOME STUFF, GET OUT AGAIN!
I MEAN WHAT IS THERE FOR ME HERE, YOU KNOW?

NATT'S RIGHT, HONEY... IT'S BETTER THAN HIM RUNNING AROUND WITH THAT AWFUL GANG...
YOU SHUT YOUR MOUTH, WOMAN! KEEP OUTTA THIS!

POPS, DON'T YOU BE TALKIN' TO MOM LIKE THAT!
DON'T YOU SHOUT AT ME, PUNK! YOU AIN'T SO BIG I CAN'T STILL WHIP YOUR ASS!

...WHAT?

1990:
DANGER KEEP OUT
WALLS, YOU STUPID, BLIND BASTARD! YOUR SHOOTING IS A DISASTER! YOU WILL EFFECT AN IMMEDIATE IMPROVEMENT OR I WILL STAMP YOUR ASS INTO THE DIRT!
AYE-AYE, GUNNY--
THE DIRT, WALLS! GET TO IT!

YOU'RE SNATCHIN' THE TRIGGER.
WHAT?
TRY SQUEEZIN' IT.

YOU HEAR ME ASKIN' YOUR ADVICE, WHITE BOY?

SUIT YOURSELF...

DAMMIT!

...
WHAT WAS THAT ABOUT SNATCHIN' THE TRIGGER?

DON'T. YOU'RE THROWIN' YOUR AIM OFF. JUST SQUEEZE IT SLOWLY.
TAKE YOUR TIME.

...DON'T KNOW HOW YOU IMPROVED SO FAST, WALLS, BUT THAT IS ALMOST PASSABLE! YOU MAY YET MAKE IT AS A RIFLE-MAN IN THE UNITED STATES MARINE CORPS!

MONAGHAN?
MM?
THANKS.

MM.

YOU PAID YOUR TAXES YET, MONAGHAN?
?

TAXES...?
YEAH, ME AN' FISHER HERE'RE COLLECTIN' TAXES. EVERY MARINE IN THE SQUAD PAYS FIFTY BUCKS A MONTH--EVERY MARINE IN THE SQUAD STAYS HEALTHY.
SO PAY UP, SQUIRT.

SURE, BUT WHEN YOU AN' FISHER NAME THE DAY, MAKE SURE I GET AN INVITE TO THE WEDDIN'.
YOU GOTTA HAVE ROCKS IN YOUR HEAD IF YOU THINK YOU CAN PULL THIS RACKET IN THE CORPS, GUTHRIE.

UNNH!

YOU'RE ONE FUNNY BASTARD, AIN'T YOU, MONAGHAN?
NUHH--!

WELL YOU BETTER UNNH!

AAW--!

BEEN MEANIN' TO HAVE A TALK WIT' THESE TWO BITCHES.

SO YOU FROM GOTHAM, HUH?
YEP.
MY MOM'S FROM THERE. I BEEN A COUPLE TIMES.

LIKE IT?
FRIGGIN' PLACE IS WORSE'N DETROIT.

IT'S GOT ITS OWN SPECIAL CHARM, THERE AIN'T NO DOUBT ABOUT THAT.
YOU A PRETTY GOOD SHOT ONNA M16, MAN. YOU BEEN AROUND GUNS A LOT?

LITTLE BIT.
BUT YEAH, GUNNY BERDINKA'S GOT ME ON THE SNIPER COURSE. THEY GOT SOME COOL EQUIPMENT THERE, NIGHT SIGHTS AN' SUPPRESSORS AN' STUFF... HELL, YOU COULD WHACK A GUY FROM A MILE AWAY IN THE DARK AN' BE HOME BEFORE ANYONE KNEW JACK ABOUT IT.

SOUNDS A LOT MORE FUN THAN DRIVIN' THIS HUNKA JUNK AROUND.
SO WHAT, YOU THINKIN' OF MAKIN' A CAREER OUTTA THIS?
STAY IN THE CORPS? NOT ME, MAN. TWO YEARS AN' I'M OUTTA HERE.
I MEAN IT AIN'T AS BAD AS I EXPECTED, YOU KNOW, BUT I DON'T WANNA BE A MARINE FOREVER. I DON'T WANNA MARCH UP AN' DOWN AN' GET SCREAMED AT FOR A LIVIN'.

HEARD THAT.
WELL, YOU GET OUT, YOU COME AN' SEE ME IN GOTHAM. I'LL SHOW YOU 'ROUND THE EVEN WORSE PARTS.

NOW THAT IS A MIGHTY TEMPTIN' OFFER...

LET'S GO, WALLS.

YOU AIN'T GONNA NEED NO SHOWER.

GUTHRIE, WHAT THE HELL YOU DOIN'? YOU GONE OUTTA YOUR MUTHALOVIN' MIND?
OH, NOTHIN' LIKE THAT, BOY. YOU JUST GOT ME A LITTLE BIT RILED.
DO IT, FISHER.

UNNH!

YOU KNOW HOW WE DEAL WITH YOUR KIND IN ARKANSAS?
BOY?

WE MAKE SURE THERE AIN'T NONE OF THAT UPPITY CRAP IN THE NEXT LITTER--
NO!!

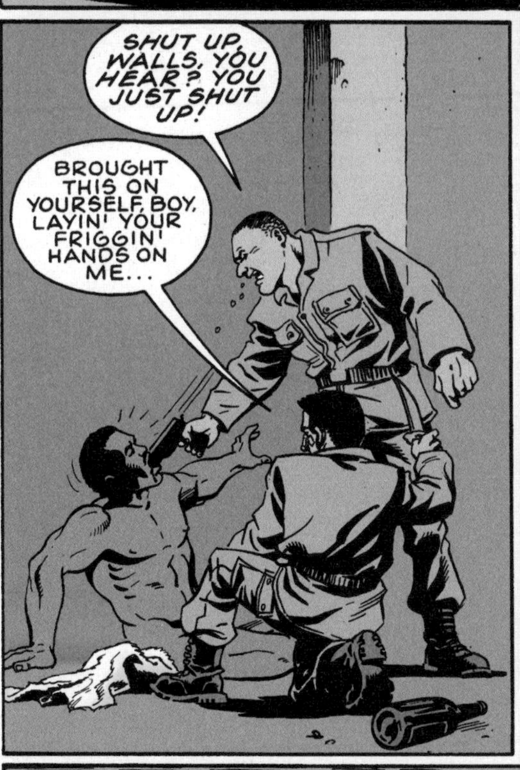
SHUT UP, WALLS, YOU HEAR? YOU JUST SHUT UP!
BROUGHT THIS ON YOURSELF, BOY, LAYIN' YOUR FRIGGIN' HANDS ON ME...

...
TOMMY.

NATT.

...SO I WAS COMIN' BACK FROM NIGHT TRIALS ON THE RANGE TO CHECK THIS THING AT THE ARMORY, AN' I SAW SOMETHIN' GOIN' ON I COULDN'T FIGURE. TOOK A LOOK WITH THE SCOPE AN' THERE YOU WERE...
THEY WERE GONNA--
THEY--

YOU COULDA WALKED AWAY, MAN. YOU COULDA JUST GONE FOR HELP.
NEVER'VE BEEN IN TIME.
YEAH. BUT I STILL KNOW WHAT YOU DONE FOR ME HERE.

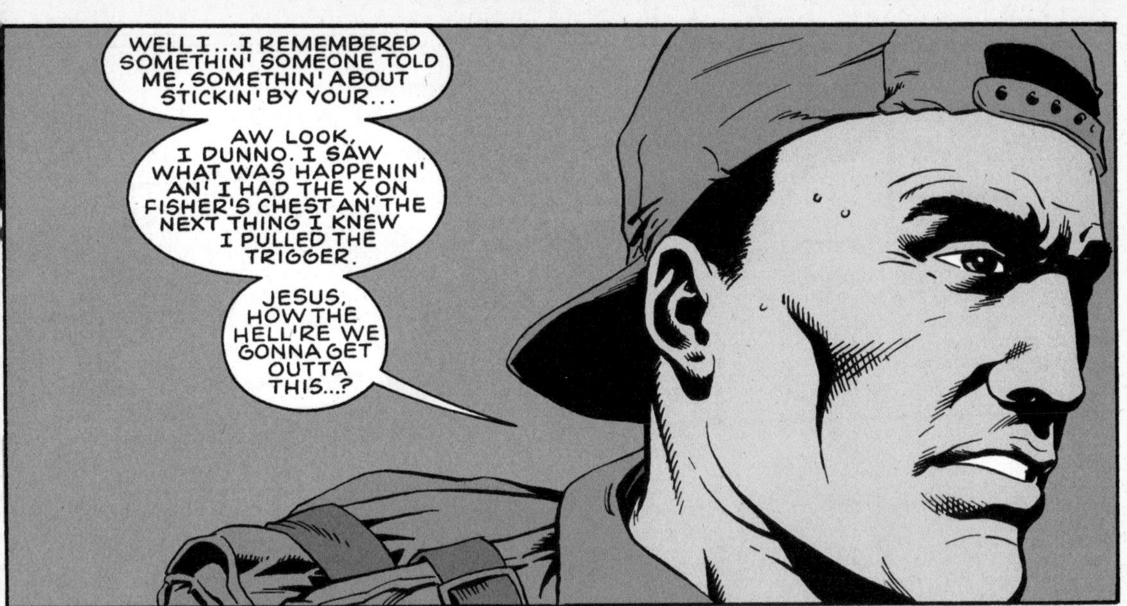
WELL I...I REMEMBERED SOMETHIN' SOMEONE TOLD ME, SOMETHIN' ABOUT STICKIN' BY YOUR...
AW LOOK, I DUNNO. I SAW WHAT WAS HAPPENIN' AN' I HAD THE X ON FISHER'S CHEST AN' THE NEXT THING I KNEW I PULLED THE TRIGGER.
JESUS, HOW THE HELL'RE WE GONNA GET OUTTA THIS...?

WELL.

YOU PICK UP THE SPENT SHELLS?
IN MY POCKET.
OKAY, WE GET RIDDA THEM AN' FISHER'S THIRTY-EIGHT. WE CLEAN UP HERE. WE KEEP THE WHISKEY BOTTLE--

'CAUSE WE GOTTA MAKE SURE IT'S OBVIOUS THEY BEEN DRINKIN', THAT'S THE FIRST AN' ONLY THING WE WANNA AUTOPSY GUY LOOKIN' FOR.
I DO GOT KIND OF A IDEA HERE, BUT...UH...

BUT FIRST WE GOTTA DIG THE BULLETS OUTTA THESE TWO FOOLS.

OH GOD, NO!
THE HORROR!

I-I-I WAS JUST BACKIN' HER OUT FOR A ENGINE TEST! I DIDN'T KNOW THEY WERE THERE!

THEY MUSTA GOT DRUNK AN' PASSED OUT BEHIND THE BRADLEY!

GODDAMMIT--!
THAT'S FISHER, WHO'S THE OTHER ONE?
GUTHRIE WAS MISSIN' AT REVEILLE, GUNNY. HE USUALLY HANGS WITH FISHER.

WHO'D HE SAY IT WAS?
GUTHRIE AN' FISHER.
OH.
THOSE POOR GUYS--!
GUNNERY SERGEANT BERDINKA, HOW-HOW CAN I EVER FORGIVE MYSELF?
I KNOW, SON, I KNOW. IT'S NEVER EASY SEEIN' MARINES DIE.

BUT I GUESS IT HELPS IF IT'S A COUPLE OF USELESS TURDS LIKE THESE TWO, HUH, GUNNY?
HMP--!

YOU ALWAYS BEEN THIS MUCH OF A WISEASS?
IT'S MY CURSE.

MAKIN' ME LAUGH LIKE THAT...
WELL, SO LONG AS WE'RE IN THE CLEAR. CORONER'S REPORT WAS POSTED YESTER-DAY, CONFIRMED THEY WERE DRUNK WHEN THEY DIED.
YES SIR, ALL OUR TROUBLES ARE OVER...

HEY, YOU GUYS HEARD THE NEWS? SADDAM HUSSEIN JUST INVADED KUWAIT!

SADDAM WHO?
WHERE THE HELL IS KUWAIT?

AW, WHO CARES...

HE SAID SEAN NOONAN SENT ME, I'M GONNA SAVE YOUR LIFE. AN' I COULD TELL HE WAS PACKIN' A FORTY-FOUR MAGNUM.
THEN I PASSED OUT.
NAN'S SLEAZY BAR

AND HE TOOK TOMMY WITH HIM?
HOW'D YOU KNOW IT WAS A FORTY-FOUR?
NOTHIN' ELSE SOUNDS LIKE THAT, HACKEN.

IT'S JUST THAT SEAN KNEW THIS COP WHO USED TO COME IN HERE, THIS BIG GUY CALLED CONNOLLY. HE CARRIED A HAND-CANNON LIKE THAT, AN' SEAN WAS ALWAYS ON AT HIM TO GET AN AUTOMATIC...

IF THE POLICE HAVE MONAGHAN, I KNOW A FED GEEK WHO CAN CHECK THEIR COMPUTER--
I NEVER KNEW SEAN HAD FRIENDS ONNA FORCE...
THEY WEREN'T EXACTLY FRIENDS. THE GUY ONLY DRANK HERE ABOUT ONCE A YEAR.

SO HOW COME TOMMY AN' ME NEVER MET HIM?
'CAUSE YOU GOT A LIFE.
I'M ALWAYS HERE.

THAT'S WEIRD, THERE'S NO RECORD OF ANY ARREST...
♪I AM BAYTOR...! ♪

SEAN'S OL' ADDRESS BOOK!
YOU THINK THE GUY TOOK MONAGHAN *HOME* WITH HIM?

ARRESTIN' TOMMY WOULDN'T SAVE HIS LIFE, THEY'D SEND HIM STRAIGHT TO THE CHAIR-- *CONNOLLY!*
ONE TWENNY-SEVEN SAINT, JESUS, THAT'S NOT EVEN TEN BLOCKS FROM HERE!
Pick up

I'M GONNA GO HAVE WORDS WIT' THIS MUTHALOVIN' COP...
ME TOO.

BUT IF TRUMAN COMES FOR MAGGIE--
IF HE HITS US WITHOUT MONAGHAN HERE WE'RE ALL DEAD ANYWAY!
GUARD HER WIT' YOUR *LIFE,* HACKEN!

HURRY IT UP, McALLISTER!
WHAT EXACTLY IS YOUR PROBLEM WITH ME?

MY PROBLEM IS I DON'T FRIGGIN' TRUST YOU. I THINK YOU WORKIN' SOME KINDA ANGLE HERE, AN' JUST 'CAUSE YOU OUT TO NAIL TRUMAN DON'T MEAN YOU GIVE A DAMN ABOUT TOMMY.
I THINK ONCE C.I.A., *ALWAYS* C.I.A...
I WISH YOU'D TELL MY EX-COLLEAGUES THAT. IT MIGHT STOP THEM TRYING TO KILL ME.
ANY OTHER WHINING YOU WANT TO DO, OR CAN WE GET ON WITH SAVING YOUR FRIEND'S LIFE?

YOU WATCH YOUR MOUTH, YOU--
SHUT UP.
I FOUND HIM.

LET'S PLAY THIS CAREFULLY. UP THE FIRE ESCAPE AND IN VIA THE DERELICT APARTMENT NEXT TO CONNOLLY'S.
LET'S JUST GET IT DONE.

WHOA.

LOOKS LIKE THE GUY'S A LITTLE PARANOID ABOUT VISITORS...
SO WOULD YOU BE, IF YOU WAS A COP IN THIS NEIGHBORHOOD--

KLIK

WELL?
I--

I THINK I GOT MY FOOT ON SOME KINDA MINE.
I THINK I ARMED IT.

IS THAT A FACT.

YOU'RE STANDING ON AN ANTI-PERSONNEL MINE. IT'LL DETONATE THE INSTANT YOU TAKE YOUR FOOT OFF IT.
I SUPPOSE THE THING ABOUT A SITUATION LIKE THIS ONE--

IS WHAT IT TEACHES YOU ABOUT TRUST.
MM?
SNAK
Closing Time: 6
GARTH ENNIS WRITER
JOHN McCREA PENCILLER
GARRY LEACH INKER
PAT PRENTICE LETTERER
CARLA FEENY COLORIST
HEROIC AGE SEPARATOR
PETER TOMASI EDITOR
HITMAN CREATED BY ENNIS & McCREA

WELL, NOW.

ISN'T THAT SOMETHING.

I TOLD YOU THIS WOULD HAPPEN. THEY'RE INSANE WITH HUNGER; THE INSTANT THE SHACKLES CAME OFF THEY TURNED ON THE FIRST FOOD THEY SAW.
WHICH IN THIS CASE WAS--
I HAVE EYES, DOCTOR.

GOOD! BECAUSE THAT'S THE SUM TOTAL OF PROJECT BLOODLINES, MR. TRUMAN! THAT'S WHAT THAT *ALIEN FILTH* YOU HAD ME PUMP INTO THOSE MEN *DOES!*
YOU THINK YOU'RE GOING TO GET SUPER-HUMANS OUT OF THIS? YOU THINK THE NEXT STEP IN HUMAN EVOLUTION STARTS WITH YOU BUILDING WHAT AMOUNTS TO A *DEATH CAMP?*

I THINK *YOU'RE* GOING TO GET SUPERHUMANS OUT OF THIS, DOCTOR. THAT, AFTER ALL, IS WHY I EMPLOYED YOU IN THE FIRST PLACE.
THAT'S WHY I EXTRICATED YOU FROM THAT STICKY BUSINESS WHERE YOU'D RAPED TWO OF YOUR STUDENTS...

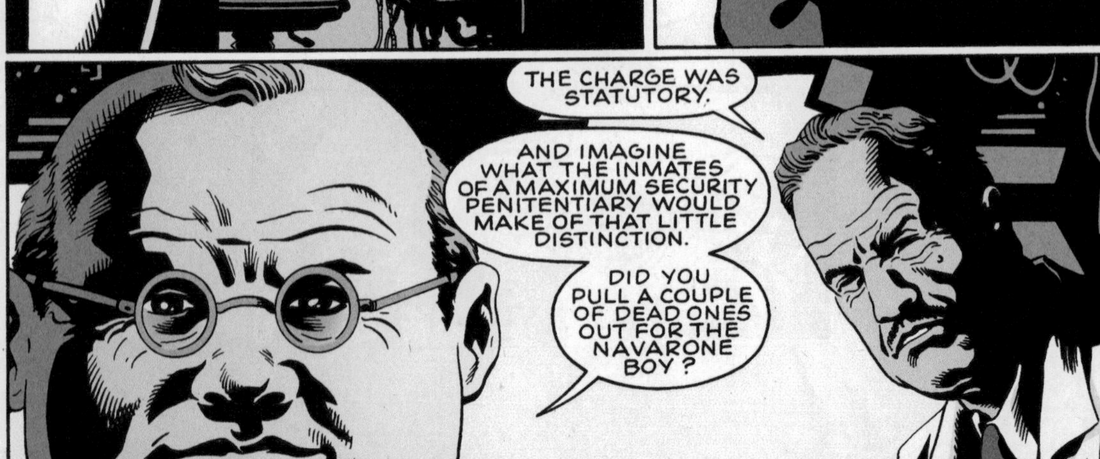
THE CHARGE WAS STATUTORY.
AND IMAGINE WHAT THE INMATES OF A MAXIMUM SECURITY PENITENTIARY WOULD MAKE OF THAT LITTLE DISTINCTION.
DID YOU PULL A COUPLE OF DEAD ONES OUT FOR THE NAVARONE BOY?

THREE OF THEM, AS PER HIS REQUEST.
THE CREEPY LITTLE BASTARD...
OURS NOT TO REASON WHY, DOCTOR. IF MARC WANTS TO PRACTICE HIS MARKSMANSHIP ON CADAVERS, THAT'S HIS BUSINESS.
HE'S THE ONE WHO'LL BE PLUGGING THAT SECURITY LEAK YOU'RE SO CONCERNED ABOUT...
WHY HIM? YOU'VE GOT AN ARMY OF C.I.A. THUGS AT YOUR DISPOSAL-- WHAT DO YOU NEED SOME BRAT FROM MIAMI FOR?
BECAUSE HE'S THE BEST THERE IS.
BECAUSE HIS OPPONENT IS THE SLIPPERIEST, SNEAKIEST, BALLSIEST, *LUCKIEST* PLAYER I'VE RUN ACROSS IN NEARLY FORTY YEARS OF BLACK OPS.
BECAUSE WHAT WE'RE DOING HERE *CANNOT* BE MADE PUBLIC, NO MATTER HOW MUCH BLOOD MUST BE SPILT TO COVER IT UP.
SO IT'S MARC NAVARONE VERSUS TOMMY MONAGHAN, TOMORROW NIGHT, ON THE DARK, DARK STREETS OF GOTHAM CITY.
I'LL HAVE A RINGSIDE SEAT.
YOU'LL BE BUSY HERE, OF COURSE.
CARRY ON.

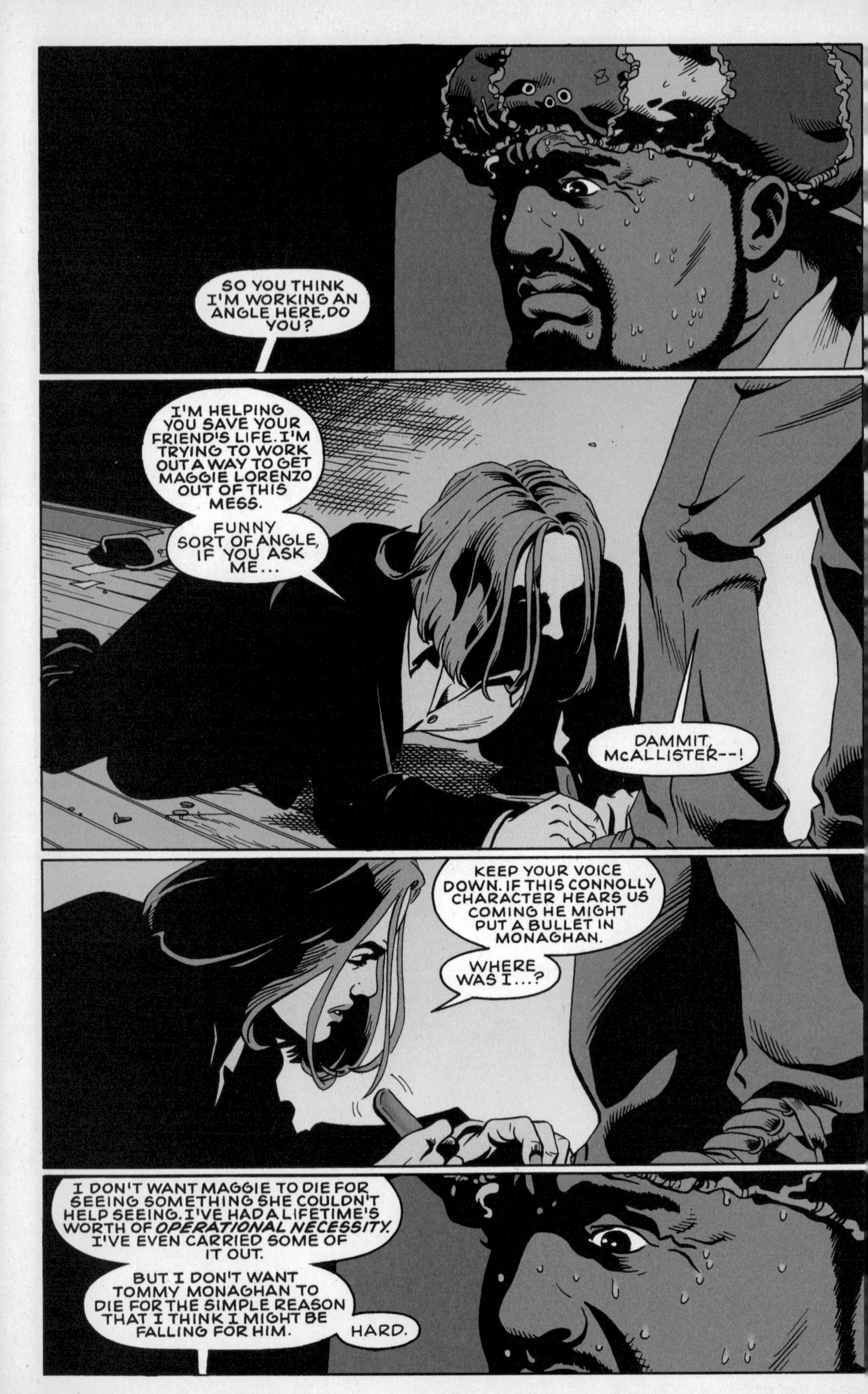
SO YOU THINK I'M WORKING AN ANGLE HERE, DO YOU?
I'M HELPING YOU SAVE YOUR FRIEND'S LIFE. I'M TRYING TO WORK OUT A WAY TO GET MAGGIE LORENZO OUT OF THIS MESS.
FUNNY SORT OF ANGLE, IF YOU ASK ME...
DAMMIT, McALLISTER--!
KEEP YOUR VOICE DOWN. IF THIS CONNOLLY CHARACTER HEARS US COMING HE MIGHT PUT A BULLET IN MONAGHAN.
WHERE WAS I...?
I DON'T WANT MAGGIE TO DIE FOR SEEING SOMETHING SHE COULDN'T HELP SEEING. I'VE HAD A LIFETIME'S WORTH OF *OPERATIONAL NECESSITY.* I'VE EVEN CARRIED SOME OF IT OUT.
BUT I DON'T WANT TOMMY MONAGHAN TO DIE FOR THE SIMPLE REASON THAT I THINK I MIGHT BE FALLING FOR HIM.
HARD.

THAT'LL BE OUR LITTLE SECRET FOR THE TIME BEING, MIND YOU.
DON'T SHIFT YOUR WEIGHT...

I LIKE HIM. HE REMINDS ME OF ME A LITTLE BIT.
I TALK ABOUT WANTING TO QUIT WHAT I DO AND HE UNDERSTANDS COMPLETELY. I'VE NEVER BEEN WITH ANYONE I CAN EVEN *DESCRIBE* MY JOB TO BEFORE. AND IT'S THE SAME FOR HIM.
I'M PROBABLY NOT MAKING A LOT OF SENSE...
I WISH.
I JUST HAVE A FEELING HE AND I MIGHT BE EACH OTHER'S WAY OUT OF THIS.
IT'S NEVER ENOUGH TO PROMISE YOURSELF YOU'LL RETIRE, YOU'RE TAKING THIS ONE LAST JOB. IT'S ALWAYS SUCH A *LIE*.

BUT PROMISE SOMEONE ELSE-- SOMEONE WHO KNOWS WHAT IT'S LIKE--
PROMISE *EACH OTHER* YOU'LL QUIT, AND GOD KNOWS WHAT COULD HAPPEN.

YOU REALLY DO LIKE HIM, HUH...?
I REALLY DO. HE'S A KILLER, BUT HE DOESN'T LET IT TURN HIM INTO A MONSTER.

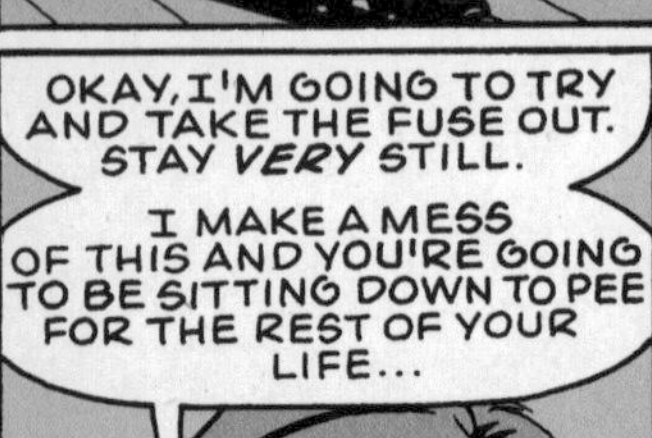
OKAY, I'M GOING TO TRY AND TAKE THE FUSE OUT. STAY *VERY* STILL.
I MAKE A MESS OF THIS AND YOU'RE GOING TO BE SITTING DOWN TO PEE FOR THE REST OF YOUR LIFE...

OF COURSE, YOU'RE GOING TO HAVE TO BE LIFTED ONTO THE JOHN TO DO IT. I'M ONLY GLAD I WON'T BE AROUND TO WITNESS THAT LITTLE DISPLAY.

YOU KNOW SOMETHIN?
YOU AN' HIM WAS *MADE* FOR EACH OTHER.

BINGO.

?
NEW PERSPECTIVE ON THE CHARGE OF THE LIGHT BRIGADE
GIBSON

NOT ONE WORD, PUNK.
WHA...?

3a
GO.

YAAAA--
WHOA!!
JESUS--!

DAMMIT!
AAH--!

HELL--

OH, CHRIST--
McALLISTER! GET HIM! GET HIM!

I'LL HIT BOTH OF YOU!
YAAACCCHH

MAGGOT--
BASTARD--

WHAT'RE YOU DOIN' HERE?
WHATHIT-- LOOCCH LICCH--

NO!!
I DON'T FRIGGIN' BELIEVE THIS--

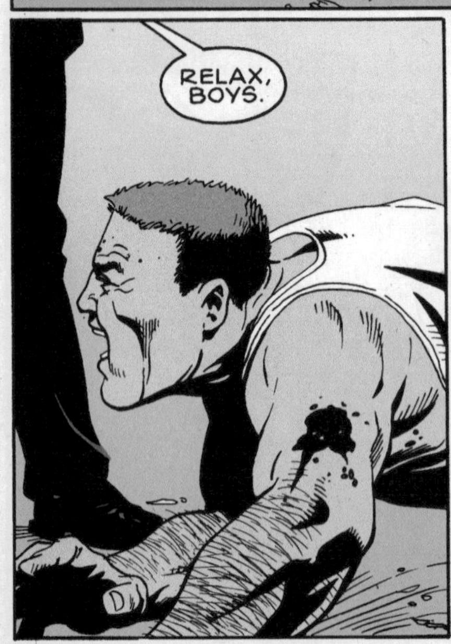
RELAX, BOYS.

IT ISN'T FUSED.
DON'T KILL HIM!

...COME AGAIN?

WHASSUP WIT' THIS FOOL, ANYHOW?

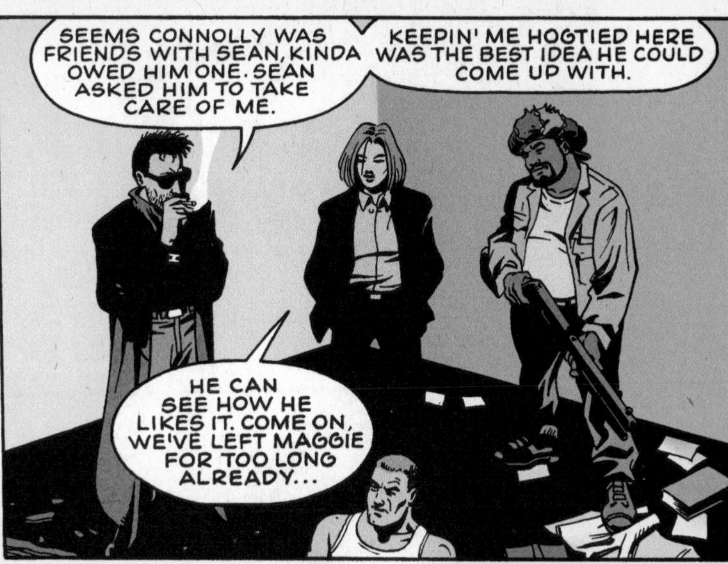
SEEMS CONNOLLY WAS FRIENDS WITH SEAN, KINDA OWED HIM ONE. SEAN ASKED HIM TO TAKE CARE OF ME.
KEEPIN' ME HOGTIED HERE WAS THE BEST IDEA HE COULD COME UP WITH.
HE CAN SEE HOW HE LIKES IT. COME ON, WE'VE LEFT MAGGIE FOR TOO LONG ALREADY...

AN' THAT'S YOUR *SOMETHIN' SPECIAL*, IS IT, PUNK?

WHAT?

...
GIMME A MINUTE WITH HIM.

SO WHAT WAS THAT SUPPOSED TO MEAN ?
IT'S SOMETHIN' NOONAN SAID.

WHEN HE CALLED ME ABOUT THIS I ASKED HIM WHAT IT WAS MADE YOU WORTH SO MUCH TROUBLE. AN' BACK THEN I DIDN'T KNOW WHAT A WORLD-CLASS BUTCHER YOU WERE, SO WHAT HE SAID TO ME DIDN'T SEEM SO STRANGE.
THE OTHER KID, HIS NEPHEW-- PAT ?
HE ONCE TOLD NOONAN HE THOUGHT YOU WERE GONNA DO SOMETHIN' SPECIAL ONE DAY.
HE DIDN'T KNOW WHAT IT WAS, BUT HE FIGURED THEY HAD TO PROTECT YOU FOR IT. JUST A FEELIN', HE SAID.
NOONAN MUSTA TOOK IT TO HEART.

SO IS THIS IT, PUNK? IS GOIN' UP AGAINST THE C.I.A. FOR SOME GIRL NO ONE'S GONNA MISS, IS THAT THE BEST YOU CAN DO ?
I'M SURE PAT AN' HIS UNCLE SEAN'D LOVE THAT, AFTER ALL THE CARE AN' HOPE THEY WASTED ON YOUR WORTHLESS ASS...

FELLAS.

YOU LISTEN, CONNOLLY.
AN' YOU LISTEN GOOD.

MAGGIE LORENZO AIN'T NOBODY SPECIAL. SHE'S GONNA COME AN' GO FROM THIS EARTH AN' MOST FOLKS'LL NEVER EVEN KNOW SHE EXISTED. ALL SHE EVER WANTED WAS TO LIVE HER LIFE WITHOUT SCREWIN' THINGS UP FOR ANYONE ELSE.
THERE ARE MILLIONS OF PEOPLE LIKE HER.

SO IN MY BOOK SHE'S DUE WHAT EVERYONE'S DUE: A *CHANCE*.
AN' SHE'S GONNA GET HER CHANCE. THE KID SHE'S CARRYIN' INSIDE HER'S GONNA GET HIS TOO, I'M GONNA FRIGGIN' MAKE SURE OF IT.
I'M GONNA KILL ANY SON OF A BITCH I HAVE TO UNTIL THAT GIRL IS SAFE--

AN' THEN I'M HANGIN' UP MY GUNS.
THAT MIGHT NOT BE GOOD ENOUGH FOR YOU, CONNOLLY, BUT IT WOULDA BEEN FOR SEAN AN' PAT NOONAN. TAKE IT FROM SOMEONE ACTUALLY KNEW 'EM.
GCPD

YOU DON'T BELIEVE WE CAN ESCAPE THE PAST, BIG MAN? YOU JUST WATCH ME.
BUT STAY THE HELL OUTTA MY WAY.

MONAGHAN!!

MAGNIFICENT AS EVER, MARC.

MARC?
THEY...

THEY LOOK AT YOU.
EVEN IN DEATH THEIR EYES ARE OPEN.
DOES IT BOTHER YOU?
I DIDN'T KNOW THEY LOOKED BACK AT YOU.
DEAD PEOPLE.

BUT NO, IT DOESN'T BOTHER ME.

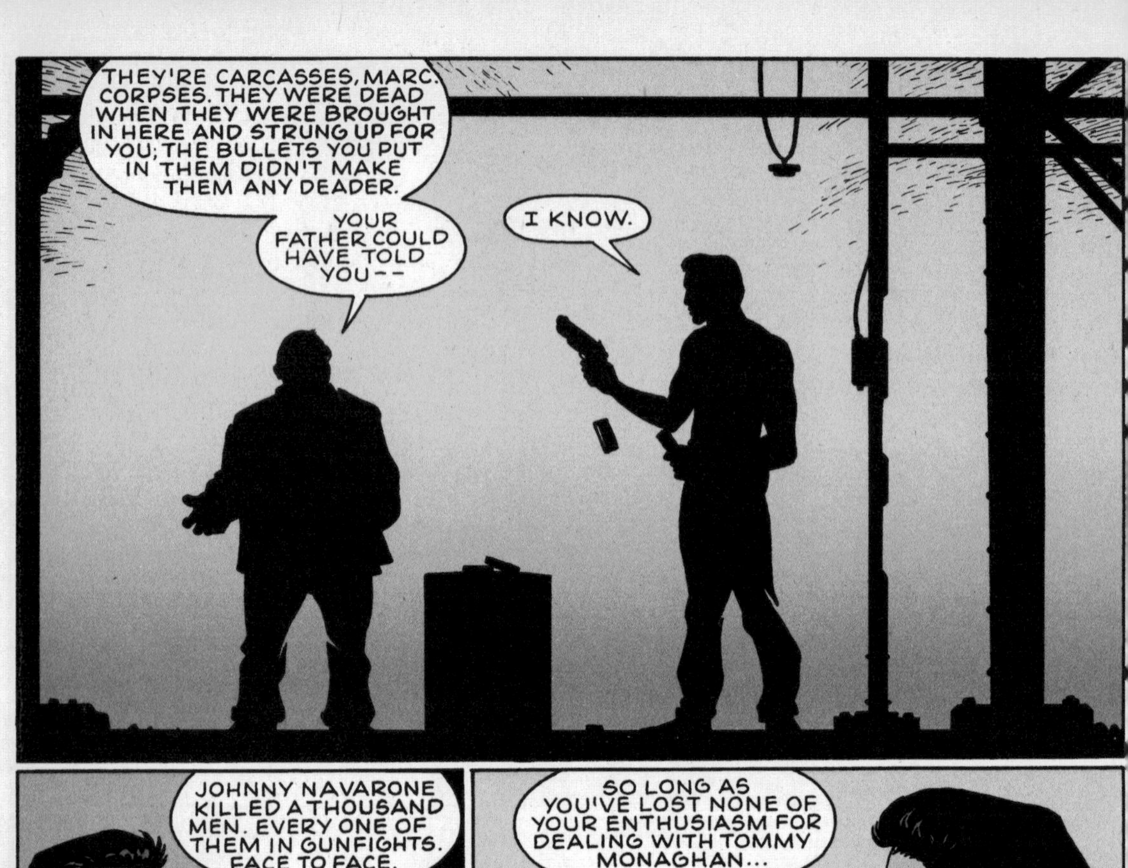
THEY'RE CARCASSES, MARC. CORPSES. THEY WERE DEAD WHEN THEY WERE BROUGHT IN HERE AND STRUNG UP FOR YOU; THE BULLETS YOU PUT IN THEM DIDN'T MAKE THEM ANY DEADER.
YOUR FATHER COULD HAVE TOLD YOU--
I KNOW.

JOHNNY NAVARONE KILLED A THOUSAND MEN. EVERY ONE OF THEM IN GUNFIGHTS. FACE TO FACE.
I INTEND TO DOUBLE THAT FIGURE, LONG BEFORE I REACH THE AGE HE DIED AT.
SO LONG AS YOU'VE LOST NONE OF YOUR ENTHUSIASM FOR DEALING WITH TOMMY MONAGHAN...
HE THREW MY TRAINING INTO CHAOS WHEN HE SHOT MY FATHER. THERE IS NO ONE I WANT TO MEET MORE.

SO: WHEN?
TOMORROW NIGHT, AT A BAR IN A LOCAL SLUM. HE AND SEVERAL COMPANIONS ARE GUARDING A WOMAN THERE.
THEY GO TOO.

OF COURSE...

IT'S JUST HUMAN MEAT, MARC.

NOTHING TO GET EXCITED ABOUT.

YOU GUYS MUSTA HAD QUITE A NIGHT...
NAN'S SLEAZY BAR

ONE TO REMEMBER, ALL RIGHT. HOW'S MAGGIE?
OKAY, I THINK. PUKED A COUPLE TIMES.

SHE SAID IT WAS *MORNING SICKNESS,* BUT I FIGURED SHE MEANT A HANG-OVER...
WHY DON'T YOU GO GET SOME SLEEP YOURSELF, HACKEN?

THANKS, BAYTOR.
I AM HE.

LEMME GUESS: WE'RE AT UP-THE-CREEK-WITHOUT-A-PADDLE DOT COM.
NOT QUITE. GOOD NEWS OR BAD NEWS?

LET'S END ON A HIGH NOTE, HUH?
MY FED PAL'S BEEN TALKING TO HIS OPPOSITE NUMBER IN THE C.I.A., WHO SAYS THEY'D BE ONLY TOO HAPPY TO THROW TRUMAN TO THE MEDIA--BUT ONLY *IF* THEY CAN BE KEPT OUT OF THE LIMELIGHT THEMSELVES.
SO NO ONE AT THE BUREAU'S ALL THAT INTERESTED IN GETTING US OUT. IF THEY CAN'T *ROYALLY* SCREW THE PENTAGON BOYS, THEN WHY BOTHER AT ALL?

SO OUTTA THE FRYIN' PAN, INTO A BIG POT OF TURDS...
HOLD ON.
THIS FRIEND OF MINE, THIS F.B.I. GUY, HE'S KIND OF A BLUE-EYED BOY. HEART IN THE RIGHT PLACE, WANTS TO DO A LITTLE GOOD, ETCETERA, ETCETERA.

HIS OFFICE CAN GET US OUT, BUT THE RESOURCES THEY CAN DRAW ON WITHOUT THE DIRECTOR NOTICING ARE LIMITED.
ONE HELICOPTER. WITNESS PROTECTION FOR *MAGGIE, ONLY,* IN EXCHANGE FOR WHAT SHE HAS ON TRUMAN--AND THAT'S IT. THEY'RE GOING TO KEEP THE COMPANY OUT OF IT.
WHICH MEANS THE THREE OF US WILL HAVE TO LEAVE THE COUNTRY.

...JESUS.
AN' THE GOOD NEWS?

DON'T GET TOO EXCITED.
THE FEDS TRACED DELIVERIES OF C.I.A. EQUIPMENT AND MUNITIONS TO A WAREHOUSE ON THE GOTHAM DOCKS. IT ALL WENT IN, DIDN'T COME OUT AGAIN, WASN'T THERE A DAY LATER WHEN THE AGENTS SEARCHED THE PLACE.

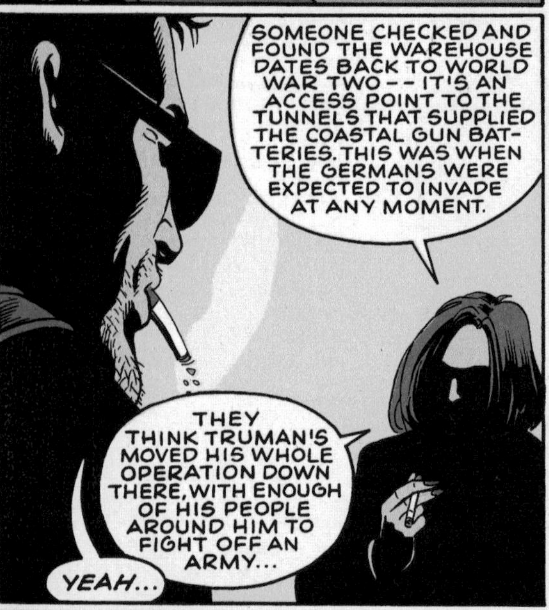
SOMEONE CHECKED AND FOUND THE WAREHOUSE DATES BACK TO WORLD WAR TWO -- IT'S AN ACCESS POINT TO THE TUNNELS THAT SUPPLIED THE COASTAL GUN BATTERIES. THIS WAS WHEN THE GERMANS WERE EXPECTED TO INVADE AT ANY MOMENT.
THEY THINK TRUMAN'S MOVED HIS WHOLE OPERATION DOWN THERE, WITH ENOUGH OF HIS PEOPLE AROUND HIM TO FIGHT OFF AN ARMY...
YEAH...

I KNOW THOSE TUNNELS. CAULDRON KIDS USED TO PLAY IN 'EM ALLA TIME, 'TIL SOME LITTLE GIRL GOT LOST AN' THE ENTRANCES WERE BRICKED UP IN SEVENTY-NINE. THEY GO ON FOREVER DOWN THERE.
TRUMAN COULDA MOVED IN AN' FIXED THE PLACE UP LIKE NEW. AN' NOBODY'DA BEEN NONE THE WISER.

BUT YOU THINK *HE* KNOWS ABOUT THE *OLDER* TUNNELS--THE BOOTLEGGIN' TUNNELS--THAT CONNECT UP WITH HIS LITTLE HIDEY-HOLE?

WE USED 'EM BEFORE, REMEMBER? AFTER THE MAWZIR THING?
YEAH... BUT...
WHAT YOU SAYIN' HERE, MAN?

TRUMAN'S OUR PROBLEM. BETWEEN HIS GOONS AN' THE G.C.P.D. WE'LL NEVER GET OUTTA GOTHAM, WITH OR WITHOUT A CHOPPER.
SO WE QUIT WAITIN' FOR HIM TO MAKE HIS MOVE, FOR THIS NAVARONE KID TO JUMP OUTTA THIN AIR AN' SLAUGHTER US ALL LIKE RATS. INSTEADA THAT *WE HIT THEM*.

SO WE GO IN UNDERGROUND AN' WE DO WHAT WE DO. SLOW AN' SNEAKY. ON 'EM BEFORE THEY KNOW WHAT'S HAPPENIN'.
WE TAKE OUT THAT ARMY OF MAGGOTS WHILE THEY'RE STILL BLINKIN' THE SLEEP OUTTA THEIR EYES, WE FIND AGENT FREAKIN' TRUMAN, WE FIND HIS LITTLE PUNK WANNABE KILLER--

AN' WE HIT THOSE SONS OF BITCHES WITH A *TON* OF NINE MILLIMETER.
THAT IS WHAT I'M SAYIN' HERE.

NO ADMITTANCE
OUT

THIS HERE IS OFFICER CONNOLLY...
CAME SNOOPIN' ROUND THE BACKA THE BUILDIN', CAUGHT CLARK HERE COMIN' OUT THE WINDOW. HADDA SAP HIM AN' THROW HIM INNA TRUNK.
YOU GONNA KILL HIM FOR US, NOONAN?

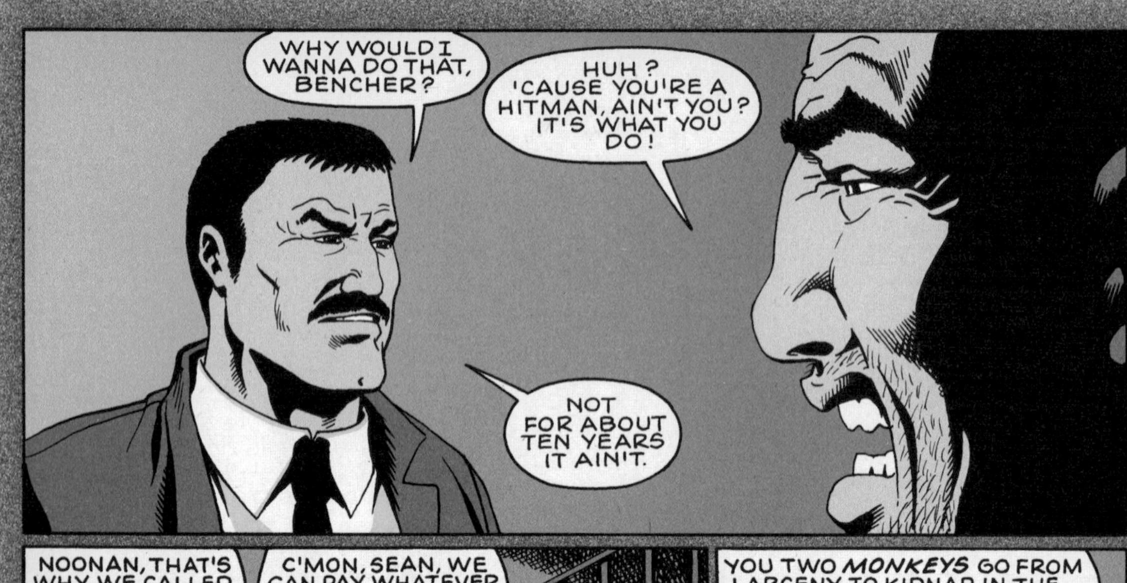

YOU TWO ***MONKEYS*** GO FROM LARCENY TO KIDNAP IN THE BLINK OF AN EYE, AN' NOW YOU WANNA TAKE IT ALL THE WAY UP TO HOMICIDE? WORSE'N THAT, YOU AIN'T GOT THE GUTS TO DO IT YOURSELF--SO YOU INVOLVE ***ME?***

GET OUTTA THE CITY, BOTHA YOU. GET OUTTA THE GODDAMN COUNTRY.

I'M LETTIN' THIS KID GO.

NOONAN! NOONAN, I'M WARNIN' YOU! IT'S GONE TOO FAR NOW, WE'RE ALL OF US IN TOO DEEP!

I SWEAR TO GOD IF YOU DON'T KILL HIM I WILL! AN' YOU ALONG WITH HIM! ***NOONAN!***

YOU STUPID FREAKIN' BASTARD, THE SON OF A BITCH'LL NAIL US ALL!!

SMART MAN, CLARK.
WAIT A MINUTE, HE'S A WITNESS-- I MEAN A SUSPECT--
STOP--!

NEW IN THE CAULDRON, SON?
WHAT? WHAT'RE YOU TALKIN' ABOUT?
YOU JUST KILLED SOMEONE, JESUS, DON'T YOU REALIZE WHAT THIS MEANS?

IT MEANS YOU OWE ME ONE.

WE GOT OUR OWN WAYA DOIN' THINGS IN THIS NEIGHBORHOOD. BUT YOU'LL GET USED TO IT.
GIVE THE BOYS AT THE PRECINCT MY BEST, OFFICER CONNOLLY.

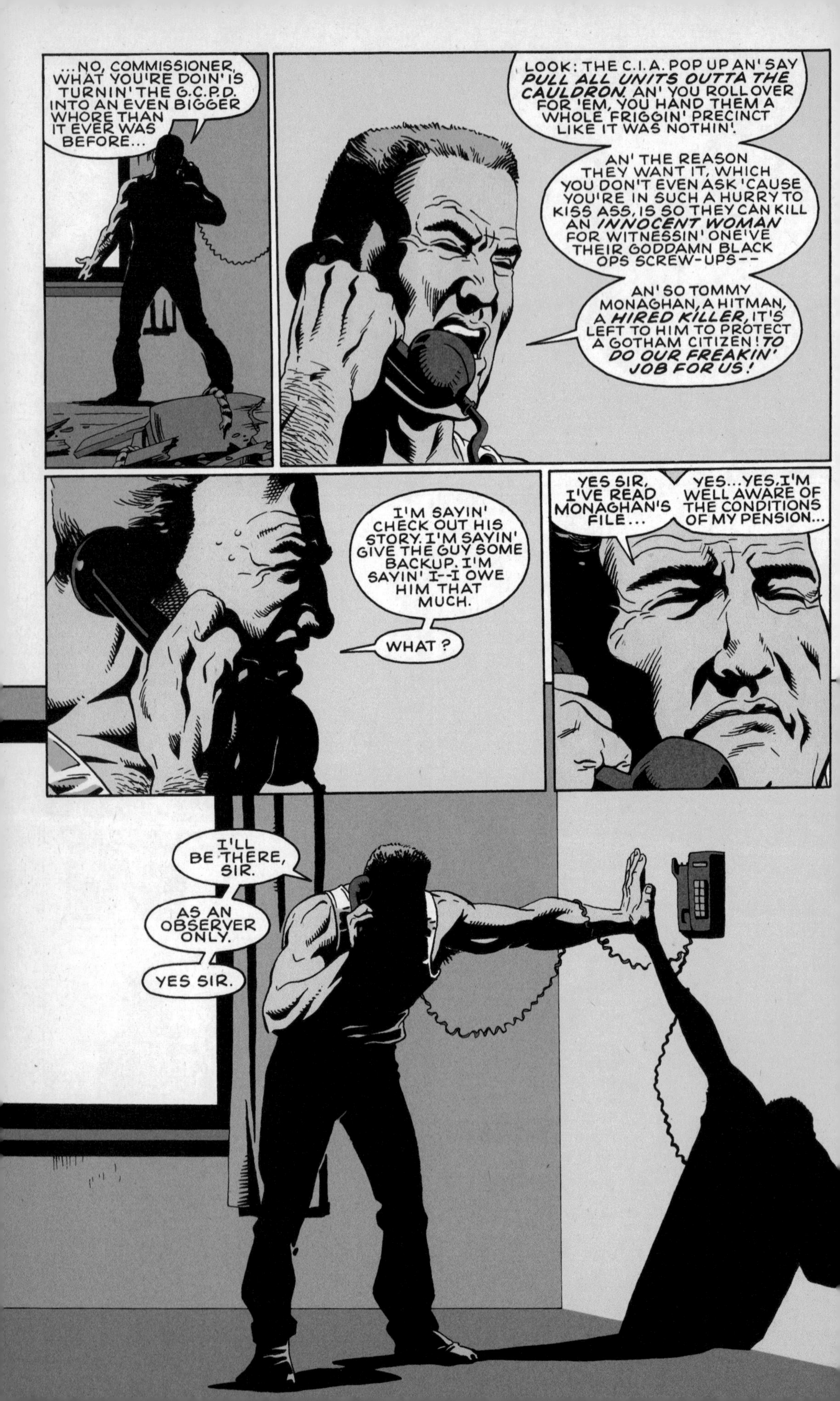
...NO, COMMISSIONER, WHAT YOU'RE DOIN' IS TURNIN' THE G.C.P.D. INTO AN EVEN BIGGER WHORE THAN IT EVER WAS BEFORE...
LOOK: THE C.I.A. POP UP AN' SAY PULL ALL UNITS OUTTA THE CAULDRON, AN' YOU ROLL OVER FOR 'EM, YOU HAND THEM A WHOLE FRIGGIN' PRECINCT LIKE IT WAS NOTHIN'.
AN' THE REASON THEY WANT IT, WHICH YOU DON'T EVEN ASK 'CAUSE YOU'RE IN SUCH A HURRY TO KISS ASS, IS SO THEY CAN KILL AN INNOCENT WOMAN FOR WITNESSIN' ONE'VE THEIR GODDAMN BLACK OPS SCREW-UPS--
AN' SO TOMMY MONAGHAN, A HITMAN, A HIRED KILLER, IT'S LEFT TO HIM TO PROTECT A GOTHAM CITIZEN! TO DO OUR FREAKIN' JOB FOR US!
I'M SAYIN' CHECK OUT HIS STORY. I'M SAYIN' GIVE THE GUY SOME BACKUP. I'M SAYIN' I--I OWE HIM THAT MUCH.
WHAT?
YES SIR, I'VE READ MONAGHAN'S FILE...
YES...YES, I'M WELL AWARE OF THE CONDITIONS OF MY PENSION...
I'LL BE THERE, SIR.
AS AN OBSERVER ONLY.
YES SIR.

Closing Time: 7
GARTH ENNIS WRITER
JOHN McCREA PENCILLER
GARRY LEACH INKER
PAT PRENTICE LETTERER
CARLA FEENY COLORIST
HEROIC AGE SEPARATOR
PETER TOMASI EDITOR
HITMAN CREATED BY ENNIS & McCREA
--THIS FACILITY HAS BEEN BREACHED--
--SECURITY TO SECTOR DELTA, THIS FACILITY HAS BEEN BREACHED--
--WE ARE UNDER ARMED ATTACK--

WE IN, GODDAMN, WE REALLY IN! KEEP POURIN' IT ON!
CHECK THE SIDE DOORS, LET'S DO SOME FRIGGIN' DAMAGE HERE!
CANTEEN!
ONE SECOND!
MR.TRUMAN, WE'VE BEEN--
MARC?
READY.

PRIORITY ONE IS *TRUMAN*. WITHOUT HIM IT'S ALL FOR NOTHING--
DOORWAY ONNA LEFT--

WHAT THE HELL IS GOING ON, WHAT'S THIS *ALERT* CRAP--
THERE!!
BARRACKS ROOM!

KEEP THEIR HEADS DOWN!
MUST BE THIRTY PLUS IN THERE--
CHARGES READY!

REMEMBER: THIS IS THE MAN WHO KILLED YOUR--
DON'T PATRONIZE ME, MR. TRUMAN.

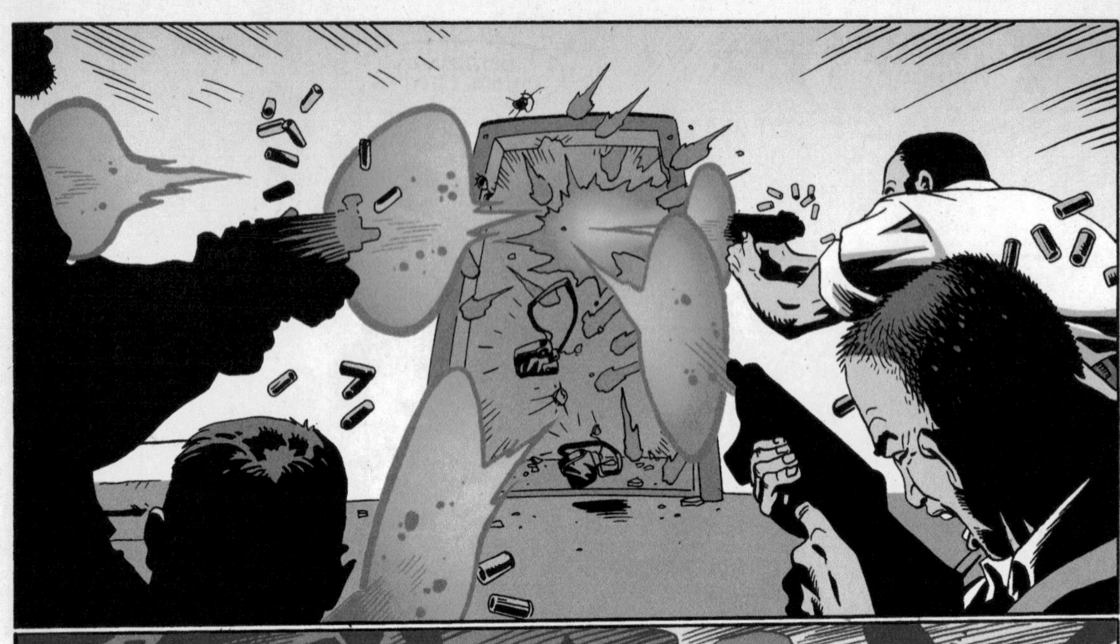

YOU TWO DON'T MESS AROUND, DO YOU?

NEVER DID.

WE SHOULD HAVE THE RUN OF THE PLACE, AT LEAST UNTIL THE REST GET UP THE NERVE TO COME DOWN HERE...
YOU SEEN THIS?

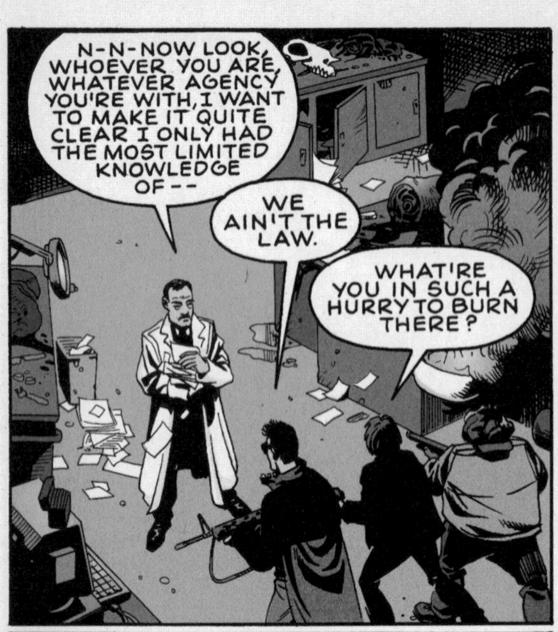
N-N-NOW LOOK, WHOEVER YOU ARE, WHATEVER AGENCY YOU'RE WITH, I WANT TO MAKE IT QUITE CLEAR I ONLY HAD THE MOST LIMITED KNOWLEDGE OF--
WE AIN'T THE LAW.
WHAT'RE YOU IN SUCH A HURRY TO BURN THERE?

JUST PAPERS, JUST--NO!
TRUMAN MAKING HOME MOVIES NOW? MM?
NO, THAT'S NOTHING! THAT REALLY IS NOTHING!

W...WAIT. DON'T WATCH THAT. I'M TELLING YOU, YOU DO NOT WANT TO SEE WHAT'S ON THAT TAPE.
PLEASE...

NO SOUND?
NO.
BE GRATEFUL.

WHAT--

WHAT *IS* THIS?

IT'S ... PROJECT BLOODLINES. IT'S WHAT IT DOES TO PEOPLE.
TRUMAN MADE ME TAPE IT.

OH JESUS, LOOK AT THAT ONE, LOOK IN HIS MUTHALOVIN' EYES! *HE KNOWS!*
THEY STILL HUMAN IN THERE! THEY KNOW WHAT THEY DOIN' AN' THEY *STILL CAN'T FRIGGIN' STOP!*

THIS IS WHAT HELL WOULD BE LIKE.

THAT WAS YOU, YOU MAGGOT SON OF A BITCH! YOU DID THAT CRAP TO MEN!
NO--!
IT WAS TRUMAN, HE MADE ME! HE WANTED METAHUMANS, HIS OWN SUPERHEROES, BUT THE BLOODLINES D.N.A. COULDN'T DO IT!
IT SPED UP THE SUBJECT'S METABOLISM TO THE POINT WHERE THEY WENT MANIC, IT TURNED THEM INTO WHAT YOU SAW! I TOLD HIM AND TOLD HIM--CROSSING ALIEN BIOLOGY WITH HUMAN, THE CHANCES OF SUCCESS WERE MINIMAL--
BUT HE JUST WOULDN'T LISTEN!
I MEAN HE'S NOT RIGHT IN THE HEAD, HE'S SICK, HE ORDERED THEM LET LOOSE ON EACH OTHER! HE WANTED IT ON FILM!
HE MADE ME TRY AGAIN, TEN MORE TEST SUBJECTS, INJECTED JUST THIS MORNING-- BUT IT'LL NEVER WORK!
IT'LL... NEVER...
WORK...
SUHBBEREEROOHHH

UHM UH SUHBBEREEROOHHH

UHM
GUHNUH SUHV UH
WUUUHHLLLD

AN' WHAT'S *HIS* SUPERPOWER, DOCTOR?

I--

UUHHH...?
UHZ LUHGZ LUHG UH JUHB FUH... FUH...

THERE'S NINE MORE GUYS BACK HERE. MUST BE THE RESTA THE TEST SUBJECTS.
ARE THEY LIKE HIM?

THEY'RE JUST DEAD.

LET'S GET THIS OVER--
TOMMY.

NO CLEAR SHOT--
ME EITHER--
LATER FOR YOU, RABBLE.

SNK

...FORGET THE SAFETY?

LEMME GUESS.

YOU NEVER POINTED A GUN AT A MAN BEFORE.

SECURITY FROM TRUMAN, WHAT IS HAPPENING DOWN THERE? HAS THE NAVARONE BOY MADE CONTACT YET?
SECURITY, ANSWER ME--
SIR, I HAVE AN ESTIMATED FIFTY DEAD HERE, AND WE'RE STILL TAKING FIRE! I WON'T KNOW ZIP 'TIL WE RETAKE SECTOR DELTA!
MONAGHAN, THAT'S A FLAME-THROWER DOWN THERE!
TRUMAN-- I WANT THAT BASTARD TRUMAN--
HEARD THAT--

TRUMAN ISN'T HERE, MONAGHAN! WE MISSED HIM! WE'LL NEVER FIGHT OUR WAY THROUGH THAT BUNCH!
WE HAVE GOT TO GO!!

ALL RIGHT, DAMMIT, POP SMOKE AN' RUN LIKE HELL--

FIRST TEAM, GO NOW! GO,GO,GO!
MR. TRUMAN, THEY'RE RUNNING, THEY'RE HEADED DOWN CORRIDOR SEVEN!
WE'VE GOT THEM, SIR! THEY DON'T KNOW IT'S A DEAD END!

...OH.
MR. TRUMAN?
THERE WOULDN'T BE ANOTHER TUNNEL DOWN HERE, WOULD THERE?
ONE... NOT MARKED ON OUR PLANS?

WELL THAT WAS A FRIGGIN' WASTE OF TIME.
'LEAST WE STOPPED THE BLOODLINES THING...

NO WE DIDN'T.
THEY STILL HAVE THEIR SAMPLE OF THE ALIENS' D.N.A. THEY'LL GET ANOTHER RESEARCHER, ANOTHER BUNCH OF UNLUCKY SONS OF BITCHES, AND THEY'LL KEEP ON GOING 'TIL TRUMAN GETS HIS SUPERHEROES...

SO THEY CAN KEEP ON *DOIN' THAT* TO PEOPLE.
WE ACCOMPLISHED NOTHING TONIGHT.

WE CERTAINLY DIDN'T NAIL TRUMAN, WHICH PUTS US RIGHT BACK TO SQUARE ONE. HE CAN COME AND GET MAGGIE LORENZO, AND US, AND THE COPS'LL LOOK THE OTHER WAY.
WHICH MEANS PLAN B: HAND MAGGIE OVER TO THE F.B.I., AND THE THREE OF US LEAVE THE COUNTRY.

AN' NOT COME BACK?
FEDS'LL PROTECT MAGGIE IN RETURN FOR HER EVIDENCE. WE'LL JUST BE THROWN TO THE WOLVES.
AN' SOONER OR LATER, TRUMAN OR NO TRUMAN, SOME CREEP AT THE C.I.A.'LL DECIDE TO TIDY UP THE THREE LOOSE ENDS...

I HAVE NOTHING.
I CAN GO.

I AIN'T NEVER GOIN' HOME. EVERY FOOL IN DETROIT THINKS I SET THE ROLLIN' SIXTIES UP FOR FIVE-OH.
GO.

I JUST WANT MAGGIE SAFE.
GO.

...THERE IT IS.

IT'LL TAKE ME A WHILE TO HOOK UP WITH THESE FED GUYS. I'LL CALL YOU WHEN I'VE GOT AN E.T.A. FOR THE HELICOPTER.
WE'LL BE READY TO GO.
BE CAREFUL. TRUMAN'LL HAVE NOONAN'S UNDER SURVEILLANCE NOW; THE INSTANT MAGGIE COMES OUT THE DOOR HE'LL BE DOWN ON YOU LIKE A TON OF BRICKS.
RIGHT.
SO... I GUESS I'LL SEE YOU ON THE CHOPPER...
AND WHERE DO WE GO FROM THERE?
WELL, UH...
WE...?
YOU CAN READ MINDS, CAN'T YOU? I KNOW YOU CAN, I SAW IT IN YOUR FILE.
YEAH, BUT IT GIVES ME ONE MOTHER OF A MIGRAINE. IT AIN'T WORTH THE PAIN, OR I'D--
IT WILL BE.

WE OUGHTA GET BACK TO MAGGIE 'FORE THEM PUNKS GET OVER THE SLAPPIN' WE GAVE 'EM.
YOU OKAY?
YEAH.

WELL, KINDA OKAY. THAT LITTLE BASTARD SCARED THE LIVIN' FREAKIN' CRAP OUTTA ME.
AH, HE STILL BITCHED OUT WHEN IT CAME TO IT.

AIN'T NOTHIN', MAN. 'CEPT MAYBE ONE OF THEM REMINDERS WE AIN'T NONE OF US IMMORTAL.
C'MON, WE'LL GO BACK TO NOONAN'S AN' HAVE A BEER.

A BEER AT NOONAN'S.
SURE.

JUST ADD IT TO THE LISTA THINGS WE'LL NEVER DO AGAIN.

ONAN'S SLEAZY BAR
YOU KNOW WHAT?

WHAT?
NUTS
NSPCC SUGAR BOX

I THINK IT MIGHT BE TIME FOR BUTCH AN' SUNDANCE.
Closing Time
GARTH ENNIS WRITER
JOHN McCREA PENCILLER
GARRY LEACH INKER
PAT PRENTICE LETTERER
CARLA FEENY COLORIST
HEROIC AGE SEPARATOR
PETER TOMASI EDITOR
HITMAN CREATED BY ENNIS & McCREA

SOAPY SUDZ!
2001
HNNF--!
LAUNDRETTE
24hr

>Living room
Bathroom

...WE OUGHTA STOP DOIN' THIS. WE OUGHTA DECIDE TO STAY AWAY FROM EACH OTHER AN' STICK TO IT FOR A CHANGE.
FOR BOTH OUR SAKES.

ARE YOU SURE ABOUT THIS, LIEUTENANT CONNOLLY?
NOONAN'S

THAT BAR'S WHERE THEY'LL BE, SON.
WHATEVER HAPPENS, HAPPENS HERE.

NOONAN'S
AN'...WE JUST STAND BY AN' DO NOTHIN'?
THAT'S THE ORDERS.

WE DO NOTHIN'. WE THINK ABOUT OUR CAREERS AN' OUR PENSIONS.
WE LET THE C.I.A. WALK INTO GOTHAM AN' MURDER A GIRL WHO'S ONLY GOT KILLERS TO PROTECT HER.
WE FORGET--WHAT WE *OWE*--

AN' WE SIT UP HERE AN' WE OBSERVE.

AW, I KEEP BEATIN' MYSELF AT TIC-TAC-TOE...!
YOU KNOW WHAT THEY CALL TIC-TAC-TOE IN BRITAIN, HACKEN? THEY CALL IT NOUGHTS AN' CROSSES.
WHY?
YOU KNOW THEM CRAZY BRITS, MAN.
MORNIN', MAGGIE...
HEY.
ALL THIS FOR ME.
I CAN'T GET OVER IT.
WELL, YOU SAW SOME BIG STUFF, KID. THESE SECRET AGENT CREEPS ALWAYS FREAK OUT WHEN THEIR SECURITY GOES WRONG, THEY ALWAYS BRING OUT THE BIG GUNS. THEY'RE PARANOID.
IT'S JUST THE STUPID WORLD THEY LIVE IN.
I MEANT YOU, TOMMY.

YOU AND YOUR FRIENDS, YOU'RE DOING SO MUCH FOR ME. YOU'VE HIDDEN ME HERE FOR DAYS, YOU'VE GONE OUT AND FOUGHT AND KILLED TO PROTECT ME, YOU'VE RISKED GETTING KILLED AGAIN AND AGAIN...
I MEAN YOU'RE HAVING TO LEAVE THE COUNTRY OVER THIS, YOU'RE TURNING YOUR WHOLE LIVES UPSIDE-DOWN! AND I-I JUST DON'T THINK I DESERVE IT, ALL THIS RISK AND LOSS...!
IT... WHAT WE'RE DOIN', IT...
IT'S JUST THE RIGHT THING, MAGGIE. GETTIN' YOU OUT, GIVIN' YOU A CHANCE TO MAKE IT.
NOT JUST YOU.
I WAS THINKING.
WHEN HE'S BORN I'D LIKE TO CALL HIM TOMMY.

YOU DON'T WANNA CALL HIM THAT, KID.
YOU'LL CURSE HIM.

BUT--
NO.
REALLY.

THAT NAME COMES FROM A COLD, USED-UP, STUPID LITTLE PLACE ACROSS THE OCEAN. IT WAS GIVEN TO ME OUTTA SPITE FOR THE SON OF A BITCH WHO SCREWED MY MOTHER. THE WHOLE GODDAMN MESS ENDED IN BLOOD.
I NEVER GOT OUT FROM UNDER IT, EITHER. ALL I'VE GOT TO SHOW FOR MY TWENTY-EIGHT YEARS IS A LONG, DARK TRAIL OF SLAUGHTER AN' KILLIN', AN' MY FRIENDS GETTIN' KNOCKED OFF ONE BY ONE.

THERE AIN'T NOTHIN' THERE TO CELEBRATE, OR TO REMEMBER.

SO DON'T, OKAY?

YOU ARE SO WRONG.

THIRTY-NINE DEAD, SEVENTEEN WOUNDED. THAT'S NOT INCLUDING THE NAVARONE BOY.
AND OUR TEAM WATCHING NOONAN'S REPORTED IN. MONAGHAN AND WALLS RETURNED THERE AT OH-FOUR-THIRTY. McALLISTER WAS NOWHERE TO BE SEEN.
GONE TO ARRANGE THEIR ESCAPE, NO DOUBT. THE TREACHEROUS LITTLE BITCH.
WELL, WE'LL HAVE TO GO AND GET THEM, THAT'S ALL THERE IS TO IT...
WH-WHAT?
MR. TRUMAN, JUST THE THREE OF THEM TOOK OUT ALMOST SIXTY OF OUR PEOPLE! AND I MEAN WITH MARC NAVARONE GONE, WHO HAVE WE GOT WHO CAN HANDLE TOMMY MONAGHAN?
OUR WHOLE OPERATION HERE IS RUINED. WE SHOULD CUT OUR LOSSES AND RUN FOR THE HILLS...!
WE STILL HAVE OVER *TWO HUNDRED* COMBAT PERSONNEL. PROJECT BLOODLINES HAS SUFFERED SETBACKS, NOTHING MORE. WE ARE NOT RUNNING ANYWHERE.
WE CAN'T.
CIA
SMARMY
WE'RE ACTING WITHOUT AGENCY APPROVAL HERE. THEY CAN CLAIM THEY'VE NEVER HEARD OF US. THEY DON'T CARE HOW MUCH OF THE GOVERNMENT THIS COULD BRING DOWN, AND NEITHER WILL THE F.B.I.
WE EITHER KILL MAGGIE LORENZO AND HER PROTECTORS OR WE -- ALL OF US, YOU, ME, EVERYONE INVOLVED -- ARE GOING STRAIGHT TO THE CHAIR. MAKE YOUR CHOICE.
THEN GET THE TROOPS MOVING.

KATHRYN, ARE YOU SURE ABOUT THIS? I MEAN ALL I CAN GIVE YOU IS THE CHOPPER, I HAVEN'T THE AUTHORITY FOR ANY OTHER BACK-UP--
I'M SURE.

WELL AT LEAST LET ME COME WITH YOU!
WHEN DID YOU LAST FIRE YOUR SIDEARM, RICHARD? BASIC?
BUT IT'S GOING TO BE INCREDIBLY DANGEROUS! YOU COULD GET KILLED DOWN THERE!

YOUR CHIVALRY'S SHOWING. PUT IT AWAY.
JUST MAKE SURE THE WITNESS PROTECTION PEOPLE ARE READY FOR MAGGIE LORENZO. AS SOON AS HER TESTIMONY'S ON RECORD I WANT HER WELL ON HER WAY TO WHEREVER.

YOU'RE A NICE GUY, RICHARD. I APPRECIATE YOUR HELP.
KATHRYN, YOU--YOU DON'T KNOW WHAT YOU'RE DOING! TRUMAN'S BOUND TO BE EXPECTING YOU! THERE'S GOING TO BE AN *ARMY* BETWEEN YOU AND TOMMY MONAGHAN!

THEN GOD HELP THEM.

YOU REMEMBER THE LAST TIME WE SAW SEAN?
SURE. 'FORE WE TOOK HACKEN AN' SIXPACK TO THE HOSPITAL.
THERE WAS SOMETHIN' I WANTED TO SAY TO HIM.
ABOUT HIM BEIN' LIKE A FATHER TO ME. TIEGEL TOLD ME I SHOULD DO IT.
AN' I WAS GONNA, I ALMOST DID, BUT HE LOOKED AT ME AN'--I FELT--AW, I JUST FELT STUPID. LIKE IT WASN'T SOMETHIN' MEN SAY TO EACH OTHER. AN' HELL, I COULD ALWAYS GET HIM ANOTHER TIME.
BUT IT AIN'T NOTHIN' TO HOW STUPID I FEEL NOW FOR HAVIN' KEPT MY GODDAMN MOUTH SHUT...
I THINK HE KNEW, TOMMY.
YOU DIDN'T HAVETA SAY IT.
WHAT'S GOT YOU GOIN' OVER YO' REGRETS, ANYHOW? 'CAUSE WE LEAVIN' TOWN?
OR YOU THINK THERE'S MORE'N GOTHAM MIGHT BE COMIN' TO A END...?

I DUNNO.
YOU EVER REMEMBER US TAKIN' ON ODDS AS BAD AS THIS BEFORE?
MMM...

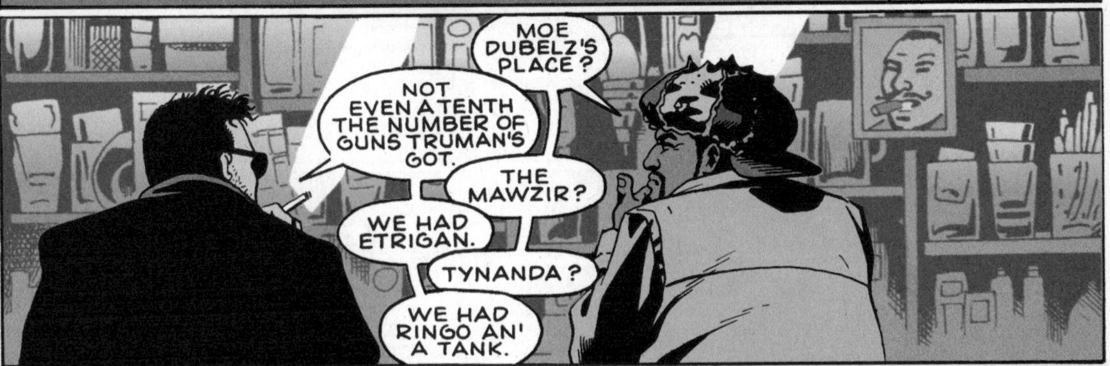
MOE DUBELZ'S PLACE?
NOT EVEN A TENTH THE NUMBER OF GUNS TRUMAN'S GOT.
THE MAWZIR?
WE HAD ETRIGAN.
TYNANDA?
WE HAD RINGO AN' A TANK.

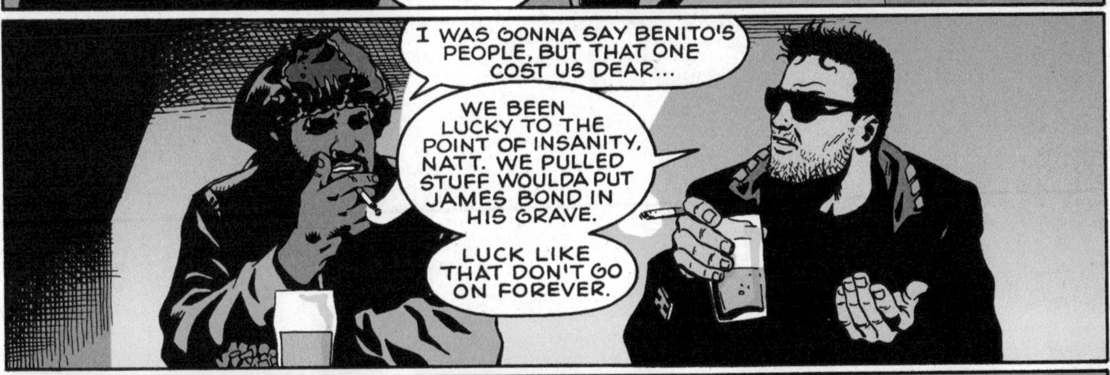
I WAS GONNA SAY BENITO'S PEOPLE, BUT THAT ONE COST US DEAR...
WE BEEN LUCKY TO THE POINT OF INSANITY, NATT. WE PULLED STUFF WOULDA PUT JAMES BOND IN HIS GRAVE.
LUCK LIKE THAT DON'T GO ON FOREVER.

NO, IT DON'T...
SO TELL ME SOME-THIN'.

WHY'RE YOU DOIN' THIS?

JUST GETTIN' YO' BACK LIKE ALWAYS, HOMES.
NATT, THIS IS PRACTICALLY A SUICIDE RUN. AN' IT'S MY FIGHT, IT'S ONE I PICKED WITHOUT SAYIN' JACK TO YOU--AN' YOU STILL STAYED, EVEN WHEN YOU SAW WHAT WE WERE UP AGAINST.
WHY?

HMH.
YOU KNOW HOW YOU ALWAYS SAID YOU WOULDN'T SHOOT NO GOOD GUYS, AN' I ALWAYS SAID YOU WAS FULL OF IT? BUT EVEN NOW, YOU CAN PROBABLY STILL SAY YOU NEVER DONE IT?
...YEAH...

WELL I GUESS I'M DOIN' THIS 'CAUSE I CAN'T SAY THE SAME THING.

HELL, NATT.
I DON'T KNOW THAT I CAN EITHER.

BEEBEEP
BEEBEEP
KLIK
HEY.
LEMME GET TWO SHOTSA BLACK BUSH, BAYTOR.

YEAH, WE'RE READY. TEN MINUTES? RIGHT.
SEE YOU.

NATT--
YOU THINK THIS PLACE IS GONNA BE OKAY?

TOMMY, THIS PLACE IS ALWAYS GONNA BE OKAY.

I'LL GET MAGGIE...
OKAY, LET'S GO.

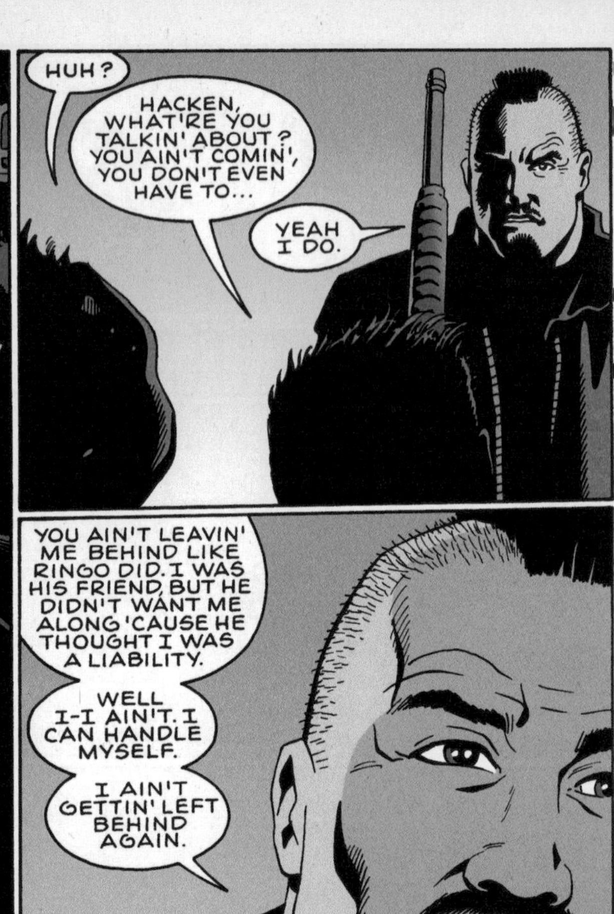
HUH?
HACKEN, WHAT'RE YOU TALKIN' ABOUT? YOU AIN'T COMIN', YOU DON'T EVEN HAVE TO...
YEAH I DO.
YOU AIN'T LEAVIN' ME BEHIND LIKE RINGO DID. I WAS HIS FRIEND, BUT HE DIDN'T WANT ME ALONG 'CAUSE HE THOUGHT I WAS A LIABILITY.
WELL I-I AIN'T. I CAN HANDLE MYSELF.
I AIN'T GETTIN' LEFT BEHIND AGAIN.

HACKEN... RINGO DIDN'T TAKE YOU WITH HIM 'CAUSE HE DIDN'T WANT YOU GETTIN' KILLED.
YEAH...?
YEAH.
HE WAS YO' FRIEND, WASN'T HE?

AAAOOW!!

HOLY JEEZ, TOMMY, SOMEONE JUST HIT ME OVER THE HEAD! DID YOU SEE WHO IT WAS?

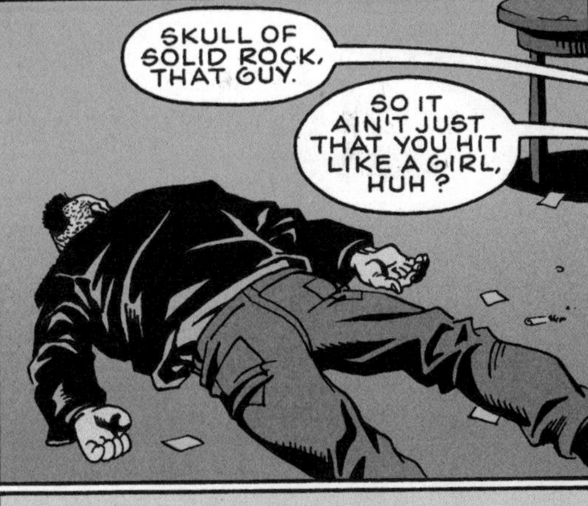
SKULL OF SOLID ROCK, THAT GUY.
SO IT AIN'T JUST THAT YOU HIT LIKE A GIRL, HUH?

BITE ME...

SEE YOU, BAYTOR!
I AM BAYTOR!
WE'LL SEND YOU A POSTCARD, DUDE! YOU CAN COME HOOK UP WIT' US!
I AM BAYTOR!!
GOODBYE, BOYS.
DID YOU HEAR THAT...?
HE... HE SAID SOMETHIN' DIFFERENT...
HE SAID SOMETHIN' DIFFERENT! HE DIDN'T SAY *I AM BAYTOR!* OH MAN, THIS IS A *FIRST!*
HOLY MOTHERLOVIN' JESUS, BAYTOR CAN ACTUALLY TALK!!

I AM BAYTOR!!

♪
DUHHH...
WUZZAT YOU WUZ SAYIN', JOE...?

NUFFING

WHAT YOU SEE, MAN?
NOT MUCH.

NOTHIN' UNUSUAL... FOUR GUYS WATCHIN' US ACROSS THE SQUARE, BUT I DON'T SEE NO RIFLES...
YOU KNOW WHAT, I THINK THE BIG GUY MIGHT BE *CONNOLLY*...

COME ON, PUNK, GET YOUR ASS OUTTA THERE...!

IF McALLISTER'S ON TIME WE MIGHT JUST--
HEAR THAT?

DOWN!!

YEEOW!
STAY LOW, KID--
FIVE MORE MINUTES AN' WE'DA BEEN FRIGGIN' CLEAR--
MR. TRUMAN, WE'VE GOT THEM PINNED! BAR AT THE CORNER OF SAINT AND PECKINPAH!
I KNOW WHERE IT IS, CRETIN. KEEP THEM THERE, OUR E.T.A. IS UNDER A MINUTE.
GET THAT ONE! GIVE 'EM MAXIMUM!
OUTSTANDING...!

ONE TO US--

GODDAMMIT, THAT SHOULDA BEEN HIS HEAD...
MR. TRUMAN, LONGSHOT HAS *SCORED!*

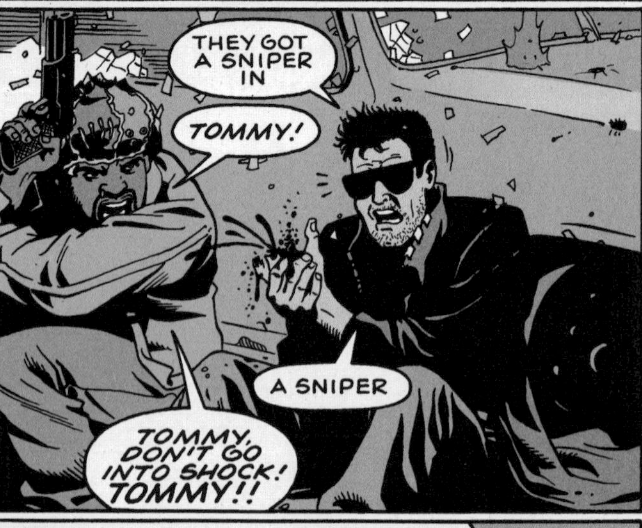
THEY GOT A SNIPER IN
TOMMY!
A SNIPER
TOMMY, DON'T GO INTO SHOCK! TOMMY!!

YOU'RE JUST IN TIME, MR. TRUMAN! WE'VE GOT THEM, THEY'VE NOWHERE ELSE TO GO!
IN AT THE DEATH.
VERY GOOD.

TOMMY! FRIGGIN' QUIT IT! WE GOTTA GET OUTTA HERE!!
THE--
THE SNIPER--

HUH?
OH JESUS!

BURN IN HELL.

THAT...
WHORE...
THEY'RE RUNNIN'!

WELL DON'T JUST STAND THERE, BRING THEM DOWN!!

WHOA--!
BLAM

MAGGOTS--!

BITCH, YOU THINK YOU BAD?!

YOU THINK YOU FRIGGIN' BAD?!!

NATT?

...TOMMY?

MONAGHAN, IT'S NOW OR NEVER! COME ON!!

RUN!!!

JUST A FEW MORE YARDS, KID--
OH MY GOD, MY DEAR LORD GOD--
WE'RE *THERE*--!
McALLISTER, THERE'S HUNDREDS OF 'EM! COME ON, FOR CRYING OUT LOUD!
ALMOST, GOD-DAMMIT--!
TOMMY!!
TOMMY--
YOU GOTTA--
KILL ME--

PERFECT.
TOMMY, KILL ME! YOU KNOW WHAT THEY DO TO PEOPLE! YOU SAW THEM THINGS, THEM ANIMALS USED TO BE MEN!
TOMMY, PLEASE. SWEET JESUS, DON'T LET 'EM TAKE ME ALIVE!!
MONAGHAN! GET ON THE CHOPPER! NOW!
HE'S GONE. HE'S FINISHED! COME ON, DAMMIT!!
FOR GOD'S SAKE GO, PUNK--!
TOMMY.
YOU DID IT FOR PAT.
PLEASE.
LOOK AFTER MAGGIE.
MONAGHAN!
PLEASE.
MONAGHAN, NO!!

MONAGHAN, DON'T YOU LEAVE ME ALONE!!!

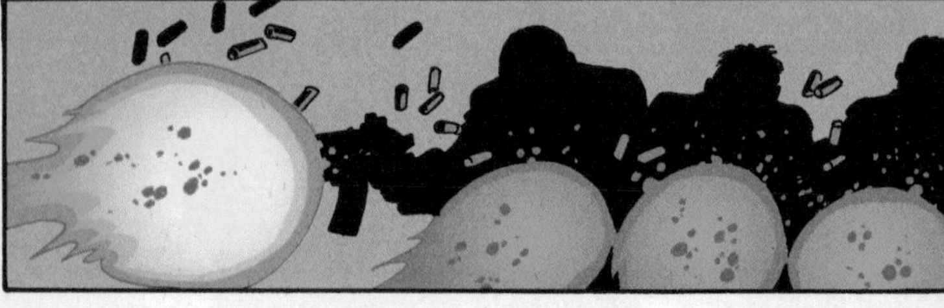

"CHARGING AN ARMY, WHILE ALL THE WORLD WONDERED."

LIEUTENANT CONNOLLY?
WHAT'D YOU SAY, SIR?

NOTHING.
G.C.P.D

WE ARE SUCH LITTLE MEN.

IDIOT.
STUPID, STUPID BASTARD.
TOMMY.

OH MAN.
WHAT'D SEAN SAY?
UH?
DREAM YOU HAD.
WHAT'D SEAN SAY?
OH YEAH.
SAID

DRINKS ONNA HOUSE, FELLAS.

THERE AIN'T NO CLOSIN' TIME.

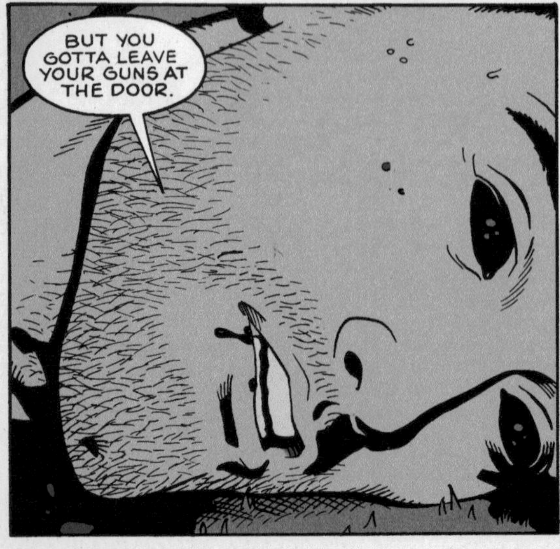
BUT YOU GOTTA LEAVE YOUR GUNS AT THE DOOR.

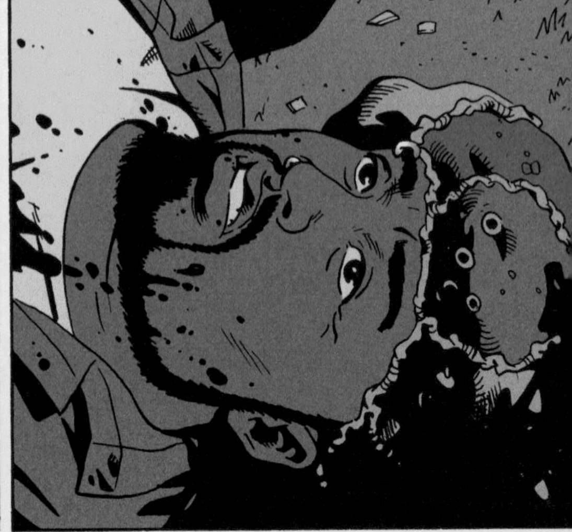

COOL.

Man, but I am gonna miss this book.

It's hard to put into words just how much I loved writing it, and the fun I had with the insanity of it, and the kick I got when someone would mention PREACHER and HELLBLAZER and so on — and then smile like we were sharing some cool little secret and tell me they liked HITMAN best of all.

My love for the underdog, I suppose. A lot of folks are amazed to see this sucker go, can't believe it never found a wider audience. Others are astonished it lasted as long as it did. What do I think? Well, five years, sixty issues. The way things are these days, that ain't half bad.

It was a singular experience to walk the world in Tommy's shoes, to visit his skewed little corner of existence four or five days out of every month. It was a blast to fill a mainstream comic book with the most mental mix of stories I could think of, so that constipated Godfathers shared a neighborhood with armies of Tyrannosaurs, and Batman stalked the night with Bueno Excellente. Best of all to write, though, when the guns had fallen silent and the last baby seal had been bludgeoned to death, were the scenes in Noonan's Bar: when Tommy, Natt, Sean, Pat, Ringo, Hacken, Sixpack and Baytor would sit in the gloomy, smoky warmth and sink a beer or ten, and leave the madness at the door. All of them, all of Tommy's Heroes, talking the most important nonsense in the world.

My most heartfelt and sincere thanks, then, to everyone who bought and supported this book. Thanks to the good folks at DC who did their bit as always, especially to Mike Carlin for his patience and indulgence, and Lateef Williams, whose kind words were always appreciated. Cheers to old mate Steve Dillon, who could never have dreamed that Dogwelder would *actually see print, for God's sake*, and also to Warren, Grant, Darick, Mal, Joe, Greg, Marks Waid and Millar, Chris Claremont, Kurt Busiek, Axel, Stuart, Tony and Amanda — all of whom know just what the right word of encouragement at the right time can be worth. Thanks also to Hugh, Gerry, Mike, Keith, Kathi (with thanks for Ignatius Haddock), Maggy, Tim (-my the Fish), Jayne, Mum and Dad, as unlikely a collection of HITMAN fans as you'd ever hope to meet. And thanks to Ruth, who makes it all worthwhile, and who it's all for anyway, really.

On to the home straight now. First, extra-special thanks to Doug Mahnke, Carlos Ezquerra, Steve Pugh, Nelson and Jimmy, whose talents meant we never had fill-in jobs on HITMAN: we had brilliant, brilliant art from start to finish. Thanks to Willie Schubert and Pat Prentice, who lettered half the book each, and Carla Feeny, who colored every single page. Looking back, I doubt I'd change a thing. Thank you Mr. Garry Leach (with a neat assist from Andrew Chiu), who's been at this game so long I doubt he could be less than perfect if he tried. To my old friend Dan Raspler: thanks for the DEMON job that kicked the whole thing off, for commissioning the series, and for your faith ("I don't know that this zombie aquarium thing is really such a good idea... ah, what the hell").

At so many times, in so many ways, Pete Tomasi has been this book's goddamned hero. He's busted his ass on this thing, taken bullet after bullet for it — without Pete's deftness of touch and careful strategy we'd have been sunk a long, long time ago. And it was just nice to work with someone who got it straight off, understands the point of view from which — really, truly, when all's said and done — *Kelly's Heroes* is the greatest movie ever made. A thousand thank-yous, Pete, and the very best of luck.

And John McCrea? Well, summing up a good, dear friend in just a few words is never easy, but... brilliant artist. Top bloke. And alchemist. Because whether my scripts were good or bad or mediocre, Johnny never turned them into anything but gold.

I've got so much work ahead of me now; all kinds of one-shots and miniseries, everything from the biggest established characters to the smallest, most obscure personal projects. I might even finally get off my ass and write a screenplay or two. But now that HITMAN's finished... I don't know.

I've got the strangest damn feeling I'll never have quite this much fun again.

— Garth Ennis

Six or seven years — including the run on THE DEMON — is a mighty long time working on one character, and now Tommy, Natt, Hacken, Baytor, Sixpack and the boys, Sean, Ringo, Pat, and, of course Tiegel and Wendy are like a group of friends who I see in the pub and shoot the breeze with. I'm sad to see them go, and I'd like to thank all of you out there for supporting this mad little book.

First off, the HITMAN crew: Garth, ol' buddy, it's been a pleasure, and I'm sure we'll work on other books until we're both in wheelchairs. Peter T., you the man. 'Nuff said.

Bad Dan, thanks for giving this book a chance — cheers, mate. Garry, you saved me from early insanity by stepping in with your stylish inks. Carla, Willie S. and Pat, thanks for your sterling work. Cheers to Stu Chaifetz, Tommy's first colorist. Lateef, all the best, mate. Tony B., you're a big ejjitt. Also the big thumbs-up to Steve Pugh, Carlos Ezquerra, and Doug (the Boss) Mahnke for drawing such fine pictures, Andrew (nice guy) Chiu for fab inks under pressure, and Bob Greenberger for catapulting me over to JENNY SPARKS.

Thanks to the following who posed for various characters: John Lawlor (Pat), Steve Fullerton, Hun (see you for lunch) Emerson, Sue Green, Maureen McTigue (thanks for the WONDER WOMAN job darlin'), Drew, Tim H-H, Rory and Sarah, Frank and Lynn, James (hello sailor) Hodgkins, Tony Lewis, Andreas Wernick, Kev, Andrew Chiu (again), Richard Coyne, Karl, Una Frickker, my brothers Steve and Jas and my Mum and Dad. Special thanks go to Rachel, who posed for just about every woman in the comic and still kept her marbles.

And to my friends Glenn and Nikki Fabry, Ruth, Nick Abadzis and Angela, Fred at Dark Horizons, Steve Dillon, Warren Ellis and Nikki, Nelson you mad sod, Davy Francis, Dave Gibbons, Ed Hilliyer and the Detonator crew, Alex Hutchinson, Patti Jeres, Joey and Connie, Marie (around the world in 80 days) Javins, Mark Millar, Jimmy and Amanda, Joe and Nancy, Darick, Axel, Stuart, the Brum Comics Contingent (beer and curry, lads), the Handsworth crew, Chris Carroll, Frank Camusso, Nigel Potter, Ben Rush, Liam and Chris, Stuart and Angela, Bryan Talbot, Bunche and once again to Rai, the love of my life.

But, of course, we still had one last story to tell. What follows is the one we somehow never could find space for in the original HITMAN run, in which Tommy and the Justice League face horrors from outer space on the dark side of the moon...

JLA

"MISTER KENT, LET ME BEGIN BY THANKING YOU FOR TAKING THE TIME TO SEE ME."

"YOU'VE BEEN VERY PERSISTENT. WHAT HAS IT BEEN, TWO YEARS SINCE YOU FIRST CONTACTED MY OFFICE?"

"TWO AND A BIT."

"I KNOW WHAT IT'S LIKE FOR A WRITER ESTABLISHING A REPUTATION. SO..."

"THIS IS AWKWARD. AH...I KNOW YOU'VE REPEATEDLY DENIED ACTING AS A LIAISON FOR SUP--"

"I HAVE TO GO NOW, MISTER KIRBY."

"SIR--I REALIZE--"

"YOU KNOW THE PARAMETERS UNDER WHICH I AGREED TO DO THIS. AND YOU WERE JUST ABOUT TO SAY THE MAGIC WORD."

"MISTER KENT, PLEASE, WAIT A MOMENT--"

"I'M AFRAID I CAN'T."

"THERE IS JUST ONE QUESTION, ***PLEASE***--"

"GOODBYE, MISTER KIRBY."

"MISTER KENT, DOES THE NAME *TOMMY MONAGHAN* MEAN ANYTHING TO YOU?"

WHAT?

ON THE DARKSIDE PART ONE

Garth Ennis writer
John McCrea art and cover
For my son, Luke, in loving memory, John.

David Baron colorist
Travis Lanham letterer
Harvey Richards asst. ed.
Peter Tomasi & Michael Siglain editors

WELL.
I THINK I'VE LEFT IT A LITTLE LATE TO CLAIM I DON'T KNOW WHAT YOU'RE TALKING ABOUT.

I'M RELIEVED TO HEAR IT. I WASN'T RELISHING THE PROSPECT OF ACCUSING A PULITZER-WINNER OF DECEIT.

NOTHING TO IT, AFTER THE FIRST FEW TIMES.
MYSELF.
ALL RIGHT, LET'S START AGAIN. YOU'RE PETER KIRBY, AND YOU'RE WORKING FOR...?

I WAS WORKING FOR A PUBLISHER OF TRUE CRIME MATERIAL--NONE OF IT VERY GOOD, IT HAS TO BE SAID. THEY WENT INTO RECEIVERSHIP NOT LONG BEFORE I FIRST CONTACTED YOU.
MY FIRST AND ONLY ASSIGNMENT WAS AS A RESEARCHER, ON A BOOK ABOUT GOTHAM CITY CRIMINAL FIGURES. NOT EXACTLY VIRGIN TERRITORY TO BEGIN WITH, BUT I WAS TOLD I HAD TO COME UP WITH SOMETHING NEW.
THE WAY I SAW IT, MY ONLY CHANCE WAS TO VEER OFF THE BEATEN TRACK A LITTLE BIT...

WHICH IS HOW I ENDED UP IN A BAR IN THE MIDDLE OF THE CAULDRON, A LITTLE PLACE CALLED ***NOONAN'S.***

IT WAS SUPPOSED TO BE QUITE SOMETHING IN ITS DAY, AT LEAST ACCORDING TO THE COPS I'D SPOKEN TO. BUT NOW IT'S JUST...DRUNKS. IT'S GUYS KILLING TIME 'TIL THEIR TIME'S UP.
THE BARMAN--WELL, I VERY MUCH HOPE IT WAS SOMEONE IN A RUBBER SUIT, BUT HE SAID HIS NAME WAS ***BAYTOR.*** HE SAID THAT QUITE A LOT, AS A MATTER OF FACT.
I WAS ABOUT TO LEAVE WHEN I NOTICED SOMETHING ODD BEHIND THE BAR.

to all the boys at Noonans Superman
GLORY

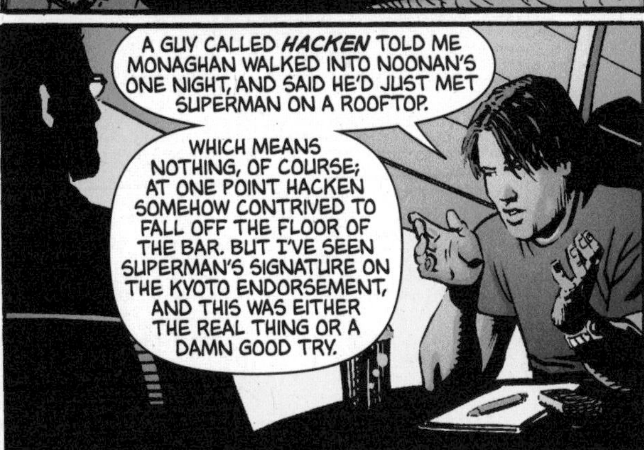

A GUY CALLED ***HACKEN*** TOLD ME MONAGHAN WALKED INTO NOONAN'S ONE NIGHT, AND SAID HE'D JUST MET SUPERMAN ON A ROOFTOP.
WHICH MEANS NOTHING, OF COURSE; AT ONE POINT HACKEN SOMEHOW CONTRIVED TO FALL OFF THE FLOOR OF THE BAR. BUT I'VE SEEN SUPERMAN'S SIGNATURE ON THE KYOTO ENDORSEMENT, AND THIS WAS EITHER THE REAL THING OR A DAMN GOOD TRY.

AND THEN, OF COURSE, THERE'S YOUR OWN REACTION JUST NOW.
HOW EXACTLY DID TOMMY MONAGHAN END UP WITH SUPERMAN'S AUTOGRAPH?

SUPERMAN GAVE IT TO HIM.

THEY MET ENTIRELY BY CHANCE. SUPERMAN HAD JUST HAD A SPACE RESCUE MISSION GO BADLY WRONG ON HIM; MONAGHAN GAVE HIM A FRESH PERSPECTIVE ON IT. *
SIR, DO YOU KNOW WHO TOMMY MONAGHAN *WAS?*
* HITMAN #34

HE WAS A HITMAN.
YES, HE WAS A HITMAN, HE KILLED ALMOST FIVE HUNDRED PEOPLE. THAT BAR, NOONAN'S--IT WAS A NEST OF ASSASSINS, AND HE WAS THE WORST OF THE LOT...!
SUPERMAN DIDN'T KNOW THAT. NOT THEN, AT ANY RATE.
BUT HE DOES *NOW?*
YOU SEE, THAT'S WHAT I CAME HERE FOR, MISTER KENT. THAT'S WHAT I'VE BEEN TRYING TO GET TO THE BOTTOM OF FOR WELL OVER TWO YEARS NOW.
THE CONNECTION BETWEEN THE GREATEST HERO IN THE WORLD AND A MURDEROUS GOTHAM THUG.

all sp

WHY DIDN'T YOU TAKE THE JOB WITH FOX?

I DO MY HOMEWORK TOO. WHY?
...WHAT THEY DO ISN'T JOURNALISM.
WHAT HAPPENED IN INDONESIA LAST JANUARY?
I BROKE THE GOLDEN RULE. DROPPED THE MIKE, WENT TO HELP THE REFUGEES.
GOT FIRED.

MISTER KIRBY.
IF I SAID I WAS GOING TO TELL YOU A STORY THAT YOU COULD NEVER USE, THAT YOU COULDN'T POSSIBLY REPEAT TO ANYONE, WOULD YOU GIVE ME YOUR WORD THAT YOU'D NEVER DO EITHER?

UH...
WHY... WOULD YOU...?

BECAUSE SUPERMAN CAN'T CONFESS.
AND I THINK HE MIGHT NEED ME TO DO IT FOR HIM.

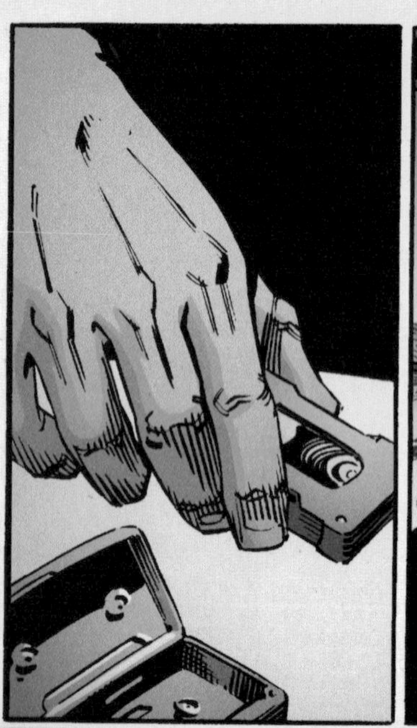

THANK YOU.
THIS IS A STORY THAT OUGHT TO BE TOLD, EVEN IF ONLY ONCE.

"THE GREATEST HERO IN THE WORLD AND A MURDEROUS GOTHAM THUG."
THERE ARE DIFFERENT KINDS OF COURAGE, MISTER KIRBY.

"THIS WAS A LONG TIME AGO."
DID YOU ABSOLUTELY HAVE TO SAY THAT TO HIM?

SAY WHAT TO HIM?
WHEN YOU WERE REVIEWING HIS REPORT ON THE TOKYO INCIDENT.
YOU ASKED IF HE'D NEUTRALIZED THE ENTIRE SWARM, HE SAID--MORE OR LESS. YOU PRESSED HIM, AND HE ADMITTED THAT SOME GOT AWAY THROUGH THE JUMP-GATE.
YOU SAID--SO ON THE WHOLE, LESS RATHER THAN MORE, THEN.
HE SHOULD LEARN TO BE SPECIFIC.
YOU WERE PRETTY COLD WITH HIM.
COME ON, HE'S BEEN DOING THIS LONG ENOUGH TO KNOW BETTER...
THEN ISN'T IT TIME TO STOP TREATING HIM AS SOME KIND OF PERMANENT ROOKIE?
HEY, YOU WANT TO TALK ABOUT COLD, GO SEE BATMAN. YOU KNOW WHAT HE TOLD HIM?
WHAT...?
"IF YOU'RE NOT GOING TO USE THE RING TO ITS LIMITS, WHY BOTHER HAVING IT IN THE FIRST PLACE?"

WHAT'S HE DOING OUT THERE, ANYWAY?
A MANNED NASA PROBE IS ON ITS WAY BACK FROM THE EDGE OF THE SOLAR SYSTEM; THE CREW REPORT SOME KIND OF REACTOR MALFUNCTION. THEY'VE ASKED TO PUT DOWN HERE RATHER THAN RISK ATMOSPHERIC REENTRY.
E.T.A. IS TEN AND A HALF HOURS. WE SENT GREEN LANTERN OUT FOR A CLOSER LOOK.
DIDN'T THE *YEAGER* HAVE REACTOR TROUBLE?
ANOTHER TRIUMPH FOR THE LOWEST BIDDER.

THE YEAGER?
THE SHUTTLE LOST ON ITS WAY TO MARS.
IT'S JUST THE FIVE OF US TONIGHT. DOUBLE MONITOR DUTY.

I WANTED A WORD ABOUT--
IT'LL HAVE TO WAIT.

BATMAN?

GO AHEAD.
I'M SCANNING THEIR SYSTEMS NOW. YOU SHOULD BE GETTING SOMETHING ANY SECOND.

RECEIVING NOW. CAN YOU SEE ANY SIGN OF THE CREW?
NOT YET. HEY, D'YOU WANT ME TO GIVE THEM A HAND? MAYBE TOW THEM IN THE REST OF THE WAY?
WAIT UNTIL--

GET THE HELL AWAY FROM THAT SHIP!

DO YOU HEAR ME?
GREEN LANTERN, ACKNOWLEDGE.
GET AWAY FROM THAT SHIP ***RIGHT NOW.***

BIG, BAD GOTHAM CITY...

YOU CALL THIS BAD? I GUESS YOU NEVER BEEN TO KABUL.
YEAH, OR BAGHDAD.
OR PECKHAM ON A SATURDAY NIGHT. WHO'S THIS BLOKE WE'RE HERE FOR AGAIN?
MONAGHAN.

TOMMY MONAGHAN.
THE ITALIANS GOT A MILLION ON HIS HEAD.

OKAY, FIRST UP IS WEAPONS PREP. THEN I'M GONNA START ASSIGNIN' SEARCH SECTORS--
WAIT A MINUTE, WHO DIED AN' LEFT YOU IN CHARGE?

I'M EX-DELTA FORCE, WHO THE HELL ELSE IS IT GONNA BE?
HEY, *I* WAS A SEAL! ***NAVY SEALS,*** DUDE!

SO GO BALANCE A BALL ON YOUR NOSE...
DROP ***DEAD***--

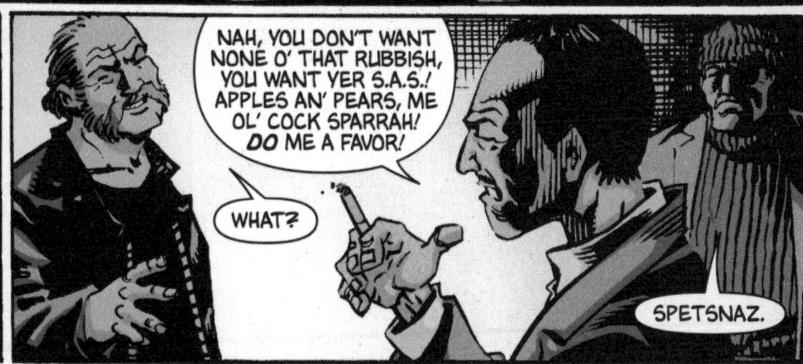
NAH, YOU DON'T WANT NONE O' THAT RUBBISH, YOU WANT YER S.A.S.! APPLES AN' PEARS, ME OL' COCK SPARRAH! ***DO*** ME A FAVOR!
WHAT?
SPETSNAZ.

HEY, GO DELTA! DELTA GETS IT DONE!
SOD OFF, YOU USELESS YANK POOF!
SPETSNAZ.

GO DELTA!
NAVY SEALS!
S.A.S.!
SPETSNAZ.

CANDYGRAM FOR MONGO--

♪
CHOOM!

TIMMY? TOMMY. THANKS FOR THE TIP, I OWE YOU BIG TIME...

UUHHHH...
NO, REALLY, THOSE GUYS WOULDA CHOPPED ME INTO DOGFOOD. LISTEN, I GOTTA GO, OKAY?
YOU TAKE CARE.

AH-AH.
WAAH--!

BLAM BLAM
TWO FOR FLINCHIN'.

DUDE, THAT IS SO GROSS--!
WHAT-- WHAT ARE THEY...?
BEFORE YOUR TIME.
IMAGINE THAT.
WHAT'S THAT SUPPOSED TO MEAN?
BE QUIET, BOTH OF YOU.
BATMAN.

THE *BLOODLINES* INCIDENT.
DEEP SPACE PARASITES OF ENORMOUS POWER AND TOTAL HOSTILITY. CAME WITHIN A HAIRS-BREADTH OF TAKING THE PLANET.
WE NEVER DID FIND OUT WHERE THEY CAME FROM.
THEY'RE ON THE NASA PROBE...?
NOT FULLY GROWN. I DOUBT THERE'D EVEN BE ROOM FOR THEM. BUT THE COMPUTER FOUND A GENETIC MATCH FROM THE SCAN YOU TRANSMITTED.
AND THE CREW ARE NO LONGER RESPONDING TO SIGNALS.
THERE WAS A SIDE EFFECT TO THE CREATURES' ATTACKS. A VERY RARE ONE.
IN ALMOST TWO DOZEN CASES, A REACTION IN THE VICTIM'S D.N.A. RESULTED IN THE DEVELOPMENT OF METAHUMAN POWER.
WE'RE NOT GOING TO HAVE TO DEAL WITH THOSE PEOPLE, ARE WE?
WE'RE GOING TO NEED AT LEAST ONE SURVIVOR, IF WE WANT TO KNOW--
WHERE ARE YOU GOING?
TWO BIRDS WITH ONE STONE.
BACK SHORTLY.

NOONAN'S
LONG TIME NO SEE...
TELL ME ABOUT IT. SO WHAT'S GOIN' ON WITH YOU BOYS?
I MADE FRIENDS WITH A DOG!
SHOOTING PEOPLE FOR MONEY.
KICKIN' ALLA BUTTSHA J.L.A. AIN'T GOTTA SHTONESH FER...
ROAD CREW crüe
I AM BAYTOR!!
TRYNNA MAKE AN HONEST LIVIN', REGRETTIN' EVERY MINUTE OF IT.
YOU KNOW, HE REALLY IS BAYTOR. LET'S HAVE A DRINK TO THAT.
LESH HAVE A DRINK... TO EVERYTHING...!

SEAN, BEFORE I FORGET, CAN YOU SEND A CASE OF BUSHMILLS OVER TO TIMMY THE FISH?
THAT THING GO OKAY?
WENT GREAT. I DUNNO HOW TIMMY FOUND OUT, BUT...
HE DOES BUSINESS WITH THE FERRETTIS. PROBABLY HEARD SOMETHING.
I EVER TELL YOU TIMMY THE FISH MADE CHEESE OUTTA HIS GIRLFRIEND'S BREAST MILK?
...SHUT UP...!
NUTS
NO, NO. SWEAR TO GOD.
WHY WOULD ANYONE--?
HE SAID HE GOT CURIOUS. YOU KNOW TIMMY, HE'S ALWAYS TINKERIN' WITH SOMETHIN' OR OTHER.
DID HE SAY HOW IT TASTED?
RINGO, YOU'RE *BUYIN'* THIS?
STRANGER THINGS HAVE HAPPENED. YOU VOMITED ON BATMAN ONCE.
YEAH, BUT I DIDN'T MAKE CHEESE OUTTA HIS--
YOU ***PUKED*** ON ***BATMAN?*** *
* IN HITMAN #1

LONG STORY. AN' IT AIN'T EVEN IN THE SAME BALLPARK AS WHAT WE'RE TALKIN' ABOUT.
IN BRITESHT DAY... IN DARKESHT NIGHT...NO EVIL SHALL ESHCAPE MY SHIGHT...

OKAY DOWN THERE, SIXPACK?
I'VE TAKENA NAME *PARALLAKSH* NOW...
NATT JOINING US TONIGHT?

OUGHTA BE. KEEPS TELLIN' ME ABOUT THIS HOT NEW GIRL HE'S BEEN SEEIN', SAID HE MIGHT--HEY, SPEAKA THE DEVIL!

HERE'S--
HERE'S--
NATT

OH, WHAT A GREAT PLACE...!

'CHOO LOOKIN' AT, *FOOL?*
GUH...UH...
MIND YO' BUSINESS! MUTHALOVIN' BUM!

YOU GET ME A MARTINI, BABY? I JUST GOTTA POWDER MY NOSE...
COMIN' RIGHT UP, ALICE HONEY.

GONNA NEED A LOTTA POWD--
SOMETHIN' TO SAY, HACKEN?

UH...I...
LOOKED LIKE YOU GOT SOMETHIN' TO SAY. YOU SURE?
Y...Y... YEAH...

SHE SEEMS REAL NICE--
AW, *MAN...!*

...'BOUT THREE WEEKS, AN EVERYTHIN' GOIN' JUST FINE. ONLY THING IS SHE WORKIN' AT INJUN PEAK, SHE A SECRETARY UP THERE...
INJUN PEAK?

THE RESEARCH FACILITY.
REMEMBER ZOMBIE NIGHT AT THE GOTHAM AQUARIUM? THE UNDEAD BABY SEALS?*
OH YEAH.
* HITMAN #14

ANYHOW, THEY DOIN' SOME KINDA TELEPORTIN' EXPERIMENT, TRYNNA ZAP A ELEPHANT FROM ONE ROOM TO THE NEXT--AN' ALICE GOES INTO THE NEXT ROOM BY ACCIDENT. STOOPID DOCTORS NEVER PUT NO SIGN UP.
AN' I DUNNO WHAT TO DO, I MEAN I *LIKE* THIS GIRL, SHE IS ***REALLY COOL...*** AN' IT'S WEIRD AN' EVERYTHIN', BUT I'M TRYNNA BE A GOOD GUY HERE...

I MEAN IF YOU WAS WIT' SOMEONE WAS CRIPPLED, OR HER FACE GOT ALL MESSED UP IN A FIRE--YOU AIN'T GONNA JUST ***RUN OUT*** ON--
SHE'S COMIN' BACK.

LOOK... I KNOW IT'S THE LAST THING YOU WANNA THINK ABOUT, BUT WE STILL GOT THAT JOB LATER ON TONIGHT...
I KNOW.
LEMME TAKE HER HOME AN' I'LL MEET YOU OUTSIDE MY CRIB AT THREE, OKAY?

NATT HAS BEEN PROMISING TO TAKE ME HERE ***ALL WEEK!***
SO WHO'S WHO?

YO, WHASSUP? THIS IS NATT THE HAT, LEAVE A MESSAGE. *BEEEP*
AW, FOR CRYIN' OUT LOUD...!
GOOD VIBES

TWO HOURS! *TWO HOURS!*

THE BIG PEG
Out of order

SOAPY SUDZ

RIGHT, YOU LAZY, DONUT-EATIN' SON OF A--
THE THING WIT' THE TRUNK...
847

DO THE THING WIT' THE TRUNK...
YEAH

MONAGHAN.
UH?

YAAAHH!!

MONAGHAN.

IF YOU GO FOR YOUR GUNS I'LL BREAK YOUR ARM.
IF YOU EVEN *LOOK LIKE* THROWING UP I'LL BREAK THEM *BOTH*.
CLEAR?

HOW ABOUT IF I JUST HANG HERE AND WET MY PANTS?
THAT WOULD BE FINE.

SO... WHAT HAPPENED THE FIRST TIME BATMAN AND MONAGHAN MET, EXACTLY?
LET'S JUST SAY MONAGHAN MADE THE LIST.
COFFEE STOP
OF COURSE, GIVEN THAT BATMAN REGULARLY HAS HIS HANDS FULL WITH THE LIKES OF RA'S AL GHŪL AND THE JOKER--TO SAY NOTHING OF HIS J.L.A. COMMITMENTS--YOU CAN UNDERSTAND WHY HE HADN'T MADE IT A MAJOR PRIORITY.
NOW, HOWEVER, THE LEAGUE NEEDED ONE OF THE BLOODLINES METAHUMANS. THE DATA IN THEIR COMPUTER WAS SCANT AND OUT OF DATE; IF THEY WERE GOING TO FACE WHATEVER WAS ON THE NASA PROBE, THEY WANTED SOME KIND OF FRESH SAMPLE.
BUT SUPERMAN DIDN'T KNOW JUST WHO BATMAN HAD GONE TO FETCH...
NO.
NOR WHAT IT WAS THAT MONAGHAN DID FOR A LIVING.
NO.
NOT AT THAT POINT, ANYWAY.
ALL IN ALL, IT PROMISED TO BE AN INTERESTING MEETING.

HOLY MOTHERLOVIN' GOD ALMIGHTY, I AM ON THE MOON!!

WHO...?
JEEZ, YOU'RE THE FLASH! AN' YOU'RE WONDER WOMAN!
TOMMY MONAGHAN, AT YOUR SERVICE! DAMN GLAD TO MEET YOU!

GREEN!
OH NO.

MY OLD BUDDY! HOW LONG HAS IT BEEN?
HEY, REMEMBER WHEN WE TEAMED UP TO TAKE DOWN THOSE C.I.A. MAGGOTS?* THE LOOKS ON THEIR FACES WHEN YOU SHOWED UP, I SWEAR TO GOD...!
UH-- YEAH-- LOOK--
W-W-WAIT A MINUTE--!
*HITMAN #S 11-12

YOU *WORKED* WITH HIM?

YOU EITHER DID OR YOU DIDN'T.
IT'S NOT AS SIMPLE AS--
YEAH, BUT YOU SEE, THERE WERE THESE GUYS--
DO YOU KNOW WHAT IT IS HE DOES?
DUDE, IT'S--IT'S GOTHAM, YOU KNOW? SOMETHING TERRIBLE ALWAYS HAPPENS TO ME WHEN I GO THERE, STUFF ALWAYS SEEMS TO GET TURNED ON ITS HEAD...
I MEAN THIS ONE TIME, OKAY, SOMEONE SPIKED MY DRINK AND I DON'T KNOW WHAT HAPPENED--ALL I REMEMBER IS THIS VOICE GOING BUENO, OVER AND OVER, BUENO, BUENO, BUENO...!
IT'S ALL VERY CONFUSING...
ARE YOU FINISHED?
DID YOU EVEN STOP TO THINK ONCE ABOUT WHAT YOU WERE DOING? ABOUT THE MORAL IMPLICATIONS OF ALIGNING YOURSELF WITH THIS MAN?
DID YOU CONSIDER THE DISGRACE YOU WOULD BRING ON YOURSELF, ON THIS LEAGUE, ON THE INSTITUTION THAT GAVE YOU THAT RING YOU'RE--
TOMMY?
TOMMY MONAGHAN?
IS THAT YOU?

GUILTY AS CHARGED. I BET YOU NEVER EXPECTED TO SEE ME AGAIN, HUH?
THAT I DIDN'T, I HAVE TO CONFESS. WHAT ON EARTH ARE YOU DOING HERE?
WELL, YOU AIN'T GONNA BELIEVE THIS EITHER, BUT I'M ONE OF THE BLOODLINES GUYS. I GOT BIT, SURVIVED IT, ENDED UP WITH SUPERPOWERS.
REALLY?
THAT IS AMAZING, WHEN WE MET IN GOTHAM I HAD NO IDEA YOU WERE ANYTHING OF THE KIND...
HOW 'BOUT YOU, HOW YOU BEEN DOIN'?
I'VE BEEN GOOD... LOOK, I WANT TO THANK YOU AGAIN FOR--
AH, 'SCUSE ME? SUPERMAN?
SORRY TO INTERRUPT...
BATMAN WANTS TO TALK TO YOU ABOUT *MORAL IMP--*
HE'S AN ASSASSIN.

I'M SORRY?
MONAGHAN. HE'S A HIRED GUN.
HE KILLS FOR MONEY; THE POWERS HE GAINED IN THE ATTACK JUST MAKE IT EASIER.
COME ON, YOU'RE MAKIN' IT SOUND WAY WORSE THAN IT IS...!
FIRST OF ALL, I GOT RULES ABOUT HOW I DO IT. I ONLY WASTE BAD GUYS, I DON'T JUST TAKE ANY CONTRACT GOIN'.
I MEAN, SERIOUSLY, IF *I'M* THE LAST THING YOU SEE ON EARTH? YOUR NEXT SIGHT AIN'T GONNA BE THE PEARLY GATES, I CAN PRETTY MUCH PROMISE YOU THAT...
WHAT WERE YOU DOING ON THAT ROOFTOP?
UH.

AAOW!

SORRY, WAS THAT TOO HARD?
WHAT THE HELL'RE YOU--

YOU TOOK ADVANTAGE OF SUPERMAN'S GOOD NATURE. I IMAGINE HE'S FEELING QUITE UPSET.
I DIDN'T MEAN TO... I MEAN COME ON, IT'S WEIRD ENOUGH I'M STANDIN' ON TOPPA SOME HOTEL AN' THE MAN OF STEEL POPS UP OUTTA NOWHERE. WHO WOULDN'T WANNA TALK TO HIM, YOU KNOW?
AN' HE'S A REALLY COOL GUY, I DON'T WANNA BUM HIM OUT BY TELLIN' HIM I'M THERE TO CLIP SOMEONE...
SO YOU DECEIVED HIM.

WELL, LIKE I SAID.
I DIDN'T MEAN TO.
WOULD YOU PUT THAT DOWN BEFORE YOU BREAK IT, PLEASE? THANK YOU.

SO WHAT EXACTLY ARE YOUR POWERS, ANYWAY?
I CAN SEE THROUGH STUFF AN' I CAN READ PEOPLE'S MINDS.
NOT VERY WELL, THOUGH; I GET THESE KILLER MIGRAINES...

EVER THINK ABOUT PRACTICING, LEARNING A LITTLE FOCUS? MAYBE IMPROVE THINGS THAT WAY?
YEAH, BUT THERE'S ALWAYS SOMETHIN' GOOD ON T.V.
LISTEN, WHY ME? THE OTHER BLOODLINES GUYS ARE SUPER HEROES, WHY NOT JUST CALL ONE OF THEM?

DON'T GET ME STARTED...
THOSE GUYS ARE LAME.
I MEAN THEY ARE *REALLY LAME.*

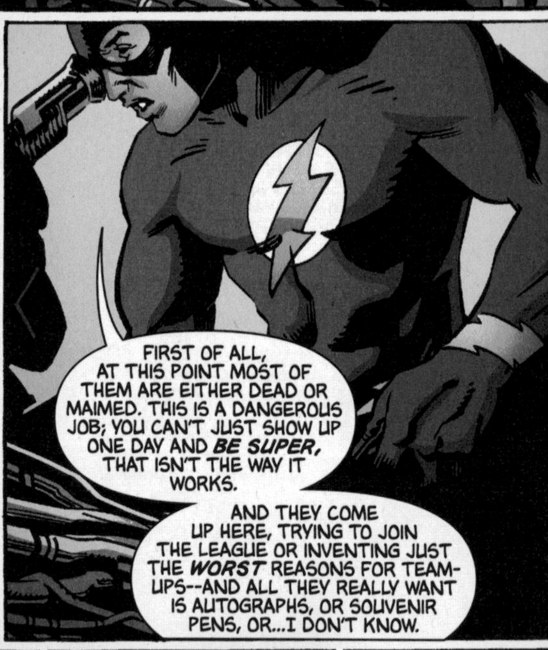
FIRST OF ALL, AT THIS POINT MOST OF THEM ARE EITHER DEAD OR MAIMED. THIS IS A DANGEROUS JOB; YOU CAN'T JUST SHOW UP ONE DAY AND *BE SUPER,* THAT ISN'T THE WAY IT WORKS.
AND THEY COME UP HERE, TRYING TO JOIN THE LEAGUE OR INVENTING JUST THE *WORST* REASONS FOR TEAM-UPS--AND ALL THEY REALLY WANT IS AUTOGRAPHS, OR SOUVENIR PENS, OR...I DON'T KNOW.

BATMAN PROBABLY CONSIDERED YOU THE LESSER OF TWO EVILS...
CHARMIN', I MUST SAY.
YOU MAKE FIRE WITH THAT THING? LIKE JUST A LITTLE ONE?
OF COURSE...

THANKS.

WE DON'T ALLOW SMOKIN IN HERE.

DON'T TRY TO FRIGHTEN ME WITH YOUR ORCERER'S WAYS, LORD V--
SHUT UP.
PROGRESS?
SOME. I CAN ALREADY TELL YOU THAT HIS BLOOD DOESN'T MATCH UP WITH THE SCAN FROM THE NASA PROBE.
THAT CAN'T BE RIGHT. THE SCAN DATA MATCHED WHAT'S IN OUR BLOODLINES FILE.
TO THE EXTENT THAT THE COMPUTER WOULD FLAG IT, YES. BUT OUR FILE SAMPLES WERE TAKEN FROM DEAD TISSUE, WHEREAS MONAGHAN IS ALIVE AND WELL.
FIRSTLY, THE BLOODLINES CELLS HE'S CARRYING ARE INERT; THEY'VE DONE THEIR JOB AND HAVE CEASED ALL ACTIVITY. THE ONES THE SCAN I.D.ED ARE DOING ANYTHING BUT.
SECONDLY, THEIR BASIC STRUCTURE IS QUITE DIFFERENT. MUTATED. EVOLVED, EVEN.
YOU'RE TALKING ABOUT A STRONGER SPECIES.
YES, I'M VERY MUCH AFRAID THAT I AM.
SOMETHING ELSE YOU SHOULD BE AWARE OF. NASA HAVE BEEN CALLING CONSTANTLY, WONDERING WHY THEIR PROBE'S GONE SILENT. WE'VE HEARD FROM THE WHITE HOUSE, TOO.
I'VE BEEN DOING MY BEST TO GIVE THEM THE RUNAROUND. DURING THE LAST BLOODLINES OUTBREAK, THE U.S. GOVERNMENT CAME WITHIN AN INCH OF LAUNCHING I.C.B.M.S.
THIS A BAD TIME TO ASK THE WAY TO THE JOHN?

THE MARS SHUTTLE, THE YEAGER, SUFFERED A REACTOR MALFUNCTION NOT LONG INTO HER MISSION. I MANAGED TO REACH THE SHIP AND HOLD THE HEAT SHIELD IN PLACE, JUST LONG ENOUGH FOR THE CREW TO ESCAPE.
THE ONLY TROUBLE WAS, I MISSED ONE OF THEM. DIDN'T SEE HIM UNTIL AN INSTANT BEFORE THE REACTOR BLEW.
"SUPERMAN'S GOING TO LET ME DIE."
"THAT'S THE THOUGHT PAUL KENNED TOOK WITH HI TO ETERNITY."
AND?
AND I WAS HAVING A GOOD DEAL OF TROUBL WITH IT, AND TOMM MONAGHAN HELPE ME.

HOW?
HE TALKED ABOUT...
IT WASN'T REALLY TO DO WITH THE INCIDENT ITSELF. I DON'T QUITE RECALL HOW WE GOT ONTO THE SUBJECT, BUT--IT WAS WHAT HE HAD TO SAY ABOUT BEING AMERICAN.

"ABOUT THE PROMISE AND THE HOPE OF IT. ABOUT DOING WHAT YOU CAN TO HELP.
"THOSE AREN'T COMMON SENTIMENTS NOWADAYS. USUALLY, WHEN YOU HEAR THEM, YOUR FIRST THOUGHT IS OF WHAT YOU'RE ABOUT TO BE SOLD."

BUT HE BELIEVED EVERY WORD.
HE IS AN ASSASSIN.
HE BELIEVED IN WHAT HE WAS SAYING. I KNOW HE DID.

HE IS AN ASSASSIN. THAT IS THE BEGINNING AND END OF THE DEBATE.
YOUR SYMPATHY, EMPATHY, HOWEVER IT IS YOU IDENTIFY WITH HIM: IT DOES NOT REFLECT WELL ON YOU AS A WARRIOR.

I'M NOT A WARRIOR.
I'M NOT A SOLDIER OF ANY KIND.

IT'S ONLY A SHORT STEP FROM THERE TO CALLING YOURSELF A *CRUSADER,* OR SOMETHING EQUALLY DUBIOUS. TOO MANY POWERFUL PEOPLE MAKE THESE SILLY DECLARATIONS-- THEN IT'S ALL *HOLY QUESTS,* OR *SACRED DESTINY...*
THAT'S GENERALLY WHEN THE TROUBLE STARTS.
IF YOU ARE NOT A WARRIOR, WHAT ARE YOU?
I'M SOMEONE WHO DOES WHAT HE CAN.
AREN'T WE ALL?
ON THIS WE SHALL AGREE TO DIFFER.
THERE IS WORK TO DO.

MAN, WHAT A HIKE JUST TO GET TO THE CRAPPER!

MIND YOU, I GUESS YOU'D WANT A BIT OF DISTANCE IF AQUAMAN HAD BEEN ON THE GUMBO OR SOMETHIN'...

OH, MAN.

HOW CAN I NOT?

E.T.A. IS NOW SIX HOURS. TO BE HONEST, I DON'T KNOW WHY WE'RE EVEN HAVING THIS ARGUMENT.
THE USUAL REASON.
ALL I'M SAYING IS THAT WE CAN'T IGNORE HUMANITARIAN CONSIDERATIONS. THE ASTRONAUTS ON THAT PROBE NEED HELP NOW. LETTING THEM LAND HERE GIVES THEM THE BEST POSSIBLE CHANCE--
AND CREATES THE RISK OF AN UTTERLY LETHAL CONTAGION, GIVEN WHAT MAY BE ABOARD. WE HAVE THE CAPACITY TO QUARANTINE THE VESSEL IN LUNAR ORBIT-- *THEN* WE CAN START THINKING ABOUT THE BEST WAY TO HELP THE CREW.
THAT'S NO GOOD, THAT JUST LEAVES THEM STRANDED OUT THERE.
THINK ABOUT IT FOR A MOMENT: A DOZEN MEN AND WOMEN, COMPLETELY HELPLESS, FACING THE PROSPECT OF *DYING IN SPACE*--
YOU'RE LETTING YOUR FAILURE WITH THE YEAGER CLOUD YOUR JUDGMENT.
I'M SORRY YOU FEEL THAT WAY.
I'M WITH SUPERMAN, NO WAY CAN WE JUST ABANDON THESE GUYS. I COULD HAVE THE SHIP DOWN HERE IN LESS THAN AN HOUR, I COULD SET UP LIKE A PROTECTIVE SHIELD AROUND IT...

NO ONE GOES NEAR THAT SHIP. NO ONE.
IF THOSE THINGS GET LOOSE DOWN HERE IT'S THE END OF US ALL.
BUT--
DUDE, AT IS SO COLD.
I DON'T KNOW, I JUST DON'T GET IT...
THAT'S BECAUSE YOU'RE A CHILD WHO'S WANDERED INTO A DISCUSSION FOR ADULTS.
WHAT DID YOU JUST SAY TO ME?
INCOMING TRANSMISSION.

IT'S FROM THEM.
HELP US--
HELP US--

THEY'RE TURNING US INTO--
SUPER HEROES

WH... WHAT...
IT'S SPEEDING UP.
MAN, DID YOU HEAR THAT VOICE?
COMING MUCH FASTER THAN IT SHOULD BE. FASTER THAN IT'S EVEN CAPABLE OF.
COLLISION COURSE.
"IMPACT IN FIVE SECONDS. FOUR. THREE. TWO."
HEH HEH HEH!
TOMMY WAS HERE

THOOOM
UH-OH.
TOMMY WAS HERE

UH?

WHOA!
TOMMY WAS HERE

...I ALWAYS SAID YOU WERE THE BEST SUPER HERO, YOU KNOW THAT? ANYTIME IT CAME UP, I SAID--GREEN LANTERN, HE'S THE MAN. HE'S GOT THE BEST POWERS, THE BEST OUTFIT, THE BEST ORIGIN, HE'S DEFINITELY THE COOLEST OF ALL OF 'EM...
YEAH, WELL--

YOU WERE WRONG.

OUTER SEALED
INNER OPEN
HELLO?
CAN YOU HEAR ME?
I'M HERE TO HELP YOU. IF ANYONE CAN HEAR ME, PLEASE SAY SO.
HELLO?

I SAID NO ONE WAS TO GO ANYWHERE NEAR IT, HE *COMPLETELY IGNORED* MY INSTRUCTIONS...
WELL, HE WILL DO IT.
I THINK THE SENSORS ARE GOING DOWN. I CAN'T GET A READING ON THE SHIP.
WHAT'D I MISS?
YOU HAVE NO PART TO PLAY HERE.
GREEN LANTERN, GET BACK OUTSIDE. I WANT THE NASA VESSEL ISOLATED.
ON MY WAY...
WAIT A SECOND.

MY POWER IS GONE.
WHAT?
I FELT IT. LIKE IT WAS SWITCHED OFF.
NOT GONE SO MUCH AS...I KNOW I CAN MOVE FASTE THAN...BUT...
IT'S LIKE I DON'T REMEMBER HOW TO DO IT, LIKE THE IMPULSE FROM MY BRAIN IS BEING *JAMMED...*

UH... I DON'T KNOW HOW TO TELL YOU THIS...
WONDER WOMAN?

DESTROY THESE.
HEY!

...I CAN'T.

IT'S AS THE FLASH SAID. I KNOW I CAN SNAP THE WEAPON LIKE A TWIG--I SIMPLY CAN'T REMEMBER HOW TO.
SOMETHING IS STOPPING ME. IT'S LIKE NOT KNOWING HOW TO TAKE MY NEXT STEP.
YOU CAN'T JUST KEEP SQUEEZING?
THAT'S WHAT I WAS AFRAID OF.

YOU WANNA SET THOSE DOWN BEFORE YOU PUT A HYDROSHOCK THROUGH THE WINDOW?
YOU'VE ALL LOST YOUR POWERS AT ONCE, SO WE CAN ASSUME THE CREATURES ARE RESPONSIBLE. THE FIRST WAVE DISPLAYED NO SUCH ABILITY: WE CAN ONLY GUESS AT WHAT ELSE THE NEW AND IMPROVED VERSION CAN DO.
THEIR NEXT MOVE WILL OBVIOUSLY BE TO GAIN ACCESS TO THE WATCHTOWER...

I JUST REALIZED SOMETHIN'. MY X-RAY VISION'S GONE.
YOU SURE?
I'M SURE.

HEY...
HEY.
FLASH, YOU STAND BY THE SENSORS. SOUND THE ALARM AT THE FIRST SIGN OF A BREACH.
THE SENSORS AREN'T WORKING, REMEMBER?
IF THEY DO GET IN, WE'RE GOING TO NEED WEAPONS...
YEAH, WELL THAT'S THE PROBLEM, *WE'RE* THE WEAPONS. AND WE'RE NOT WORKING.

HEY!!
SUPERMAN'S STILL OUT THERE, AIN'T HE?
EVERYONE'S POWERS'VE FAILED. HE'S OUT THERE IN TOTAL VACUUM.

WHAT ABOUT SUPERMAN?
WHAT THE HELL'RE WE GONNA *DO?*

ON THE DARKSIDE PART TWO

Garth Ennis writer
John McCrea art and cover
David Baron colorist
Travis Lanham letterer
Harvey Richards asst. ed.
Peter Tomasi & Michael Siglain editors

UH... SOMETHIN' HERE YOU MIGHT WANNA TAKE A LOOK AT...

CREW OF THE PROBE.
RIGHT, SO WHERE'S SUPERMAN?
HE'LL HAVE TO LOOK AFTER HIMSELF.
HE'S STUCK OUT THERE WITHOUT HIS POWERS, REMEMBER?
WITH OR WITHOUT THEM, THERE ARE FEW PEOPLE MORE CAPABLE. AND WE HAVE PROBLEMS OF OUR OWN.
I DON'T LIKE THIS. EVERYONE'S SUPERPOWERS FAIL AT ONCE, THEN THE WATCHTOWER'S SYSTEMS START GOING DOWN, THEN *THEY* DECIDE TO WALK IN. NO ATTEMPT AT COMMUNICATION, EITHER.
YOU SHOULD BE ABLE TO RAISE THEM, FLASH.
SO IS IT THE BLOODLINES THINGS DOIN' THIS?
YOU HAVE NO PART TO PLAY HERE, MONAGHAN. I TOLD YOU THAT ALREADY.
YOU'RE A PRISONER. WHEN WE'RE DONE WITH YOU HERE, YOU'LL BE HANDED OVER TO THE G.C.P.D. AND JAILED FOR MULTIPLE MURDER.
IN THE MEANTIME, MAKE SURE YOU STAY OUT OF THE WAY.
YOU KNOW, YOU DON'T HAVE TO BE SUCH A--
LEVEL ONE AIRLOCK JUST OPENED.

THE CODE?
WASN'T USED. THE DOOR JUST OPENED FOR THEM.
C.C.T.V. IS OUT, I CAN'T SEE WHO'S DOWN THERE.

"BUT I THINK I CAN TAKE A GUESS."

ELEVATOR'S ON ITS WAY UP.
PREPARE YOURSELVES.
WE--WE HAVEN'T GOT OUR POWERS, MAN! WE'RE GONNA HAVE TO GO HAND-TO-HAND!

HAS ANYONE GIVEN ANY THOUGHT TO WHAT MIGHT BE UNDER THOSE SUITS?

♪
THE ORIGINAL BLOODLINES CREATURES WERE HUGE...
BUT COULD TAKE HUMAN FORM.
SO NO ONE'S GOING FOR, UH, JUST A BUNCH OF NASA DUDES WANTING HELP WITH THEIR BUSTED SPACESHIP?

THIS IS IT--
QUIET.

NASA

SHOW YOURSELVES.
DO IT NOW.

OH, GOD.

NO...
NO PRIZES FOR GUESSING WHO THOSE ARE FOR.

BLAM
BLAM
MONAGHAN!!
THOSE ARE PEOPLE, DAMN YOU! HOLD YOUR FIRE!
WHAT'RE YOU, INSANE? YOU WANT ONE OF THOSE FRIGGIN' THINGS ON YOUR HEAD?
HOW THE HELL DID THEY GET POWERS--?

THE MESSAGE, REMEMBER?
HUH?
THEY'RE TURNING US INTO SUPERHEROES?

WE GOTTA GET OUTTA HERE!
THEY'RE BETWEEN US AND THE ELEVATOR-- GET DOWN--

ONLY WAY IS STRAIGHT THROUGH 'EM! GET READY!
YOU FIRE THOSE GUNS AGAIN AND I'LL--

IT'S OKAY, THEY'RE SET TO STUN!
BLAM
BLAM
BLAM
BLAM
MONAGHAN!!

INTO THEM!
THE HOSTS ARE STILL HUMAN--!
KRAK
DON'T YOU THINK I KNOW THAT?
OLD SCHOOL, GREEN!
I CAN'T BELIEVE THIS IS HAPPENING TO ME...!
BATMAN, WATCH YOUR SIX!

BATMAN!
KRAK
MAN, THE ONE GUY USED TO NO POWERS--!
THE ONE GUY WE REALLY NEED! COME ON!
I CAN'T HOLD THEM BACK!
I--
OH NO.

WH-WH-WHAT DO WE--?
BRING HIM ANYWAY!
MOVE!
BLAM

THEY'RE SHOOTING AGAIN! COME ON!
BLAM
BLAM

DOORS!
NEVER BE IN TIME!
TAKE HIS BELT OFF! GIVE IT TO ME!

CHARGES. PLASTIQUE AND PHOSPHORUS.
THROW IT!

THOOM

GOOD SHOOTING!
CAN'T THEY CONTROL THE--
I TORE OUT THE HARDWIRING. WE'RE GOING DOWN ON HYDRAULIC BACKUP.

EEYEW, I TOUCHED IT!
CHILL, GREEN.
WHAT'RE WE GONNA DO ABOUT HIM, ANYWAY?

ALIVE.
THEY NEEDED THE SUITS TO GET HERE. EFFECT CAN'T BE FATAL TO THE HOST, AT LEAST NOT STRAIGHTAWAY.
IT'S ON HIM PRETTY TIGHT...
THEY AIN'T BULLETPROOF. MIGHT JUST FALL OFF IF I SHOOT IT.
KILL BOTH
ONE DIES TWO DIE
IT TALKS...
OR... *THINKS*...
NO MATTER HOW, WE HEARD IT.
WE RETREAT TO THE WATCHTOWER'S LOWEST SUBLEVEL. LEARN WHAT WE CAN FROM THIS CREATURE.
THEN WE RETAKE WHAT IS OURS.
ARE WE THERE YET?
WHAT?
ARE WE THERE YET?
WHAT'RE YOU--?
I WAS THINKIN'.
WHEN YOU WERE A KID YOU MUSTA DRIVEN YOUR FOLKS CRAZY WITH THAT.

WHERE ARE WE?
UNDER AQUAMAN'S TANK.
IS THIS THING GOING TO TALK AGAIN OR NOT?
SO DO YOU GO ROUND EVERY DAY AN' FEED HIM?
IT ONLY SPOKE BECAUSE IT FEARED DYING.
MM.
SO IT DID.
KILL BOTH
ONE DIE T--
YEAH, WE GOT THAT.
WHAT IF I JUST MAYBE SHOT PARTA YOU OFF? LIKE THIS BIT, RIGHT WHERE IT MEETS YOUR BIG FLOPPY SACK THING?
DUDE, DOESN'T THIS KIND OF BOTHER YOU? I MEAN IT'S LIKE... *TORTURE...*
HE DOESN'T MEAN IT.

YES HE DOES--!
ALL RIGHT, BUT SHE DOESN'T. AND SHE'S THE ONE CALLING THE SHOTS.
YEAH, BUT... I DON'T KNOW.
SOMETHING ELSE I WAS THINKING: DOES IT SEEM WEIRD TO YOU THAT WE'RE SWEATING THIS--
YOU'RE SWEATING THIS.
YEAH, OKAY. BUT ISN'T IT STRANGE THAT THERE ARE GUYS IN THE MILITARY, THE U.S. MILITARY, WHO SERIOUSLY MESS DUDES UP JUST TO FIND OUT THE TIME--AND WE'RE PROTECTING THE ENTIRE PLANET, AND WE, LIKE, WET OURSELVES IF ONE OF OUR BAD GUYS GETS A SCRATCH?
LIKE THIS, LIKE TORTURED. OR KILLED. YOU KNOW WHAT I MEAN?
THAT'S THE WAY WE DO THINGS IN THE J.L.A. GO JOIN DELTA FORCE OR SOMETHING, IF YOU'RE SO KEEN TO PLAY HARDBALL.
HEY, I'M THE ONE WHO WAS GETTING BOTHERED IN THE FIRST PLACE, REMEMBER?
WELL THEN IT SOUNDS LIKE YOU'VE ANSWERED YOUR OWN QUESTION...
I WAS JUST ASKING HOW YOU FELT ABOUT-- OKAY, FORGET IT! FINE!
FINE!
FINE.
MONAGHAN--!

I DID NOT TELL YOU TO DO THAT!
YOU DIDN'T TELL ME ANYTHIN'! WHAT, AM I ON THE TEAM NOW, OR SOMETHIN'?
NO MORE
NO MORE
I'LL HANDLE THINGS FROM HERE.
...TWO HOURS SINCE WE HEARD FROM SUPERMAN. YOU DON'T THINK...?
OF COURSE NOT. I'M A LOT MORE CONCERNED WITH WHAT THEY'RE THINKING IN THE WHITE HOUSE RIGHT NOW.
I MEAN IF THEY EVEN GET A SNIFF OF WHAT'S LOOSE UP HERE...
COME ON, THEY'RE NOT GONNA NUKE US...!
HEY, MISTER YAKAMOTO, CHECK OUT THE BIG SHINY AEROPLANE UP THERE.

EARTH.
OH, MAN...!
WHAT ELSE, I SUPPOSE.
THEY'RE A SUBSPECIES, LESS POWERFUL BUT MORE INTELLIGENT. INFILTRATION RATHER THAN OPEN ASSAULT.
THE...POSSESSION CAUSES A BRIEF COMA, AFTER WHICH TIME CONTROL IS COMPLETE-- ALBEIT WITHOUT FULL COORDINATION. NEXT, D.N.A. IS EFFECTIVELY REWIRED, TRIGGERING METAHUMAN POWER IN THE HOST. EXACTLY WHAT KIND IS UP TO THE PARASITE.
UNLESS THE HOST
SO... THEY GIVE ONE OF THE ASTRONAUTS SOME SORT OF ADVANCED TELEPATHY, ALLOWING THEM TO BLOCK OUR POWERS... ANOTHER ONE GETS, WHAT, ELECTRO-MAGNETICS? GIVING THEM THE RUN OF THE WATCHTOWER SYSTEMS...
THE OTHERS GET LASER-VISION, OR BIOWEAPONS OR MORPHING ABILITIES-- IT'S LIKE SOME KIND OF FACTORY, OR SOMETHING...
TELL YOU THE FIRST THING WE OUGHTA DO, IS TIE HIM UP TIGHT.
HUH?
AS IT IS, HE CAN WIPE THE FLOOR WITH THE WHOLE LOT OF US. YOU IMAGINE WHAT HE'LL BE LIKE WITH POWERS?
NOW WHAT?
SHE'S HANDLIN' THINGS FROM HERE, GREEN.

THE ENEMY'S INTENTION IS O GAIN CONTROL OF THE WHOLE LEAGUE.
THEY'LL USE THE TELEPORTERS TO TAKE US TO EARTH, WHERE OUR TASK WILL BE BLANKET GENOCIDE. AT THE SAME TIME, A BREEDING POPULATION WILL BE ESTABLISHED HERE ON THE MOON.
IT'S WORKED FOR THEM ON A HUNDRED DIFFERENT WORLDS.
MONAGHAN AND I WILL RETURN TO THE CONTROL ROOM, WHERE WE'LL TRY TO SUMMON ASSISTANCE-- SUPERHUMAN ASSISTANCE. WE CAN'T ALERT CIVILIAN AUTHORITIES, FOR THE REASONS ALREADY DISCUSSED.
WHY JUST YOU TWO...?
WE ARE TRAINED WARRIORS. WITHOUT YOUR POWERS YOU ARE MORE HINDRANCE THAN HELP.
HEY, DIDN'T YOU SEE THE OL' RING-STINGER BREAKIN' HEADS WITH HIS TRUSTY CHAIR?
WE CAN'T RISK HAVING ONE OF THEM LOOSE BEHIND US. IF BATMAN REGAINS CONSCIOUSNESS, DO WHAT YOU MUST.
IT'S RING-SLINGER...
AIN'T THAT WHAT I SAID?
THEY'VE CUT POWER TO THE ELEVATOR.
MEANIN'?
THERE'S A SERVICE LADDER IN THE WALL OF THE SHAFT.
AND?
NINE HUNDRED METERS, STRAIGHT UP.
SWELL.

YOU WANNA--
SLOW DOWN--
A LITTLE--?

CIGARETTES.
WHERE DID YOU LEARN YOUR CRAFT?
COUPLE YEARS INNA MARINES.
AND THIS IS HOW YOU CHOOSE TO USE IT?

THEY TEACH YOU GUNS, BOMBS AN' SLITTIN' THROATS. WHAT AM I GONNA DO, DRIVE A CAB?
IT SEEMS A COLD, DARK, GRIM THING.
A KILLER'S LIFE.

IT HAS ITS MOMENTS...

WHAT WAS THAT?

AAAH--!
DAMN!

NO CLEAR SHOT! WATCH IT, YOU GOT NUMBER THREE COMIN' DOWN!
MONAGHAN! LISTEN TO ME!
KNOCK THAT ONE OFF YOUR BACK!

CAN'T!
THEY ARE ENOUGH TO TAKE US BOTH! AND THEN IT'S OVER!
KEEP GOING, MONAGHAN!
KEEP FIGHTING!!
23

DON'T GIVE UP!!
GUTSY BROAD.
...HHHH.
THANK YOU, GOD.

LONG MAY YOU LOOK AFTER THE IRISH.

"SLOW DOWN THERE, BOBBY. GET YOUR BREATH BACK."
"CAN'T, SIR. CAN'T. WE JUST RECEIVED A PRIORITY CALL FROM *NASA.*"
"THEY HEARD FROM THEIR PEOPLE ON THE PROBE YET?"
"NO, SIR, THEY HAVEN'T. WHAT THEY HAVE DONE IS ANALYZED SOME OF THE DATA THE PROBE SENT BACK, BEFORE IT COMMENCED ITS RETURN JOURNEY."
"AND...?"
"THE CREW FOUND A SMALL ASTEROID OUT BEYOND PLUTO, SPENT A COUPLE DAYS EXPLORING IT. ELEMENTS IN ROCK SAMPLES SUGGEST EVIDENCE OF THE *BLOODLINES* CONTAMINATION."
"THAT'S...IS THAT THOSE THINGS THE SUPER-PEOPLE TOOK DOWN IN NINETY-THREE?"
"YES, SIR."
"AND--GENERAL KELLY, DO I RECALL A REPORT ON THAT BUSINESS--"
"THE ONE I WROTE, YES, SIR. ENTITLED *GLOBAL DEVASTATORS.*"
"OH, LORD. AND THE PROBE CRASHED ON THE MOON, SINCE WHICH TIME WE'VE BEEN UNABLE TO RAISE THE JUSTICE LEAGUE'S LUNAR WATCHTOWER."
"THAT'S CORRECT, SIR."
"I DREAD TO ASK, GENERAL..."
"MISTER PRESIDENT, IT WILL TAKE US A LITTLE OVER AN HOUR TO RE-TARGET A DOZEN MINUTEMEN ON THE WATCHTOWER. I RECOMMEND WE DO SO WITHOUT DELAY."
"YOU...REALLY THINK...?"
"IF THE LEAGUE IS DOWN, WE'RE NEXT. WE CAN LAST PERHAPS A DAY WITH CONVENTIONAL FORCES, SIR; ONE WEEK AFTER THAT THE PLANET WILL LOOK LIKE RWANDA."
OH GOD.
DO IT.

HOLY--
YAAAAHH!!
BIG GUY'S NOT ALL HE SHOULD BE--
I HOPE--!

AAAH--
DAMMIT--
SUPERMAN!
BLAM
BLAM
COME ON!
YOU GOTTA
BE IN THERE!
SUPERMAN!
YOU'RE
SUPERMAN!
BLAM
BLAM
YOU! ARE!
SUPER!
MAN!
BLAM
H
HUH

HHAAARRRGH!!
SHRIPP
BLAM
GOD ABOVE.

CAN'T GET WARM.
TOOK EVERYTHING I HAD.
JUST CAN'T.
THEY AIN'T MEANT TO COME OFF LIKE THAT. PROBABLY WOULDA KILLED ANYONE ELSE.
IT TOLD THE OTHERS WHAT I WAS DOING. TELEPATHY, OR...SIMILAR...
LISTEN: BATBOY'S K.O.ED WITH ONE OF THE THINGS ON HIM. WONDER WOMAN TOO, IF SHE AIN'T SPREAD ALL OVER THE ELEVATOR SHAFT.
FLASH AN' GREEN ARE USELESS. THE ASTRONAUTS ALL GOT TURNED INTO SUPERGUYS; ONE OF 'EM CAN SWITCH YOUR POWERS OFF JUST BY THINKIN' ABOUT IT.
I'M SUPPOSED TO HIT THE CONTROL ROOM AN' CALL FOR HELP--EXCEPT THAT'S WHERE THEY ARE, ALL WITH BRAND NEW SUPERPOWERS AN' THE THINGS STUCK ON THEIR HEADS.
AN' THE WHITE HOUSE IS PROBABLY ABOUT TO NUKE US, TOO. HOW'S YOUR DAY BEEN GOIN'?
BARELY KEEP MY EYES OPEN. CAN'T DO A THING TO HELP YOU.
TOOK ME THE MOMENT I BOARDED THE SHIP, SO UNFORGIVABLY STUPID...
COME ON, MAN.
KNOCK IT OFF.

I GOTTA GO. THE THINGS GET BATS AN' THE SUPER-HOTTIE MOVIN', THAT'S GONNA BE GAME OVER.
YOU FOLLOW ON WHEN YOU CAN, OKAY?
WAIT.

GOTHAM.
WHY DIDN'T YOU TELL ME?
EVERYTHING YOU SAID. ABOUT ME. ABOUT THE COUNTRY.
AND YOU'RE...

I DUNNO.
I THINK I TOLD YOU...YOU CAN'T HELP WHAT PEOPLE ARE GONNA BELIEVE ABOUT YOU. SOMETHIN' LIKE THAT.

I GUESS YOU CAN'T HELP WHO'S GONNA BELIEVE IN YOU, EITHER.

INCOMING
12 MINUTEMAN I.C.B.M.
SUGGEST DEFENSE:
SUPERMAN
GREEN LANTERN
MARTIAN MANH NTER
RECOMMEND IMM TE ACTION
INCOMING

I AM ALL OUTTA IDEAS...

BLAM
BLAM
BLAM
BLAM
BLAM
BLAM
BLAM
BLAM
FWASSSH
PA-ZOW
TZZZZ
BLAM
BLAM
AH, YOU MAGGOTS--!

NASA
BLAM
BLAM
YAAAH!
MY POWER JUST CAME BACK.
HEY...!

WHERE YOU GOIN'?
HUH?
YOU LITTLE PUKES ARE TELEPATHIC, RIGHT? SO TELL YOUR PALS TO GET THE HELL OFF BATBOY--
AND ANYONE ELSE THEY GOT--
BLAM
OR I DO THIS ALL DAY.
BLAM
NO MORE
NO MORE

MONAGHAN? DO WE HAVE COMMS?
WE GOT INCOMIN' MISSILES, MAN! THE NUKES ARE IN THE FRIGGIN' AIR!
ON MY WAY.
NAAAH--!
THIS IS THE FLASH FOR J.L.A. WATCHTOWER CALLING NORAD, SENDING ON CHANNEL YANKEE-NINE:
EMERGENCY CODE SILENT NIGHT, I SAY AGAIN, SILENT NIGHT-- ACKNOWLEDGE, OVER?
WHAT...?
I'M TELLING THEM WE'RE IN CONTROL. IF THEY GO FOR IT, THE WARHEADS WILL BE DEACTIVATED MID-FLIGHT.
YOU KNOW, IF I WAS SUPERMAN OR BATMAN, THEY WOULDN'T EVEN WAIT TO ASK THE WHITE HOUSE...
ACKNOWLEDGED
YESSSS...!
MONAGHAN?
WHAT DID YOU DO HERE?

WHAT THE HELL DO YOU MEAN, MURDER?
I MEAN A DOZEN NASA PERSONNEL, ALL OF WHOM DIED AT YOUR HAND.
I DON'T BELIEVE I'M HEARIN' THIS! THEY TOOK ALLA YOUR POWERS AWAY, THEY HAD CONTROL OF THE WATCHTOWER, THERE WERE NUCLEAR MISSILES INCOMIN'--
I MEAN COME ON, WHAT WOULD YOU GUYS'VE DONE...?
NOT KILLED ANYONE. WE'RE THE JUSTICE LEAGUE OF AMERICA.
YEAH, BUT I'M NOT, AM I? I AIN'T NO SUPERHERO VERYTHIN' ALWAYS ORKS OUT FOR, OR A GENIUS COMES UP WITH IDEAS NO ONE ELSE CAN!
I'M JUST SOME SCHMUCK FROM THE CAULDRON! AN' I DID THE ONLY THING I COULD THINK OF!
THE MISSILES' FLIGHT TIME WAS WELL OVER--
SO WHAT? WHAT'S THIS IDEA I SHOULDA HAD, WITH ALL THE EXTRA TIME I HAD TO THINK?
YOU GUYS'D STILL A' BEEN OUTTA THE PICTURE, IT'D STILL A' BEEN ME AGAINST THE THINGS!
PERHAPS IF I WAS ABLE TO SPEAK IN COURT...
COURT?
OFFICIALLY, THE ASTRONAUTS DIED IN THE CRASH. ANY RECORD OF WHAT WENT ON HERE--AND OF ANY DECISIONS TAKEN IN WASHINGTON--HAS BEEN SUPPRESSED AT THE REQUEST OF THE U.S. GOVERNMENT.
WHATEVER TESTIMONY YOU MIGHT PROVIDE WOULD THEREFORE BE INADMISSIBLE AT MONAGHAN'S TRIAL--WHICH, OF COURSE, WILL ONLY COVER THE THREE HUNDRED PLUS MURDERS HE'S COMMITTED IN GOTHAM CITY...

ARE YOU SURE YOU'RE UP TO THE JOURNEY? IT HASN'T EVEN BEEN TWO DAYS...
I WANT TO BE DONE WITH THIS.
UNBELIEVABLE, *UNBELIEVABLE...!*
DO NOT THINK YOU HAVE FOUND REDEMPTION BY YOUR ACTIONS HERE.
DUDE, YOU GOTTA SEE THINGS FROM--
AW, YOU KNOW WHAT? SAVE IT.

MAN, THEY TOOK YOUR SMOKES?
UH-HUH.

AN' THEY CALL THEMSELVES THE JUSTICE LEAGUE...
YOU BOYS ASK FOR THIS ONE SPECIAL?

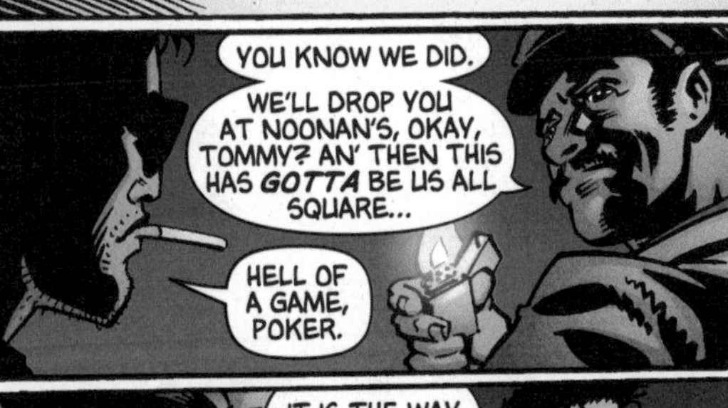
YOU KNOW WE DID.
WE'LL DROP YOU AT NOONAN'S, OKAY, TOMMY? AN' THEN THIS HAS GOTTA BE US ALL SQUARE...
HELL OF A GAME, POKER.

IT IS THE WAY YOU PLAY IT, MY FRIEND.
NOONAN'S'LL DO JUST FINE, FELLAS. LET'S TAKE THE SCENIC ROUTE.

WE GOT A WHILE 'TIL CLOSIN' TIME.

WELL, I...
I THINK I SEE WHY THIS CAN'T GO ANY FURTHER...
THE SURVIVING CREATURES?
KEPT ON ICE.
WAIT A MINUTE, STOP-- I CAN'T--
YOU'RE SAYING THIS HAS BEEN KEPT UNDER WRAPS BY THE GOVERNMENT? HOW? WHAT'S TO STOP THE LEAGUE FROM--
AN UNDERSTANDING WAS ARRIVED AT.
IT WAS POINTED OUT THAT THE LEAGUE--WHILE INCAPACITATED BY SURPRISE ATTACK--FAILED TO PREVENT THE MURDERS OF TWELVE NASA ASTRONAUTS. THAT THOSE MURDERS HAD IN FACT SAVED THE LEAGUE FROM CERTAIN DEATH.
THAT COULD BE MADE TO LOOK VERY BAD; JUST AS THE MISSILE LAUNCH COULD FOR THE GOVERNMENT. HENCE THE UNDERSTANDING.
IF CONSPIRACY'S YOUR THING, I'D SAY THAT'S A PRETTY GOOD ONE. BUT IT ISN'T REALLY THE POINT.
D'YOU REMEMBER WHAT I SAID WHEN I BEGAN THIS STORY?
THAT THERE ARE DIFFERENT KINDS OF COURAGE...?
WHAT WAS SUPERMAN DOING WITH THE LIKES OF TOMMY MONAGHAN, WASN'T THAT WHAT YOU WANTED TO KNOW?

HERE ARE HINGS THAT UPERHEROES ANNOT DO.
"BATMAN WOULD HAVE UND A WAY TO N BY TACTICS; SUPERMAN, ROBABLY BY FORCE. THE ESULT WOULD HAVE BEEN COMPLETE SUCCESS AND ZERO BODYCOUNT.
"BUT THEY WERE OUT OF ACTION, NEUTRALIZED. IT ALL CAME DOWN TO SOMEONE NEITHER MORE POWERFUL THAN A LOCOMOTIVE, NOR BLESSED WITH THE SKILLS OF THE WORLD'S GREATEST DETECTIVE.
"IT TOOK A DECISION NO SUPERHERO IS EQUIPPED TO MAKE. IT TOOK THE *UNTHINKABLE.*"
THAT'S HOW TOMMY SAVED THE J.L.A..
YOU'RE TALKING OUT MORAL OURAGE...
I'M TALKING ABOUT SHEER, UNADULTERATED, UNIMAGINABLE MORAL COURAGE.
IT'S NINETEEN FORTY-FIVE. YOU'RE HARRY TRUMAN. DO YOU DROP THE BOMBS ON NAGASAKI AND HIROSHIMA, OR DO YOU DROWN THE HOME ISLANDS IN THE BLOOD OF UNITED STATES MARINES?
I CAN'T ANSWER THAT. NOR CAN SUPERMAN.
EVEN BATMAN WOULDN'T KNOW WHERE TO START WITH THAT ONE.

DID THEY EVER MEET AGAIN?
NO.

SUPERMAN FELT THAT AN INJUSTICE HAD BEEN DONE. HE'S BEEN CALLED *RIDICULOUSLY FAIR;* TRUE, PERHAPS, BUT HE NEVER STOPPED WONDERING IF HE COULD SET THINGS RIGHT.
WHICH IS A MOOT POINT, BECAUSE TOMMY DIED SIX YEARS AGO IN GOTHAM CITY. SOME BUSINESS WITH THE C.I.A. THAT NO ONE EVER WANTED TO EXPLAIN.*
*HITMAN #60

I DON'T KNOW, MISTER KIRBY. YOU WANTED A STORY--TOMMY MONAGHAN'S JUST MIGHT BE ONE WORTH TELLING.
YES, IT MIGHT.
IT JUST MIGHT.
MISTER KENT, YOU TOOK ME INTO YOUR CONFIDENCE BECAUSE YOU SAID THAT SUPERMAN CAN'T CONFESS.
IT FOLLOWS THAT HE CAN'T RECEIVE ABSOLUTION, EITHER, SO I OFFER THIS WITHOUT COMMENT.
"THE DRUNK I MET IN GOTHAM, *HACKEN*--HE TOLD ME SUPERHEROES WERE A JOKE IN NOONAN'S BAR. IDIOTS IN UNDERWEAR, YOU KNOW THE SORT OF THING.
"AND MONAGHAN AGREED, EXCEPT--"
EXCEPT FOR SUPERMAN. HE ALWAYS SAID IT.
RIGHT TO THE ENDA HIS LIFE, HE'D RAISE HIS GLASS TO THAT PICTURE OVER THERE, AN' HE'D SAY--

"SUPERMAN'S OKAY BY ME."

DAYDREAMING.
NIGHT-DREAMING NOW, ON THE DARKSIDE LONG BEFORE I KNOW IT.
I SHRUG MYSELF AWAKE, GO HYPERSONIC OVER THE ALEUTIANS.

UP HERE, WHERE THE AIR IS RAZOR-THIN.
WHERE MEN BELIEVE THEMSELVES INVISIBLE.
I TAKE A LAST, SHARP, FROZEN BREATH--

AND HOLD IT.

THE SEAS ARE SAPPHIRES, THE ELDS AND FORESTS EMERALDS. THE HIMALAYAS GLEAM LIKE DIAMONDS.
THE STRANGE BLUE WORLD TO WHICH MY FATHER SENT ME.

IF YOU KNEW HOW YOU ARE LOVED, NOT ONE OF YOU WOULD RAISE A HAND IN RAGE AGAIN.

IN GOTHAM, IN THE CEMETERY AT SAINT JACK'S, THE GRAVE IS BUT A MARKER. DULL AND MUTE.
OFFERING NO TESTIMONY.
AFTERWARDS, REPAIRS WERE FINISHED QUICKLY. THE WHOLE BLACK BUSINESS WAS FORGOTTEN, BRUSHED AWAY.
I ASKED FOR ONE SMALL CORNER TO BE LEFT, A LENGTH OF MOONBASE WALL THAT THREATENED NO ONE.
I WAS SMILED AT, DARKLY. BUT INDULGED.
AND IT'S HERE THAT I COME WHEN I OFFER A PRAYER...

TO THE LORD FOR THE SOUL OF A KILLER.
TOMMY WAS HERE
THE END

The Hitman/Lobo crossover that became THAT STUPID BASTICH! was originally scheduled to be published as HITMAN ANNUAL #2 with art by John McCrea. Presented here for the first time are McCrea's pencils for the opening page.